CONFLICT IN STUART ENGLAND

A. Whitney Griswold

W. N.

Oxford 1955

CONFLICT
IN
STUART ENGLAND

Essays in honour of
WALLACE NOTESTEIN

edited by

WILLIAM APPLETON AIKEN

and

BASIL DUKE HENNING

ARCHON BOOKS
1970

ISBN: 0-208-01029-7
PRINTED IN THE UNITED STATES OF AMERICA

CONTENTS

CONTENTS

6

FOREWORD

THIS volume was planned by William Appleton Aiken, Professor of History at Lehigh University. He chose the theme of the book, secured the contributors and had edited several of the essays before his sudden death on September 26th, 1957. Thus I have only finished what was well begun by a fine scholar and my good friend.

BASIL D. HENNING

Wallace Notestein

*

Hartley Simpson

THE authors of these articles, adept in combat and conflict, were introduced to the political turbulence of the seventeenth century under congenial auspices. They remember fondly the intellectual companionship and warm friendship of Wallace Notestein.

Cicero remarked that the authority of those who teach is often an impediment to those who desire to learn. We who studied with Notestein might wonder that such a relationship between student and teacher need occur. Mastery of his field was the only authority he invoked, and that he wielded through the art of conversation. We do not remember 'Note' as a teacher barricaded by a class-room desk, and indeed, except when lecture courses made it mandatory, he dispensed with the classroom. No mere classroom hour could contain him; he had too much to impart, too much to share, to explore, to test by other minds. Conversation and discussion began in the classroom, possibly, but soon it was being continued on the library steps, along campus walks, over the luncheon table, in his apartment or yours as he sifted and sorted his reading and thinking long into the night. His zest in scholarly activity was convincing; historical scholarship came to life in his discourse, jovially illuminated from a memory retentive of the pertinent and ready with the apt, authentic citation out of recondite sources. Before many months you would find yourself crossing the Atlantic with him, working beside him in the British

Museum, tracking down manuscripts in a country house or parish chest, taking long walks through the English countryside while he talked of politics, poetry, manners, agriculture and churches, and reminiscing about English folk through the centuries over beer in a village inn or a London pub. His art of relating Britain and its people to their historical and scholarly remains has been mastered by few of his contemporaries, and almost certainly by no other historian from this side of the Atlantic in his time. Like a philosopher of old his academy was wherever he was; his students dropped in as their affairs permitted to pick up news of the profession and renew the lively discourse on which they had come to depend.

There is much talk these days about the scholar-teacher which every school should produce and every student strive to become. Notestein is a scholar-teacher, precisely because he is nothing like the paragon described in pedagogical tracts. In some respects he is typical of scholar-teachers of his generation whom we honour, but typical only to that degree. The attribute which primes a distinguished scholar-teacher is one that is clearly always left out of the fanciful descriptions—his own character and individuality. Notestein is our remembrancer that a scholarly career is most happily lodged in gentle human qualities. His character, independence, intellectual vigour, scholarly method, routine of work and life cannot be trapped in a formula. Students pay him the tribute of knowing better than to suppose they can imitate him, but from his character and method they have learned, though he never bothered to preach it, that a good teacher must be genuinely himself. These days it is the fashion in certain quarters to be disdainful of the fact-grubbing of scholarship. Notestein always believed in the hard manual labour of scholarship and has been quite unashamed of the toil of research. Here he set his students the first example in scholarly integrity. Wherever they may be working, even those in non-academic pursuits, they are honest craftsmen.

Notestein's teaching and scholarship have been strongly influenced by indoctrination in constitutional history he received from his old teacher, George Burton Adams. Yet Notestein ventured into history by way of literature, and his doctoral dissertation, *A History of Witchcraft in England 1558–1718*, might be said to mark his transition from an academic career in literature to one in history. His study of constitutional history has not been concerned primarily with political theory or the strictly intellectual analysis of constitutional law and thought. Early in his scholarly career he became interested in the origins of the parliamentary conflict. Maitland, McIlwain, and Pollard were demonstrating that the emergence of the modern parliamentary constitution could be explained intelligently only by first understanding the function of parliament and the constitution as the men of the Tudor and Stuart age construed it. This had been attempted, however, only through interpretation of passages in public documents, contemporary treatises on law and institutions and polemic tracts. Notestein perceived that one major source of contemporary and raw thought on the constitution, parliamentary diaries, had been only scantily exploited. Some had been used and a few published by Gardiner and other historians in the nineteenth century, but it was Notestein who conceived that the record of the parliamentary struggle could be restored to its context by as complete a collection of those diaries as could be recovered by diligent hunting. It was he who worked out the principles for editing them, and it was through his study of separates and similar compilations that the nature of the composition of some of the sources of parliamentary reports and their degree of reliability and authenticity was revealed. Some of these parliamentary diaries he has edited, others have been edited by his students. *The Winning of the Initiative by the House of Commons*, the Raleigh Lecture to the British Academy in 1924, presents Notestein's conclusions at mid-career after analysis of a crucial period in the development of the conflict that led to civil war. There he emphasized the importance of the tactics of procedure. That lecture and the diaries have justified his conviction that painstaking, scholarly reconstruction of the record of Stuart parliaments would modify and extend significantly work being done on many aspects of the history of the period. Historians in many fields of Tudor and Stuart history have drawn upon this material, and *The Winning of the Initiative* has stood the test of time.

To many it seemed that Notestein was completely absorbed in parliamentary history, but his students sitting in his study while he paced up and down, tossing a pencil and talking about the character of the English people from medieval to modern times, were hearing the rehearsal of a synthesis of social and institutional history which fascinated him. He had always been interested in the evidence men left of themselves as exponents of the culture of their time, in personal diaries, letters, family papers, in parish records and quarter sessions records, on the stage and in the churchyard. Using these and numerous other sources, he has adapted the technique of the short study known as a character, widely in vogue in the seventeenth century to describe persons, institutions, types, attributes, even things like newspapers and inns, to the delineation of English people who were representative of their station and culture. *English Folk* is a collection of a few of many similar studies to which Notestein has devoted much research and thought. His own ancestry, his enjoyment from boyhood in reading Scottish ballads, history and literature, and his satisfaction with the acute Angles who went north inspired foraging for the ideas that took form finally in the *Scot in History*, again a character study of a nation. *The English People on the Eve of Colonization 1603–1630* is still in this genre. If men and women of the seventeenth century could read it, they would recognize it as a character of the English people of their time; and in this book you have Notestein's fully developed concept of the inseparability of man and institution.

Wallace Notestein is Sterling Professor Emeritus of English History at Yale University. He began his teaching career at the University of Kansas and was Professor of History at the University of Minnesota and at Cornell University before coming to Yale. As much beloved by those who know him in England as in America, he was an Associate Member of All Souls 1931–2, and Fellow of Balliol and Eastman Professor at Oxford in 1949–50. He holds honorary degrees from Wooster, Harvard, Birmingham, Glasgow, Yale and Oxford. By acclaim he stands as professor-at-large to a host of men and women on both sides of the Atlantic who never were enrolled as his students but who received in abundance his counsel, aid and encouragement.

The following Oration was delivered by the Public Orator in presenting the recipients of honorary degrees at a Convocation held at Oxford University on Saturday, July 12th, 1958.

Degree of D.Litt.

WALLACE NOTESTEIN, M.A., Balliol College

Sterling Professor of English History at Yale University 1928–47; George Eastman Visiting Professor at Oxford 1949–50.

Salutate, Academici, hospitem Americanum qui semper elaboravit ut duo nostri populi in dies inter se fiant coniunctiores. quamquam quid dico 'hospitem'? hic enim abhinc novem fere annos beneficio Georgii Eastman Professoribus nostris adnumerabatur eodemque illo tempore libentissime nos coniugem eius Magistrorum in ordinem honoris causa adscripsimus. porro autem non adeo Americanus est ut non glorietur aliquando se materno genere Scoticae esse prosapiae; nec tamen adeo Scoticus ut nos Anglos non amet—immo gaudet nostra quoque rura urbesque peragrare. quaerit peragrando quae sint ubicumque, quaeque fuerint, vivendi condiciones; penetrat omnem ruris angulum, vir sua ipsius bonitate habitantibus commendatus; studet cognoscere locorum pariter hominumque naturam. hac munitus scientia nunquam se brevibus unius aetatis finibus continuit, mavult tamen rerum scriptor in saeculo p. Chr. n. septimo decimo aevoque superiore versari. hinc ei docere placuit quemadmodum regendae civitatis auctoritatem senatores Britannici, sive Parliamenti concilium inferius, sibi primum vindicarint; hinc eruere atque edere illa diaria Caroli prioris sub regno conscripta quae morem omnem senatorium eius aetatis

13

illustrant; hinc ostendere quae tum fuerint instituta nostratium cum primum trans mare Atlanticum plurimi migraverint.

mitto *Scotorum* eius *Monumenta,* mitto *Veneficarum Historiam*; unum hoc addo, neminem unquam liberalius doctrinae suae copias consortibus studiorum commodasse.

praesento vobis Wallace Notestein, Historiae Britannicae in Universitate Yaleana Professorem Emeritum, ut admittatur honoris cause ad gradum Doctoris in Litteris.

An Analysis of Major Conflicts in Seventeenth-Century England

*

Willson H. Coates

I wish to acknowledge my indebtedness to University of Rochester colleagues in history, John B. Christopher and Harry J. Benda (now of Yale University), and in English literature, Joseph Frank, and to other friends in the historical profession, Jack Hexter, and Charles and Kate George. Shown an earlier version of this essay, they have offered suggestions and criticisms which I have not invariably followed but for which, along with their encouragement, I am grateful. I wish also to thank J. Salwyn Schapiro and Hayden V. White who gave their characteristically gracious consent to my using some sentences or phrases I had written for our jointly projected introduction to the intellectual history of Western Europe since the Renaissance. I wish to thank the late William Appleton Aiken and Basil D. Henning for their suggestions and helpfulness in their capacities as successive editors of this volume.

BECAUSE British history from its beginnings to 1776 is also, in a genuine sense, early American history, British historians have long recognized that their history is a natural sphere for Anglo-American co-operation. Miss Veronica Wedgwood has generously spoken of the superior capacity for detachment which Americans can bring, especially to the seventeenth century. Whether or not Americans deserve this tribute, I have noticed that in absorbing the evidence of recent scholarship the conservative British have shown themselves to be more receptive and thorough than the presumably adaptable Americans. A notable instance of this was the stubbornness with which many American scholars clung to old views about the 'Lancastrian experiment', and a 'Tudor despotism' which supposedly brought about a long parliamentary decline. To this generalization about the obduracy of American scholars there have, of course, been many exceptions, Mr Wallace Notestein being a conspicuous one. It is, however, with an awareness of this cultural lag that I approach the subject of this essay. I know that British readers may be justified in feeling that enough for the present has been said and written in recent years on the aetiology of the Great Rebellion, but I am proceeding, nevertheless, with another transatlantic analysis.

To many historians the conventional answers to basic questions about the familiar and dramatic conflicts of seventeenth-century England seem no longer to be adequate. Apart from Marxian dogmatists and extreme Tory apologists, however, those who have attacked or abandoned the tenacious Whig tradition about the Great Rebellion and the Glorious Revolution have been alternately precise and tentative about the new interpretations to which they could commit themselves. When Mr Lawrence Stone in his summary of the Tawney hypothesis said 'that the shift in the relative proportions of the national income held by the different classes of society was the basic cause of the upheavals of the mid-seventeenth century is now clear beyond reasonable doubt', he expressed himself with an historical certitude to which he has not subsequently adhered.[1] The participants in seventeenth-century

English historical studies generally feel, as one would in any healthy intellectual enterprise, that the refinement of well-substantiated views, and the search for further clarification and for new evidence which may change those views, must go on.[2]

This is in the spirit of S. R. Gardiner who made no pretensions to finality even though his monumental work is both authoritative in its narrative and confident in its moral judgments. Since his time, beginning with the indefatigable and immensely learned Sir Charles Firth, the roster of historians lured into historical research in seventeenth-century England is an illustrious one. A long list of scholars would have to be named if we were to include all who have amplified our knowledge of that period, especially of the administrative, religious, literary, economic and social aspects. The resulting increased cognition has come from neo-Tory approaches, from new psychological insights, from increased awareness of economic factors, from pertinacious researches of all kinds including those into local history and family connections, from a determination to employ the historical imagination in seeing the seventeenth century 'from the inside', and, perhaps, from the almost agonizing relevance of seventeenth-century problems and dilemmas to those of the twentieth century.

Not all of this extensive historical activity has a bearing on the major conflicts of seventeenth-century England; and from those treatises which are pertinent to this theme only a few are being selected here for consideration. Since these are directly or implicitly assaults on the long-dominant Whig point of view, it would be appropriate to begin with a brief statement of the Whig conceptual framework. The Whig interpretation which Mr Herbert Butterfield denigrated more than twenty-five years ago was, even then, with its contrasting patriots and tyrants, a caricature of what any reputable historian in the Whig tradition would present as history.[3] According to the more sophisticated Whig point of view the major conflict of the seventeenth century, although it undoubtedly involved a struggle for power, was essentially a war of ideas concerning religion and politics which rent families and divided members of the ruling gentry class. The seventeenth century was the crucial period in the emergence of constitutional government and of religious and intellectual freedom in England. Whether or not such a result was the intent of the Puritans, the Parliamentarians, the Cromwellians or the Restoration Whigs, it was—partly because powerful opponents of their particular views survived—their main historical achievement. Among the assaults on this Whig historical reconstruction I propose to discuss first, not Mr Hexter's 'storm over the gentry', but a preliminary zephyr that has been barely recorded. It occurred at a meeting of the American Historical Association in December 1940 when the late Alexander Thomson of Wesleyan University presented a paper, not subsequently published.[4] The thesis of this paper, amalgamating neo-Tory, Marxian and other ingredients, is neatly summarized in its opening paragraph:

> The English civil war of the seventeenth century was a struggle in which two different conceptions of society came to grips. One was a view of society as functional, according to which the various groups and individuals in the population performed their own special functions for the good of the whole. This idea was derived from the Christian common-wealth of the Middle Ages; it survived the separation from Rome, and it received the approval of the Tudor and Stuart monarchy and the blessing of the Anglican Church, the two instruments that had the responsibility for seeing that these functions were adequately carried out. The other conception was a newer one. It had been quickened by the commercial revolution and abetted by the Protestant reformation. It was of a society composed of individuals who had no functions to perform but who had only rights which the State existed to protect. Though the responsibility of the State to the people was implied, this newer conception did not go the whole way towards democracy and individualism. For the rights to be protected were chiefly those of individuals who possessed property in land. Hence it has been called a freeholders' conception of society. Though this idea was thrusting itself forward in England before the Civil War, the war hastened and secured its acceptance.

Mr Thomson went on to say of the gentry: 'Whatever their origins and their interests, in their mode of life they reflect the conflict or combination of the two conceptions of society which were competing for pre-eminence in England.' In order to maintain and improve their resources 'the gentry were led to emphasize the newer conception of society at the expense of the older'. 'Forgetful of their functions, they thought almost exclusively in terms of their rights.' In the Long Parliament they struck down 'the instruments of prerogative government which the Tudors and Stuarts had utilized to carry out their scheme of a functional society'. During the Civil War and Interregnum 'the gentry probably suffered more as individuals and eventually gained more as a class than any other group in English society'. Many of the new owners of estates 'were interested primarily in squeezing from them all they could obtain. Even the old gentry were forced by the financial set-backs of the war and by the continued high level of taxation to get all they could out of their land. The commercial spirit therefore completely conquered the country-side ...' Because the Privy Council of the Restoration 'never took up again the social policy of the old, the squire indeed may be said to have emerged from the purgatory of the Star Chamber into an economic paradise. He emerged into a social and political paradise as well. For the restored monarchy existed at his sufferance. If this fact was not immediately clear, it became so after 1689 when the gentry-dominated Parliament by the Bill of Rights and the other Acts of the revolution settlement set a trap powerful enough to catch the most ambitious king.'

I trust that the foregoing excerpts do justice to a well-formulated analysis which, among other merits, gives a plausible explanation of how a section of the gentry could be so unequivocally associated with puritanism in 1640 and so eager to make terms with the monarchy and Church at the Restoration. There are, however, many questionable implications or assumptions in Mr Thomson's thesis.[5] The Civil War is represented as an effort of the gentry to destroy the functional concept of society which was restraining the freeholders' concept. By clear implication the war was not regarded by Mr Thomson as a struggle of liberal forces against arbitrary government. But the peculiar way in which English liberties have evolved is precisely by the enunciation in general terms of the particular rights of a dominant or rising social class. It may be that the seventeenth-century revolution was a triumph for constitutional government in the interests of the gentry class, but it was none the less a triumph for constitutional government. Moreover, in the tone of Mr Thomson's historical revisionism there is an unmistakable tendency to employ a realistic inter-pretation of the conduct of the gentry and an idealistic interpretation of the conduct of the monarchy. If the struggle for rights and liberties is depicted as being waged by the gentry with the aim of achieving unchecked social and political power, it should not be implied that the broader social justice for which the absolute monarchy seemed to stand was any more genuine than the claim of the gentry that they stood for the rights of the subject and the interests of the nation as a whole. Mr Thomson asserts that 'It was the measure of the failure of the first two Stuart monarchs that their policy of social justice got mixed up with purely personal and fiscal considerations and became entangled in religious controversy.' Thus the fiscal and religious policies of the Stuarts are made incidental and unfortunate rather than fundamental and deliberate.

In addition, Mr Thomson assumes that under the freeholders' concept of society the gentry, which really comprised a new landed aristocracy with or without noble titles, was more brazen than the old aristocracy when the functional concept had prevailed. But was there really any difference between the two societies in the desire of the upper class to rule and maintain its ascendancy? Did not the feudal nobility equate its special interests with the good of society as much as the gentry? The functional order may have been regarded as a necessary social cement in the Middle Ages and in the Tudor and Stuart periods, but was it not also a convenient fiction for the aristocracy? Did it not imply acquiescence by the lower orders to their status in society? Furthermore, did not such a subservient attitude continue to be normal, and even have a renewed vitality, in the England of the Restoration period and later? Questions may be raised, too, about the vigorous maintenance of the functional concept by the Stuart monarchy. At best the benevolence of the Government was spasmodic. Were the granting of monopolies to Court favourites and the sale of peerages expressions of the functional concept?[6] Although there was, indeed, between the later Middle Ages and the eighteenth century a perceptible change in the attitude towards property which may be legitimately designated as a shift from the functional to the freeholder concept, the monarch and his courtiers were as much contaminated by the change as anyone else, while the continuation of the unpaid governmental services of the gentry after the Restoration suggests that the freeholders' concept had not made a complete triumph.[7]

Finally, the Thomson thesis seems to be predicated on the assumption that the gentry *wanted* the transformation of English society from a functional to a freeholders' concept of it and that they were in a position to control events to achieve this end. Actually when the parliamentary gentry had to make their crucial decision in 1641 whether or not to be satisfied with the Long Parliament's reforms, they could not possibly have envisioned the outcomes of 1649, 1653, 1660 or 1688. How *did* the parliamentary gentry conceive of their role at the time the major decision for civil war was made? They had, of course, no intention of encouraging social revolution or political democracy, but, as previously suggested, their claim to represent the people was no more a pretence than that of the King to be the defender of the people's liberties. It is quite clear that the London populace spontaneously supported the parliamentary point of view while the parliamentary leaders candidly welcomed this support.[8] Undoubtedly many of the gentry on the parliamentary side, deeply resenting as they did Laud's meddlesome policy, were political rather than religious Puritans, but whatever their motivation they were, in their opposition to episcopacy, really representing at the time the views of the most politically conscious section of the lower classes. The popular basis for seventeenth-century royalism was different from, not any more genuine than, the popular basis for parliament and puritanism.

By far the most formidable assault on the Whig version of the English Revolution was made in 1941 by Mr R. H. Tawney,[9] drawing on his profound knowledge of economic history. He could hardly have anticipated the now celebrated controversy subsequently conducted mainly in the pages of the *Economic History Review*.[10] This erudite disputation among economic historians has, not for the first time, dramatically revealed that, *pace* Marx, there never could be *the* economic interpretation of history. In the preoccupation of the disputants with the anatomy of aristocracy, the rising gentry and the declining or 'mere' gentry, the Whigs seem to be the forgotten men; but actually, if either Mr Tawney (assisted by Mr Stone) or Mr Trevor-Roper (assisted by Mr Cooper) is to be declared the victor, it is not the jousting adversary so much as the Whig interpretation that would be the vanquished.

A memorable inquest into these scintillating contentions was witnessed by those historians who attended the session on 'The

Gentry: 1540–1660' at the American Historical Association meeting in St Louis, December 1956. Of the three papers then delivered, Mr J. H. Hexter's 'Storm over the Gentry' is the most directly pertinent to our present purpose. Since this paper, in all its scholarly gaiety and pungency, and with elaborations of its argument, was subsequently published in *Encounter*,[11] it needs no summary here. I am substantially in agreement with Mr Hexter's critique, and am concerned here with developing a line of criticism which was only one of his subsidiary purposes.

Mr Tawney finds, as James Harrington did before him, 'the cause of political upheaval in antecedent social change',[12] but he does not bring his hypothesis to its point of contact with the most decisive events it is intended to explain. Let us assume for the moment that, whether Mr Tawney is giving an exposition of Harrington or presenting his own economic interpretation (which is essentially an elaboration of his view of Harrington),[13] he is describing a social transformation that really took place in England between 1540 and the end of the seventeenth century. When the nobility is bought out by the rising gentry class 'but will not abdicate its privileges', then there is 'an interlude of dislocation. The only possible remedy for the resulting disorders is the reconstruction of political institutions in accordance with the requirements of the changed social structure.'[14] This diagnosis could apply to the Restoration of 1660 or the Revolution of 1688, but not to the Scottish resistance of 1637 or to the situation in England in 1640, in 1641 or in 1642. In another passage, however, 1642 is clearly implied. The Tudors, Mr Tawney says, 'haunted by the fear of feudal revolts', fostered the rising middle class and its instrument the House of Commons; but Elizabeth's Stuart successors 'lacked the arts by which she had beguiled the monster... It was not the Civil War which had destroyed the old régime, but the dissolution of the social foundations of the old régime which had caused the Civil War.'[15]

In his version of the Tawney hypothesis Mr Stone attempts to be more precise about its application to the course of events, but he ends by exposing its limited application. In his first version in 1948 he describes the conflict between the English aristocracy and the rising gentry, merchants and lawyers as so critical that 'A revolution, peaceful or violent, as chance and personality might dictate, had become quite inevitable.'[16] His article in 1952 ends with a fuller explanation of 'the rise of the gentry' at the expense of both the very large landowners and of the peasantry. This shift, 'coupled with the growth of higher education, of administrative experience in the shires and political experience at Westminster, led to the emergence of the House of Commons as the most powerful organ in the State, and the overthrow in 1640–1 of a system of monarchy that offended its religious and constitutional beliefs, its interests and its prejudices; ... the Civil War was fought between two not unevenly matched sections of this middle landowning group.'[17] In other words, the revolution mentioned in Mr Stone's previous article is now accomplished 'peacefully', but the victors decide to have a civil war—as casually as if they had chosen teams for a soccer match.

The awkwardness of this historical verdict has since been implicitly recognized by Mr Stone, who apparently no longer thinks 'the great political struggle' can be explained primarily in economic terms.[18] The kind of dispassionate research which Mr Stone himself has encouraged has tended to make both of the contending economic interpretations inconclusive.[19] Moreover, the classic view of the English Civil War has gained new and overwhelming support in the books on the Long Parliament published by Mrs Keeler and Messrs Brunton and Pennington.[20] Confronted with the detached researches of the two young English scholars, Mr Tawney in his introduction to their book writes with the candour and generosity expected of him. 'As far', he says, 'as the membership of the House of Commons, with which alone the present work deals, is concerned, the inference from the figures contained in it is plain. It is that the division between Royalists and Parliamentarians had little connection with diversities of economic interest and social class. Till equally comprehensive evidence to the contrary is adduced, that conclusion must stand.'[21] He also says that 'Only a charlatan will dogmatize on the welter of conflicting motives which find their agonizing issue in the choice of allegiances in a civil war.'[22] Mr Tawney has never dogmatized, but, quite understandably, he could not resist reverting to his hypothesis in this way: 'In the legislation of 1641, which wound up the old régime, and which future Royalists and Parliamentarians alike supported, economic interests played, as the tenor of the measures passed suggests, an important part. It is possible that similar motives were a power in the second stage, which saw the final rupture of the following year. If so, however, the evidence required to establish that conclusion still remains to be brought to light.'[23]

This is, indeed, a modest claim for Mr Tawney to make for his hypothesis, but it also reveals that he has never unequivocally connected the basic causal factors he postulates with the successive major events themselves. In his preoccupation with an under-lying motivation he fails to ask some of the important questions pertinent to the historical reconstruction of a crowded period of decisive history like that of 1637 to 1642. If any of the cardinal decisions had been made in alternative ways, not only the subsequent train of events but quite possibly the ultimate resolution of seventeenth-century conflicts would have been different. If Laud had understood the Scots better there would have been no Bishops' Wars and thus no particular reason for further English Parliaments under Charles I. If Strafford had been able to prevail upon Charles to keep the Short Parliament there would in all probability have been an ultimate Royalist majority in the House of Commons.[24] The Grand Remonstrance could not have been passed, and the Civil War, if it had occurred at all, might well have had a different outcome. During the first few months of the Long Parliament, when the impotence of the monarchy was exposed and the reforming Royalists were, except on religious questions like that presented by the Root and Branch Petition, not yet distinguishable from the Parliamentarians, there was no possibility of civil war. That in this phase, when the Tudor balance of the constitution was being altered, 'economic interests played an important part', together with political and religious factors, has always been recognized in the traditional Whig accounts of the reaction against Stuart methods of taxation. In dealing with the next phase, however, when men had to make up their minds in one of the fateful moments in English history, Mr Tawney all but abandons his hypothesis. If the hypothesis is of little use in explaining the reluctant decisions to face up to civil war, then it has surely failed to account for the English Revolution of the seventeenth century.

Has Mr Trevor-Roper established a closer connection between *his* hypothesis and the events it is intended to explain? In his articles on the gentry, he has not.[25] It is the economically and politically frustrated rather than the rising section of the gentry that are, for Mr Trevor-Roper, the core of the English revolutionary movement from the beginning of the organization of the parliamentary party in the Long Parliament to the triumph of the Cromwellians. These 'mere gentry' as he describes them lacked the competence to organize what Mr Trevor-Roper himself has called the 'only great revolution' in English history, and the hypothesis about them is wholly inapplicable to the succession of events in the years of decision.[26]

Mr Trevor-Roper tells us that the plight of the declining gentry bred a country-house radicalism which could lead either to the Catholic desperation of the Gunpowder Plot or to Puritan Independency.[27] The historical irresponsibility of this kind of diagnosis deserves to be 'anatomized' in the Trevor-Roper manner. Historical antecedents of Puritan Independency are, of course, to be found in the decades before 1640. Mr Haller has shown how English Puritanism, confined by the Church Establishment but without the theocratic discipline of Geneva or Scotland, manifested through some of its spokesmen the free spirit which other Puritan advocates were disposed to put under Presbyterian restraint. Thus in pulpit and press under the Anglican dispensation before 1640 can be seen traits of the Independency which was to have its brief triumph in the mid-seventeenth century.[28] But whether one accepts Mr Haller's concept of the Independents or takes Mr Trevor-Roper's shabby view of them, this day of victory would have eluded them had not those crucial decisions—from the resistance of the Scots in 1637 to, let us say, the Self-denying Ordinance of 1644—been made substantially as they were made. These are the years when Mr Trevor-Roper's hypothesis is flagrantly irrelevant, whether one is thinking of declining gentry or Puritan Independents; for neither group, identified with the other or not, could be conceived as controlling events until the English Revolution had at least begun to assume its more radical phase.

Mr Trevor-Roper would have us believe that the Independents, who originated from the 'mere gentry', transformed the political manœuvring of 1641 into civil war and social revolution. Yet who, at the time when the party division in the Long Parliament had become irreconcilable, were the Five Members singled out by the King for culpability amounting to treason? Of the two hot-heads, Haselrig, to be sure, became an Independent, but this was despite his considerable wealth, and Strode, though probably the lowest in financial standing of the five, made manifest his willingness to suffer grievously for the cause in which he believed.[29] As for the three responsible leaders, Pym had large holdings in Somersetshire, besides colonial and other investments, Hampden was 'one of the richest gentlemen in England', and Holles, though only the second son of an earl, had 'ample resources'.[30]

Once there was no retreat from civil war the dynamics of the English Revolution changes the historical problem of causation. But even during the Civil War and Interregnum, when Mr Trevor-Roper's theory might be presumed at last to come into its own, it explodes innocuously, as far as the Long Parliament is concerned, against the hard substance of the Brunton-Pennington findings. It is true, these scholars admit, that the 'Recruiters' elected to the House of Commons since 1642, and the winnowing and sifting which effected the Rump, 'reduced the proportion of old parliamentary families and increased that of the men who seized the opportunity offered by the exceptional conditions'. Yet 'Independency was perceptibly, but only just perceptibly, stronger among the new members than among the old'. The conclusion is that 'the men who abolished the monarchy and the House of Lords and passed the Navigation Act did not find themselves doing these things because they were as a whole different in origins and interests from those who had left Westminster in 1642 or 1648'.[31] A swing to the left in the predominant membership of at least some, perhaps all, of the county committees from the leading families to the lesser gentry is hardly equivalent to Mr Trevor-Roper's contention.[32]

Both Mr Tawney and Mr Trevor-Roper, making use of their insights into economic and social forces, have come to grips with some basic historical motivations. Yet turning from their essays to Miss Veronica Wedgwood's complex analysis of the years 1637–47 in *The King's Peace* and *The King's War*, or to Mr William Haller's *Liberty and Reformation in the Puritan Revolution*, is like moving from a kind of scholastic world of twentieth-century economic history to a modern penetration into seventeenth-century realities.[33] This is not to disparage the dialectical methods of Mr Tawney and Mr Trevor-Roper. Hypotheses like theirs fulfil a high purpose if they are designed to exhume buried historical facts, to expose new historical relationships, to stimulate new approaches to further historical investigation. Moreover, they would not be so fruitful if they were not based, at least during the period of disputation, upon strong convictions. Ordinarily, however, it should not be assumed that univalent historical hypotheses are suitable instruments for explaining complex historical events, as Mr Tawney and Mr Trevor-Roper well know but did not make explicit in the course of their controversy. Hypotheses positing single causes may reveal facets hitherto obscured, but major historical changes can be successfully analysed only on assumptions of multiple causation and the intricate interdependence of a succession of events.

The implication should be allowed to stand that plausible historical hypotheses, if they do not bear the burden put upon them by their proponents, should none the less be absorbed into historical thinking rather than refuted and then forgotten. There *were* rising gentry and there were declining gentry in seventeenth-century England, and they should be fitted into the patterns of conflict. Perhaps a new synthesis of all well-grounded interpretations is now possible,[34] but my purpose in this essay is a less ambitious one. I suggest, at least as an analytical procedure, that a distinction be made among three categories of conflict in seventeenth-century England—first, the continuous social conflict which has concerned the economic historians; second, the traditionally conceived ideological conflict of the 1640s resolved in 1688; and third, the conflict aroused by the short-lived radical democratic and Utopian movements. To what extent these different categories affected one another remains a debatable matter, but in the present state of our historical knowledge it would, I submit, make for historical clarification to treat them as autonomous categories.

Concerning the precise nature of the first and most prolonged conflict, economic historians have yet to agree among themselves as to whether the aristocracy was declining or just being renewed in the English fashion, or whether new methods of estate management were of major consequence before the eighteenth century, and so on; but about the price revolution of 1540 to 1640—as about many aspects of the expanding commerce, industry and banking, the disposal of monastic and crown lands, the shifting ownership of property among the aristocracy, the gentry, the merchants and industrialists, the yeomen—much has come to be known. These vast social changes, as Mr Tawney has demonstrated, were, at least in some measure, recognized at the time. Since, however, men were articulate about them with varying degrees of personal grievance, contentment or detachment, they did not leave an unambiguous record.

Although three hundred years later the lineaments of that social revolution are still not entirely clear, attributes that have a bearing on our present inquiry are quite evident. The social revolution consisted of a multitude of events over a long period of time. Innumerable shifts in property divided members of a class, cut across the well-demarcated class lines and effected new combinations of interests. Litigation was a normal expression of the animosities of this complex social conflict. Mr Tawney's gibe about the London commercial magnates who scrambled for confiscated estates in the Civil War and Interregnum and discovered 'that as a method of foreclosure war was cheaper than litigation',[35] may well be true. But he is too good a scholar to say that these magnates launched the Civil War in order to enter upon 'properties long mortgaged to them'. It is possible that the social revolution of the economic historians increased the acerbities of the Civil War, but the myriad conflicts of that revolution were not amenable to large-scale organization. Only a mammoth coincidence of gambling instincts could have led to a plan for securing social ascendancy by the clash of arms. Thus, in a recognized historical sense, the social revolution was a silent one.

It was also a completely successful revolution, but its triumph was not signalized by any manifestly important single historical event. In the realm of economic and state theory its victory is revealed in the all but uncontested sway of the doctrines of mercantilism in the later seventeenth century. The series of Acts of the Long Parliament, signed by the King in 1641 and never to be repealed, come nearest to reflecting the political success of the social revolution, but there are many other factors that brought about this establishment of constitutional royalism. To most of the victors in the social revolution both the Restoration of 1660 and the Revolution of 1688 were eminently satisfactory, but this fact hardly explains these events.

The traditionally recognized overt conflicts of the seventeenth century constituting our second distinct category were the issues which men thought they were arguing about and thought they were fighting about at the time. Although personal ambition and desire for power cannot be disentangled from genuine divergences of opinion, what essentially divided Parliamentarian from Royalist, Puritan from Anglican, Whig from Tory, was a difference of conviction about the royal prerogative, the judiciary, the role of Parliament, the character of the Established Church. The triteness of this view does not diminish its historical validity. Although essentially this concept of the English Revolution corresponds with the nineteenth-century image of it, a restatement now should not only give fuller recognition to the indispensability of the Tory role in affecting the nature of the ultimate Whig resolution, but should also be made within the larger context of the other seventeenth-century conflicts.

Further considerations bearing on this neo-Whig view make up the concluding part of this essay, but it should be restated here that the realignment of the Royalists and Presbyterians in the Second Civil War to take a stand against the Cromwellians was not a new type of conflict as compared with the First Civil War, but rather a shift in the line of demarcation between the contestants. In opening the way to power to the more radical wing of the revolutionary party, the English Revolution was exhibiting characteristics that have become familiar to students of revolutions,[36] but it was not fundamentally altering the English social structure. Those in command of the struggle in England on both sides, whether in Parliament or in the armies, still were men who had a 'stake in the country', Ireton's euphemism for men of property.

Very different, as is well known, was the real class conflict that loomed up in the mid-seventeenth century, and that constitutes our third category. To both contestants at any stage of the second category of conflicts the rising demands from the lower classes were ominous, and they gave some substance to the Royalist charge that Parliamentarians, and *a fortiori* the Cromwellians, were stirring up the masses. The Leveller movement was, nevertheless, *sui generis* even if the Cromwellians did give it its chance. Twentieth-century researches have greatly expanded our knowledge of the emergence in the mid-seventeenth century of democratic and pre-industrial Utopian thinking. Indeed, the rivalry between the political Levellers and Diggers like the Utopian Communist Winstanley, startlingly foreshadows the ideological conflict between democracy and communism of the twentieth century. Thus a fourth category of seventeenth-century conflict presented itself, but it needs no more than passing mention, for both of these popular movements may be regarded as in the tradition (if that is the right word) of English radicalism that goes back at least to the fourteenth century and the medieval couplet: 'When Adam delved and Eve span, who was then the gentleman?' Behind both movements, too, there was undoubtedly social and economic discontent.

The assumption, however, that the economic determinists have in these historical phenomena a convincing case is not well-founded, for the Lollard movement, the Peasants' Revolt of 1381, and the periodic subsequent uprisings, some of them the consequences of enclosures, did not in any instance produce any such extraordinary and full-blown documents as those of the Levellers and the Diggers. Perhaps there had been for a long time, below the surface deference of the lower classes to their social superiors, an endemic economic discontent which was manifested in those periodic outbreaks; but if so it had not been sufficient to be articulated in democratic ideas or social welfare schemes. And there is no new economic grievance in the mid-seventeenth century such as to warrant the assumption that the prodigious outpouring of the presses came primarily from economic causes.

This social revolutionary movement was, unlike those in our two other categories, premature and hopeless, and it was completely crushed. Moreover, the conflict while it lasted was of an entirely different order. As compared with the individual acts that constitute the conflicts under the first category, it consisted of overt and concerted actions of groups or masses of men. It was not, like the conflicts under the second category, an ideological and power struggle that could be resolved late in the seventeenth century by an accommodation among the possessing classes. It can, with our historical hindsight, be considered a logical extension of the principles of the parliamentary party, but the real question for the mid-seventeenth-century historian is why such radical democratic and social ideas should have had a venture at all, albeit an abortive one.

The explanation is to be found in the complex set of political, intellectual and social circumstances which permitted the free and vigorous criticism in England of authoritarian views in religion and politics. Projected into that situation was that unique, multiform brand of Protestantism, English puritanism. The original Protestant Reformation had varied and contradictory consequences, but it has often been pointed out that the ultimately logical consequence of the Reformation was democracy. On the other hand the logical consequences of an idea can easily become lost in the complicated interplay of historical forces. Such was not the fate of that multi-class phenomenon, English Puritan Independency, for the Civil War made it possible for the Independents to operate with fruitful verbal bellicosity. Large numbers of them were concentrated in the New Model Army of Cromwell. Army life need not be intellectually stultifying, for it provides, above all, ample time—and for an army of religious zealots this meant unlimited possibilities—for disputation when all were together. Thus the formulation of democratic ideas was natural, coming as it did from those who had long believed that a voluntary association of Christian believers could constitute themselves into a church. The vision of a democratic society was as fleeting as it was remarkable. The Levellers were dispersed or repressed, the tide soon turned against all radical experimentation, and fear of popular movements consolidated the Restoration aristocracy. Before the end of the century John Locke was to expound a conservative version of Leveller doctrines, but for the time being it was as if that generation, terrified by its intellectual offspring, had willing recourse to infanticide.

Only a full treatise can reveal in all their complexity the motivations of the men who took sides in the conflicts summarily analysed in the foregoing paragraphs.[37] For the purpose of this essay it is proposed instead (at the risk of leaving part of the scaffolding of my historical reconstruction standing) to conclude with some general considerations of the historical problem of human motivation, especially applied to seventeenth-century England and the patterns of conflict that have been designated.

History would be an impossible area of human reflection if there were no recurrent attributes of human nature. On the other hand, the recognition of the sense in which human nature is not always the same is surely a major component of what we call historical-mindedness. It is altogether probable, for example, that a measure of economic determinism can be more adequately substantiated in an era of economic awareness like the twentieth century than in the seventeenth century. Because the Western phenomenon of humanitarianism has intervened between the seventeenth century and the twentieth century, we are more prone to public indignation over acts of human depravity than were seventeenth-century Englishmen or Continental Europeans. At the same time we are more accustomed to thinking in terms of naked power politics than the seventeenth century, when both politics and economics were just emerging from their subordination to theology, and when Machiavelli, in disputation if not in practice, could still be dismissed as immoral. Thus it was that although Thomas Hobbes exerted an influence on other thinkers, and his generation had a horrified fascination for the sharp cutting-edge of his mind, he had no disciples who avowedly thought or acted as he described his fellow-men. Thus, too, the hesitant absolutist monarch, Charles I, and the reluctant dictator, Oliver Cromwell, bear only faint resemblances to their twentieth-century totalitarian counterparts.

The emergence, during the course of the seventeenth century, of politics and economics as independent disciplines, as well as the scientific revolution and other factors, combine to complicate the problem of determining human motivation in that century. This was the time when the growth of quiet scepticism contributed, together with the religiously devout advocacy of toleration, to religious freedom. Yet it would be entirely false to assume that the apparent religious motivation of intelligent men in that century was only an expedient cloak, or that religion was often a species of cant. To say that men unconsciously acted primarily in their economic interests even though they thought in religious or moral terms is to get involved in a kind of historico-psycho-analytical mysticism. Mr Tawney himself says that his hero, James Harrington, a mid-century proponent of toleration, 'habitually underestimates the dynamic power of religious conviction'.[38] In Charles I's time, in Miss Wedgwood's view, 'The overwhelming majority of the King's subjects, whatever their doctrines, their education or their interests, were simply and sincerely religious ... The desire to believe and the capacity to believe were still almost equally strong.'[39]

If, then, the intrinsic power of religious conviction may be assumed as an important, possibly a determining, factor in the conflicts of the seventeenth century, the problem in dealing with each of the three categories of conflict is to assess the extent to which religion was qualified by, or fused with, other motivating forces. In the above discussion of the category of premature conflict, the broad outlines of an answer are implied. Those responsible for suppressing the democratic movement were spontaneously defending their total concept of religious, political and social order, whereas the original driving force of the democratic movement itself was largely religious. Effective use, however, was also made by the leading Levellers of ideas like that of natural law, which have a classical-medieval origin, and of selected constitutional rights and traditions, as well as of fictional versions of English history. Furthermore, economic discontents and particular circumstances are essential parts of any analysis of the Levellers whose leaders displayed an uncommon sense of practical politics and expedient tactics and reached an essentially rational and secular outlook in their political thinking. But since the Leveller movement never really got beyond the realm of ideas it is only the ephemeral persuasiveness of those ideas to a still religious age that constitutes the main historical problem.

The first category of social conflict discussed in this essay had, on the other hand, strong economic roots and resulted in a permanent social change that is closely related to the emergence of modern Western capitalism. The connection between this economic development and the Protestant Reformation brought out by Max Weber[40] has been the subject of an extensive literature to which the contribution of Mr Tawney will surely remain a great historical interpretation.[41] Mr Tawney's important qualifications of the Weber hypothesis, modified further by recent researches,[42] leave open the question whether religion was an original factor in promoting the great economic changes of the sixteenth and seventeenth centuries.

At the very least, however, it can be said that, whatever changes there were in economic thinking and practice, to most men in that age it was imperative that an adjustment be worked out in religious and moral terms. There have, of course, always been some men who did not require moral sanction of their single-minded devotion to the accumulation of wealth. This is implied by the very emphasis of theologians on moral considerations in economic life. The Protestant Reformers intended to re-enforce these traditional considerations rather than to provide an ethical justification for the unabashed worldliness of the new business enterprise; but it was never their purpose to encourage cloistered virtues or to turn away from the stream of events. Moreover, there were many reasons why the new wealthy classes in England should want to be associated with Protestantism even while religious leaders excoriated them for their greed. There is no doubt that Calvinism, exerting a pervasive influence in England far beyond strictly Puritan circles, had inadvertently provided, with its emphasis on the virtues of prudence, industry and frugality, appropriate ideological tools for the accumulation of capital wealth which often quickly became landed wealth.[43] Once the new ways of accumulating wealth became almost as respectable as the old aristocratic ways of spending it conspicuously, the economic conflict we are here concerned with was well advanced. In this process the incipient weakening of religious motivation is patent, but the still dominant Protestant spirit in seventeenth-century England of necessity had made it a moulding factor in economic conflict and change.

Finally, it does not require much probing to find the religious element in the category of the traditionally conceived conflict in seventeenth-century England. There is no doubt that social and economic interests, and motives of expediency, accompanied the struggle for power, but since these considerations could operate with equal effectiveness for either side within any social class they were not determining. The central historical problem is the relationship of what were undoubtedly the two main factors, the religious and the political. By what they said men made it quite clear in the crucial year of decision 1641, and in 1688, that they were concerned with both religion and politics, although by the later date men were obviously more secular-minded. In the earlier year, because of the prevailing identification of Church and State, it is often difficult to distinguish among religious, political and constitutional reasons for decision or action. In the case of John Pym, as I learned many years ago from Mr Notestein, there seems to have been a greater preoccupation with religion in his earlier career than at the time of his leadership in the Short and Long Parliaments. It is possible that the religious fervour of that still inscrutable mind did not decline so much as the political instinct developed. In any case a close study of Pym's expert manœuvring in 1640–1 reveals that in him politics now preponderated over religion and that he shared with Charles I, as Miss Wedgwood puts it, 'an intense political fanaticism'.[44] This is consistent with his deep understanding of the Puritan zeal which, for many of his followers, made political radicalism easy to espouse so long as it served religious ends. Sir Simonds D'Ewes is a special case, though probably not an isolated one; for when it came to the Grand Remonstrance and the clause concerning the King's employment of councillors which 'the Parliament may have cause to confide in', his anti-episcopal religious ardour prevailed over his devotion to political precedent, allowing only a reluctant conclusion that his 'heart and vote went with it in the main'.[45]

Thus, although there would have been no civil war without the emotionally charged religious conflict between Puritan and Anglican, *either* political *or* religious considerations were overriding for individual Parliamentarians, and many ways of resolving or fusing religion and politics were in operation. A corresponding variety of motives existed, of course, among the Royalists, although there was less religious intensity on their side. During the whole course of the Civil Wars, shifting associations and increasing or diminishing enthusiasms disclose the relative potency of religious and political allegiance among the contestants.

CITATIONS

Where an American edition is cited the date of British publication follows in brackets if known.

[1] Compare the quoted statement, from *Economic History Review*, XVIII, 1948, 1, with Mr Stone's letter in *Encounter*, XI, No. 1, July 1958, 73–4.
[2] This attitude is reflected by Mr Stone (*Economic History Review*, Second Series, IV, 321) when he calls for an end to polemics and a continuation of dispassionate research. In his 'Recent Interpretations of the Civil War' (*History*, XLI, 67–87) Mr Christopher Hill asks many provocative questions and points to lines of historical inquiry which could be fruitfully pursued.
[3] *The Whig Interpretation of History*, London, 1931. Cf., on Whiggism, R. W. K. Hinton in *History Today*, IX, No. 11, November 1959, 720–8, and J. G. A. Pocock in *Encounter*, XI, No. 4, October 1958, 69–70. I should add that in general I have the highest regard for Mr Butterfield's historical writing.
[4] A few points in Mr Thomson's paper are briefly noted in *The American Historical Review*, XLVI, No. 3, 1941, 535–6. I have a full typewritten copy of the paper.
[5] In the critique which follows I have drawn on the notes I used in commenting on Mr Thomson's paper at the session of the American Historical Association in December 1940, but those notes have here been extended and elaborated.

[6] Mr Charles R. Mayes has recently demonstrated (*Journal of Modern History*, XXIX, 21–37) the significance of the sale of peerages in what he calls 'the growing corruption and declining integrity of the monarchy'. See also the same author's 'The Early Stuarts and the Irish Peerage' in *The English Historical Review*, LXXIII, April 1958, 227–51.
Mr G. E. Aylmer, in his 'Attempts at Administrative Reform, 1625–40' (*Ibid.*, LXXII, 229–59) in effect implicitly challenges Mr Thomson's view that a functional concept prevailed at all in the medieval and Tudor periods. Mr Aylmer says (p. 230) that features of the early Stuart administrative system 'conformed to the pattern of centuries', and that one of these features was 'the treatment of offices under the Crown as pieces of semi-private property with little notion of the public service about them or their holders'. In this and other articles (*Bulletin of the Institute of Historical Research*, XXXI, No. 83, 58–67, and *Economic History Review*, Second Series, X, No. 1, 81–93), Mr Aylmer shows how the early Stuart preoccupation with monarchical finances proved to be self-defeating and led to 'the dual victory of oligarchy and constitutionalism'. See also Mr Robert Ashton's article *ibid.*, 15–29.

[7] In using the word 'contaminated' in this sentence I am accepting Mr Thomson's value judgments for the sake of the argument. Actually I do not think there is historical evidence for value judgments which put the old English aristocracy on a higher moral plane than the gentry. Nor is there sufficient evidence for the converse view which seems to be held by Mr Christopher Hill; *vide* p. 347 of his *Economic Problems of the Church*, Oxford, 1956. Medievalists, as well as historians of the Tudor and Stuart periods, would surely take exception to the statement that 'In all spheres of life the sixteenth and seventeenth centuries saw replacement of divine right by contractual theories, of arbitrary authority by reason.' Despite this and other passages open to criticism (see note 34, below), this book is a work of the first importance.

[8] Whether the parliamentary leaders actively solicited it is, I think, still debatable. (See my Introduction, xxxii–iv, *The Journal of Sir Simonds D'Ewes*, New Haven, 1942 [Oxford, 1942].) Miss Veronica Wedgwood, however, clearly implicates Pym and his parliamentary associates in stirring up the London populace which she seems to regard as both fickle and easily excitable (*The King's War*, 31–3, 37, 57). I do not see the conclusive evidence for this view in her specific citations, although she may have found new evidence in the Oxford D. Phil. thesis by Mrs Valerie L. Pearl concerning London in the Civil War period. (This work is not yet generally available to scholars, but Miss Wedgwood was given access to it.) On the other hand, the most unlikely possibility is presented in the converse view maintained by Mr Brian Manning that 'urban and peasant mass movements' crystallized 'the political situation' and precipitated 'critical events' (*Past and Present*, No. 13, April 1958, 69–70).

[9] 'Harrington's Interpretation of His Age', Raleigh Lecture, *Proceedings of the British Academy*, XXVII, 199–223; 'The Rise of the Gentry', *Economic History Review*, XI, 1–38.

[10] It was obviously Mr Lawrence Stone, in his 'The Anatomy of the Elizabethan Aristocracy' (*Economic History Review*, XVIII, 1948, 1–53) rather than Mr Tawney, who first provoked Mr Trevor-Roper. The subsequent interchange was as follows: H. R. Trevor-Roper, 'The Elizabethan Aristocracy: An Anatomy Anatomized' *Economic History Review*, Second Series, III, 1951, 279–98; Lawrence Stone, 'The Elizabethan Aristocracy—A Restatement', *ibid.*, IV, 1952, 302–21; H. R. Trevor-Roper, 'The Gentry, 1540–1640', *ibid.*, Supplement, 1953; R. H. Tawney, 'Rise of the Gentry: A Postscript', *ibid.*, VII, 1954, 91–7.

[11] X, No. 5, May 1958, 22–34; XI, No. 2, August 1958, 75–6. Mr Hexter acknowledges his use of Mr J. P. Cooper's criticism of Mr Tawney's technique of counting manors (*Economic History Review*, Second Series, VIII, 377–89. The session of the American Historical Association, presided over by Mr Alan Simpson, is briefly summarized in *The American Historical Review*, LXII, 751–2. Mr W. R. Emerson's paper on 'The Machinery and Methods of Estate Management', evidently based on dispassionate research, gave substantial, though admittedly incomplete, grounds for believing that the early seventeenth century may have been 'the golden age of the great landowner'. Mr Perez Zagorin's paper on 'The Social Interpretation of the English Revolution' has since been published in *The Journal of Economic History*, XIX, 376–401.

[12] *Proceedings of the British Academy*, XXVII, 1941, 200.

[13] Mr J. G. A. Pocock, in Chapter VI of his *The Ancient Constitution and the Feudal Law: A Study of English Historical Thought in the Seventeenth Century*, Cambridge, England, 1957, challenges Mr Tawney's interpretation of Harrington. Mr Pocock's subtle reinterpretation of Harrington is, I think, quite convincing. See also 'Ideology Hunting: the case of James Harrington' by Judith N. Shklar in *The American Political Science Review*, LII, 662–92.

[14] *Proceedings of the British Academy*, XXVII, 210.

[15] *Ibid.*, 211–12.

[16] *Economic History Review*, XVIII, 1.

[17] *Ibid.*, Second Series, IV, 320.

[18] See his letter cited above, note 1.

[19] Some recent examples of this kind of research are to be found in Mary E. Finch, *The Wealth of Five Northamptonshire Families, 1540–1640*, Oxford, 1956; Patrick McGrath, *Merchants and Merchandise in Seventeenth-Century Bristol*, Bristol, 1955; Joan Thirsk, 'The Sales of Royalist Land During the Interregnum', *Economic History Review*, Second Series, V, 188–205, and 'The Restoration Land Settlement', *Journal of Modern History*, XXVI, 315–28; Margaret Priestly, 'London Merchants and Opposition Politics in Charles II's Reign', *Bulletin, Institute of Historical Research*, XXIX, 205–19; A. R. Batho, 'The Finances of an Elizabethan Nobleman: Henry Percy Ninth Earl of Northumberland', *The Economic History Review*, Second Series, IX, 433–50.

[20] Mary Frear Keeler, *The Long Parliament, 1640–41: A Biographical Study of its Members*, Philadelphia, 1954 (see especially pp. 21–32); D. Brunton and D. H. Pennington, *Members of the Long Parliament*, Cambridge, Mass., 1954 [London, 1954] (see especially pp. 19–20, 176–85). More recently Mr Paul H. Hardacre's *The Royalists during the Puritan Revolution*, The Hague, 1956 [London, 1956], supports the view that peers, gentry and merchants were each divided among themselves. Mr Maurice Ashley doubts that the Brunton-Pennington book disposes of the ' "class" element' in the Civil War (*The Greatness of Oliver Cromwell*, London, 1957, 37, note 6), but his own analysis of what brought on the Civil War (pp. 87–8) is centred on the two familiar issues concerning the Church and the King.

[21] *Op. cit.*, XIX.

[22] *Ibid.*, XVII.

[23] *Ibid.*, XXI.

[24] See C. V. Wedgwood, *The King's Peace 1637–1641*, London, 1955, 326, 363, 365–6; Keeler, *op. cit.*, 9–10. My own incomplete researches suggest that of the approximately one hundred and sixty members elected to the Short Parliament who either did not stand or were defeated for the Long Parliament, a significantly larger proportion was potentially Royalist than those members of the Long Parliament who had not been elected to the Short Parliament. Moreover, among the total membership of the Long Parliament the proportion of classifiable Royalists is lower than among those members (about three hundred and thirty) who had been elected to both Parliaments. Only a small additional number of potentially staunch Royalists in the House of Commons of November 1640 would have been needed to swing more of the political waverers to their side.

[25] This excludes, of course, the bulk of Mr Trevor-Roper's most distinguished writing, but it includes, besides the two articles cited above (note 10), Chapters XXVII and XXIX in his *Historical Essays*, London, 1957. I agree with Mr Hexter's tribute to Mr Trevor-Roper (*Encounter*, x, No. 5, 30–1), but find the Trevor-Roper biography of Laud and several other essays concerned in one way or another with the English Revolution (*op. cit.*, Chapters XX, XXVIII, XXX, XXXIV, XXXV, XXXVII) more persuasive than the articles under discussion.

[26] On this vulnerable aspect of Mr Trevor-Roper's theory, Mr Christopher Hill's criticism (pp. 73–4) of the article 'Recent Interpretations of the Civil War' cited above, note 2) is particularly effective. But Mr Hill does not apply the same test to Mr Tawney, although he charges Mr Hexter with failing to hold the balance between the two scholars (*Encounter*, XI, No. 1, 76).

[27] 'The Gentry 1540–1640', *Economic History Review*, Supplement 1953, 39; 'The Country-House Radicals, 1590–1660', Chapter XXVII in the *Essays*.

[28] William Haller, *The Rise of Puritanism*, New York, 1938 [Oxford, 1938], *passim*.

[29] See Keeler, *op. cit.*, 213, 355, and *D.N.B.*

[30] *Ibid.*, 202, 220, 318–19. Cf. G. E. Aylmer's article in *History*, XLIV, 228–40.

[31] Brunton and Pennington, *op. cit.*, 52, 37, 182–3; see especially Chapters II and III. Mr George Yule in his *The Independents in the Civil War*, Melbourne, 1958 [Cambridge, England, 1958], pays his respects to the Trevor-Roper hypothesis, but on balance he comes much closer to the Brunton, Pennington and Haller points of view.

[32] See especially D. H. Pennington and I. A. Roots, *The Committee at Stafford 1643–1645*, Manchester, 1957, xvii–xxiv. See also A. H. Dodd, *Studies in Stuart Wales*, Cardiff, 1952, Chapter IV; A. M. Everitt, *The County Committee of Kent in the Civil War*, Leicester, 1957, 21–7.

[33] Neither of these historians challenges the classic view of the Civil War, but Miss Wedgwood puts a new emphasis on foreign policy as a factor in the irreconcilable division. See also her 'The Causes of the English Civil War' in *History Today*, V, No. 10, 670–6, and her letter in *Encounter*, XI, No. 5, November 1958, 81.

[34] Mr Christopher Hill's alliterative synthesis of 'Protestantism, patriotism, parliamentarism and property', made in his *Economic Problems of the Church*, Oxford, 1956 (p. 343), is not reconciled with his conclusion (p. 352) that it was only the 'bourgeois revolution that succeeded'. More recently, in his *Oliver Cromwell 1658–1958*, he concedes that the political and constitutional revolutions succeeded as well.

[35] *Economic History Review*, XI, 10.

[36] Mr Crane Brinton in his *The Anatomy of Revolution*, New York, 1938, 1952, 1957 [London, 1953], a book of considerable scholarly courage, takes, in Chapter VI, a very different view from that of Mr Trevor-Roper of the political competence of the English revolutionary extremists.

[37] Since this is not a bibliographical essay no attempt is made to list such treatises. For the category of premature conflict, however, the bibliographical task on a selective basis has been accomplished by Mr Joseph Frank in his *The Levellers*, Cambridge, Mass., 1955 [Oxford, 1955], the text of which is a perceptive study of the evolving convictions of John Lilburne, Richard Overton and William Walwyn. For Winstanley see the introduction by George H. Sabine to his edition of *The Works of Gerrard Winstanley*, Ithaca, New York, 1941 [Oxford, 1941]. Mr Haller's aforementioned *Liberty and Reformation in the Puritan Revolution*, New York, 1955 [Oxford, 1955], encompassing the Levellers and with a special emphasis on Milton, is the outstanding comprehensive treatment of Puritan thinking and inner conflict for the years 1640 to 1649. See also James Fulton MacLear, 'Popular Anti-clericalism in the Puritan Revolution', *Journal of the History of Ideas*, XVII, No. 4, 443–70.

[38] *Proceedings of the British Academy*, XXVII, 221.

[39] *The King's Peace*, 76.

[40] *The Protestant Ethic and the Spirit of Capitalism*, New York, 1930 [London, 1930]. Those who read this book carefully and supplement it with some chapters in *From Max Weber: Essays in Sociology*, New York, 1946, are not so likely as some critics to view the Weber hypothesis as wholly unfounded.

[41] *Religion and the Rise of Capitalism*, New York, 1926, 1952 [London, 1929].

[42] See, besides Mr Hill's aforementioned book, Mr Charles George's 'English Calvinist Opinion on Usury, 1600–1640', *Journal of the History of Ideas*, XVIII, No. 4, 455–74.

[43] The fact that there were not only early Calvinists but seventeenth-century Calvinists who were anti-capitalist does not, of course, invalidate this statement.

[44] *Op. cit.*, 437.

[45] *The Journal of Sir Simonds D'Ewes* (1942), 185. I have analysed D'Ewes's dilemma on pp. xli–ii.

King James I and Anglo-Scottish Unity

★

David Harris Willson

This paper was made possible by a research grant from the American Philosophical Society to which the author is happy to express his indebtedness. The paper was read on July 9th, 1957 at the Anglo-American Conference of Historians in London.

A FEW hours after Mary Queen of Scots gave birth to her only son she took the child in her arms, drew back the coverlet to show its face, and said to those about her: 'This is the son whom I hope shall first unite the two kingdoms of Scotland and England.' Thus from the moment of his birth Prince James, who became a king at the age of thirteen months, embodied the Scottish hope that the house of Stuart would follow the house of Tudor upon the English throne. He was taught from childhood to regard the union of the Crowns as the primary goal of his policy and to value at its proper worth the great prize that might one day be his. Not that he required much instruction along these lines. As he became aware of the dangers, the humiliations and the poverty of a Scottish ruler, he often looked wistfully across the Border to the wealth and tranquillity of England. 'Saint George surely rides upon a towardly riding horse,' he once wrote sadly, 'where I am daily bursten in daunting a wild, unruly colt.'[1] With all his soul he yearned for the English succession, and the history of his reign in Scotland prior to 1603 gives ample proof that the union of the Crowns was his constant preoccupation and that it came as the culmination of many years of thought and effort.

Yet to consider King James as merely a crafty politician grasping at a great prize is quite to misjudge his character. He was a man who could be fascinated by lofty ideals and sublime aspirations; and no ideal attracted him more strongly than that of unity, in the sense of universal agreement and concord. Of this worship of unity one could cite many examples. In 1583, at a time when the Scottish nobles were torn by something more than their normal feuds, he had voiced his youthful ambition to 'draw his nobility to unity and concord, and to be known to be a universal king, indifferent to them all'.[2] Throughout his life he placed great faith in leagues and alliances; and perhaps the most Olympian of all his dreams was that of uniting Protestants and Catholics once more in one universal Church. In his first speech to the English Parliament in 1604 he went out of his way to remind his hearers that Henry VII had united the houses of Lancaster and York and that he, as Henry's descendant, perpetuated that union. He often spoke of Henry as a symbol of union between England and Scotland, for Henry had arranged the marriage upon which Stuart claims to England rested. Henry had believed himself a descendant of King Arthur, proclaimed by legend the ruler of all Britain; and James also, before 1603, had called himself a new Arthur about to unite the kingdoms. Thus the union of the Crowns represented his greatest worldly ambition and also one of his great ideals.[3]

Let us follow his thinking one step further. The sense of glorious triumph and achievement, which followed his accession to the English throne, led him to regard that event as a step in the unfolding of some divine plan; and he considered himself the instrument through which God was promoting the union of the realms. He told the English Parliament that union with Scotland was a blessing 'which God hath in my person bestowed upon you ... Hath He not made us all in one island, compassed with one sea and of itself by nature indivisible? ... And now in the end and fullness of time united in my person, alike lineally descended of both the Crowns.' Again James spoke of 'that blessing which it hath pleased God to reserve to our person, namely the blessed union, or rather reuniting, of these two mighty, famous and ancient kingdoms'. Thus he believed that by some divine dispensation the union of the realms was inherent in him, complete and perfect in his royal person. 'What God hath conjoined let no man separate. I am the husband and all the whole isle is my lawful wife; I am the head and it is my body; I am the shepherd and it is my flock. I hope therefore that no man will think that I, a Christian King under the Gospel, should be a polygamist and husband to two wives; that I being the head should have a divided or monstrous body or that being the shepherd to so fair a flock should have my flock parted in two.'[4]

It is not surprising, therefore, that after the union of the Crowns James's mind turned at once to the establishment of a larger union, complete, indivisible and lasting. The scope of his thinking was indeed remarkable. He wished nothing less than a perfect incorporating union of the realms. He would have one people, alike in manners and institutions, united in one common allegiance and obedience to one king. He would have one system of law for both kingdoms, one Parliament, one faith, one baptism, one language, one monarchy under one imperial Crown. He told the Speaker of the House of Commons in 1604 that 'his wish above all things was, at his death, to leave one worship to God; one kingdom entirely governed; one uniformity in laws'.[5] The names of England and Scotland should disappear in the name of Britain; the Borders should be erased and become the middle shires; and these shires, since they were in the very midst of the realm, 'the navel or umbilic of both kingdoms', should be made as tranquil and law-abiding as any other part of his dominions.[6] When he came to England in 1603 he brought with him so many of his Scottish Privy Councillors that Scotland was all but denuded of a Government, and it was believed he might establish one single Council for both kingdoms. He considered the appointment of Archbishop Bancroft as primate of all Britain, which would have been a cruel blow to the Scots. He quickly issued a new coinage stamped with legends expressive of unity.[7] Indeed, if King James had had his way, he would have established a union far more perfect than was achieved in 1707. The intensity and devotion with which he fought for union and the tenacity with which he clung to his purpose are also remarkable. 'We know'—so runs a State paper—'that the King doth passionately affect the perfect uniting of both the realms.' And Robert Cecil spoke of the union as 'that work which is so much desired by his Majesty'.[8] Union was the King's own policy, for which he received little encouragement from others. Yet by sheer determination and strength of will he drove the reluctant statesmen and Members of Parliament of both nations to concentrate for years upon a project which most of them regarded with marked distaste.

The King had other motives besides that of fulfilling the will of God. He was greatly impressed by the increased strength and security which would come to both nations through closer union. He was sincerely anxious to draw the two peoples into one. Now that they were 'joined together and under one head', he wrote in 1603, 'as they have been of long time past in one religion and language, and one common habitation in one island disjoined from the great Continent of the world, our princely care must be extended to see them join and coalesce together in a sincere and perfect union, and, as two twins bred in one belly, love one another as no more two but one estate'.[9] The Englishman 'that doth not

45

love a Scotchman as his brother, or the Scotchman that loves not an Englishman as his brother, is a traitor to God and to the King'.[10] And James would be alike to both in utter impartiality. He also entertained less lofty motives. A perfect union, he wrote to the Scottish Privy Council, would augment the grandeur and strength of his estate. It would bring honour and reputation to his name to have it effected in his time.[11] Above all, it would solidify the allegiance owed to him by his subjects. In 1604 he asked the Commons for an Act declaring that the two peoples 'are now, by the great blessing of God, and to the perpetual weal of both the nations, [united] under one allegiance and loyal subjection, in me and my person, to my person and my posterity for ever; and that thereby, that which accresceth to me and mine, and to the weal and strength of the subjects of both countries, may be rightly conceived and [clearly] understood by all men.'[12]

Had the King lived less in a world of his own, often remote from reality, he would have known that the two kingdoms were not ready for the close and perfect union he proposed. They were sharply distinct and separate in almost every way. The Reformation, it is true, had drawn them together, yet it might well be argued that in 1603 the Churches of the two kingdoms were not approaching each other but were moving apart. Contacts between the peoples were very limited; the Englishman and the Scot, far from loving each other at the King's command, were much more inclined to mutual dislike and suspicion; and the old hostility was not far below the surface. It flared out fiercely in Scotland in 1587 when Elizabeth laid violent hands upon a Scottish queen. The enemies of Mary Stuart as well as her friends in Scotland assumed that her execution would be followed by war with England; and there might well have been such a war had James VI been a less peaceful sovereign.[13] The Scots who came to England with the King in 1603 did not make a good impression. They were apt, in the first flush of their triumph, to be arrogant and pushing. James declared shortly after his arrival that he had done all in his power to prevent those 'offences or affronts which naturally do arise between several nations at their first joining in society and conversation'. He had commanded the great Scottish lords to keep a tight rein upon their servants. And yet, James added, 'we do hear of many insolencies reported to be committed by our nation of Scotland to our English subjects'.[14] The English, on their side, regarded the Scots with cordial dislike. There were disorders in Berwick, due to 'the inveterate passions of the two nations who, convening here daily, engender new occasions of distaste'.[15] There were quarrels in London; and, to James's horror, a number of duels were fought between Englishmen and Scots.

The Scottish courtiers who surrounded the King fell into two groups. The first consisted of a handful of councillors and favourites, the trusted advisers or the intimate companions of the King: George Home, Earl of Dunbar, the King's principal Minister for Scottish affairs, who for a time was Chancellor of the Exchequer and Master of the Wardrobe in England; Edward Bruce, lay Abbot of Kinloss, a judge in Scotland, whom James made Master of the Rolls; Ludovick Stuart, Duke of Lennox, outranking all the English nobility; John Gordon, made Dean of Sarum as a reward for his writings in praise of union; Sir Thomas Erskine, later Earl of Kellie, Captain of the Guard and Groom of the Stole; Sir John Ramsay, Earl of Holderness, who when he sulked in France in 1620 was wooed to England once more by a royal gift of seven thousand pounds. To these, among others, should be added the numerous Murrays, including John Murray, Groom of the Bedchamber, so potent a favourite that he was able to bring to the King's attention the suits of the Scottish officials in Edinburgh. The marked deference paid to him by the greatest men in England indicates what it meant to be a Scottish favourite of the King.[16] Not many of the Scots held high office; but they easily obtained pensions, grants and gifts of land and money, and they held those coveted places in the Bedchamber and in the Privy Chamber which brought them into daily contact with the King. Hence they had opportunity to solicit patronage for others as well as for themselves. The great majority of the suitors who thronged the Court, knowing that they could not hope to obtain an audience with the sovereign, turned to great courtiers as intermediaries who had the power to bring requests for patronage to the King's attention. For such assistance suitors were ready to pay handsomely; and there is no doubt that the Scots reaped a golden harvest.

Competition at Court for privilege and office of all kinds was constant and furious. The easy success of the Scots, who were new-comers in a market already overcrowded, aroused the bitter jealousy of the English courtiers, especially when a Scot received an office taken from an Englishman. Sir John Stanhope, the Vice-Chamberlain, for example, seldom came to Court after James told him to his face that he 'could not be at quiet' until he had bestowed his office upon a certain Scot. 'Many such like wrestlings there are with the old servants, tho' most of them carry a certain show of contentment and conformity to the King's pleasure.'[17] This jealousy of the Scots was at first a courtiers' quarrel, but it broadened into a national grievance, with sharp repercussions in Parliament, as the excessive generosity of the King and the empty state of the Exchequer became generally known.

Below these councillors and favourites there was a larger group of Scots who held minor positions about the Court, men such as Alexander Douglas, Keeper of the Council Chamber; or David Ramsay, Clockmaker Extraordinary to the King; or Abraham Abercromy, Sadler to the Prince; or Sir Patrick Home, Governor of the Poor Knights at Windsor; or Sir James Sandilands, Gentleman Usher of the Privy Chamber, who obtained a grant of old debts which proved to be much more lucrative than had been supposed; or Thomas Reid, Latin Secretary; or Sir William Stewart, Master of his Majesty's Bears, Bulls and Bandogs. These men were not naturalized by Parliament, as were the great favourites, but they could obtain letters patent of denization rather easily. The King 'was generous, and the right could sometimes be purchased. Thus Francis Bothwell, a cup-bearer to the King, was given a grant in 1604 to compound with thirty aliens for letters of denization.[18] In exploiting his privilege he doubtless turned first to his own countrymen. There were few Scots in England outside the Court. James attempted to keep undesirables from leaving Scotland and to send them home if they came south. No Scot was to come to England in order to collect debts owing to him from the King, 'there being no sort of importunity more ungracious to his Majesty'.[19] Francis Bacon expressed the opinion in the Commons in 1607 that except for some persons of quality about the King and some other inferior people depending upon them, the number of Scottish families resident in England was extremely small.[20] There was a handful of Scots in the English Church and a handful at the universities. But intermarriage was largely confined to a few great matches at Court, and the mingling of the nations had scarcely begun.

When James first came to England he assumed that the establishment of a perfect union would be a simple matter. He issued a proclamation affirming his intention to complete it quickly. He 'thought good to publish ... that with all convenient diligence ... he would make the union to be perfected. And in the meantime, he commanded all his subjects to hold both the two realms as presently united, and as one realm and kingdom, and the subjects of both the realms as one people, brethren and members of one body.'[21]

But he discovered shortly that the perfect union he had in mind would be a work of time; and gradually his noble dream began to fade away. Cecil advised him to begin cautiously by asking the Parliaments of both kingdoms to appoint commissioners to deliberate together upon measures for closer union.[22] Bacon wrote two pamphlets upon union, of which the first was a prudent warning to the King that great developments come slowly.[23] James's Scottish councillors, though prepared to obey his commands and to push his measures through the Scottish Parliament, were quite without enthusiasm, while the Kirk, fearful lest union would increase the influence of the English Church in Scotland, was actively hostile.[24]

Hence, when the English Parliament met early in 1604 it was presented with no comprehensive plan for immediate and perfect union, but with two more modest proposals. James asked, in the first place, for parliamentary sanction to assume the royal style of King of Great Britain.[25] Britain, he said, was the true and ancient name which God had given to the island, it was a symbol of the union already achieved and an omen of closer union to be wrought hereafter. How sublime was the King's self-confidence! The ruler of a small and remote kingdom, he had suddenly been exalted to the throne of a realm far wealthier, more potent and more advanced. Yet he was asking that realm to abandon its ancient name and to merge itself with a nation disliked and disregarded. The Commons refused to alter the name of England. To cross the rose with the thistle might well produce a monster. James had talked of the Ancient Britons, but had not the Ancient Britons been savages and worshippers of devils? The Commons feared that an alteration in the name of the kingdom would abrogate the laws and necessitate their re-enactment, an opinion in which the judges concurred despite great pressure from the

King.[26] Nor would the laws passed in the future by the English Parliament be binding upon all Britain. James appeared to accept this defeat, announced that he would not alter his style, and pressed for his second proposal, the appointment of commissioners of England to treat with commissioners of Scotland in preparing measures for closer union. The commissioners were voted though with obvious reluctance.

The session of 1604 had the unfortunate result of exasperating tempers all round. James sent a sharp letter to the Commons on May 1st. It was the letter of a disappointed man who believed he was advocating a sound and noble policy, only to have it frustrated by fools and knaves. The Commons, he wrote, 'transported with the curiosity of a few giddy heads, [appeared willing] to spit and blaspheme in God's face by preferring war to peace, trouble to quietness, hatred to love, weakness to strength and division to union; to sow the seeds of discord to all their posterities; to dishonour their King; to make both him and them a proverb of reproach in the mouths of all strangers, and of all enemies to this nation, and enviers of his greatness'.[27] He brought the session to an end in July with another angry speech. 'Look not that I will sing a palinode, whatsoever hath been spread to distaste this union. I am not ashamed of my project, neither have I deferred it out of a liking of the judges' reasons or yours.'[28] Animosities had been increased in both countries. Lord Balmerino, the Scottish Secretary, wrote to Cecil: 'No one will think that the present alteration of the name was worth so long and dangerous a dispute, which has exasperated some sores that the best physicians of both our States will be troubled to cure.'[29] And although the Scottish Parliament obediently passed an Act appointing commissioners, the Scots carefully safeguarded the 'fundamental laws, ancient privileges, offices, rights, dignities and liberties of this kingdom'. Their commissioners were expressly forbidden 'to treat, confer, deliberate, or do anything that in any manner of way may be hurtful or prejudicial to the religion presently professed in Scotland [or to the] Acts of Parliament made in favour of the same religion.'[30]

It became highly desirable, therefore, that the consultations of the English and Scottish commissioners, to be held in London in October 1604 should be as harmonious as possible; and if harmony was to be achieved the debates should be confined to matters which offered good hope of agreement. Once more the King reduced the scope of his policy. A month before the commissioners began their meeting he had been insisting that they discuss the union of the kingdoms into a single monarchy and the reduction of the two Parliaments to one.[31] But the topics debated by the commissioners were much less heroic; and the King was now content to say that a small beginning with the applause of all parties would give the impression that the union was making headway and would ease its future progress.[32] It is perhaps significant that just as the commissioners opened their debates, James assumed by proclamation the royal style of King of Great Britain, despite his promise to the Commons. He had a great desire, he said, to be called that which he was. It is possible that he made concessions regarding the extent of the commissioners' debates in return for the shadowy triumph of the change in his style.

The commissioners debated four things: repeal of hostile laws— that is, laws of each country aimed at the other; mutual naturalization; a commercial treaty looking towards free trade; and improvement of justice along the Border. These points became the programme of the Government and were offered to the English Parliament as a basis for legislation in 1606 and 1607.

The hostile laws were repealed without question, but the rest of the programme met with a subtle, intense and constant opposition. The articles concerning commerce were completely refused. English merchants and shipowners protested violently that they would be ruined by the competition of the Scots. This was rather absurd, yet it was true that the establishment of closer commercial ties between the two kingdoms presented numerous problems. The Scots enjoyed special rights in France, customs and taxes were lower in Scotland than in England, and the two countries were at such different levels of economic development that their interests often clashed.[33] The recommendations of the Government concerning trials on the Borders were also refused.[34] The King asked for extradition of criminals; but the Commons believed that an Englishman sent to Scotland for trial would be given short shrift by a Scots jury, and extradition was expressly forbidden.[35]

The debates on the naturalization of the Scots in England had a curious history. The commissioners had made a distinction between persons born in Scotland before James's accession to the English throne (the ante-nati) and persons born afterwards (the post-nati). The ante-nati were obviously aliens and the commissioners recommended that they be naturalized by statute with the reservation that they should not hold high office in England. The post-nati, on the other hand, since they had been born in the King's allegiance, were held to be naturalized by common law throughout his dominions and to be capable of holding any office. The Commons, however, refused to accept the ruling that the post-nati were naturalized by common law. In the remote past, it was argued, naturalization might have depended upon allegiance, but in modern times it should rest upon an Act of Parliament. Hence the Commons made no distinction between ante- and post-nati; both were aliens as things stood and both should be debarred from the full rights of English citizens. The Commons listed the places for which the Scots were to be eligible and those for which they were not. But how could the prerogative be bound where Parliament imposed restrictions? And how could Scots who drew revenues in England be held to the payment of English taxes and to the fulfilment of English service? The Commons moved slowly to the conclusion that there was but one way—to make the Scots subject to English law. It was to be a true subjection. The Scottish Parliament should disappear. So should the Scottish law; and the Great Seal of England should have equal authority in both kingdoms. These ideas appeared in the debates during March and April 1607. Doubtless they were expressed more sharply because Sir Edwin Sandys, an opponent of the Government, had replaced Bacon as the principal spokesman for the Commons in the long and elaborate conferences which were being held with the Lords. On April 28th Sandys moved that the work of the commissioners of 1604 be abandoned and that new commissioners be appointed to prepare what he called a perfect union.[36]

Here was more than a touch of irony. The Commons now talked of a perfect union, while the King was committed to the imperfect union of the commissioners. James's behaviour in the early part of the session had been quite correct; and on March 31st he had pleaded the cause of union in an eloquent and persuasive speech, one of the best he ever delivered in Parliament. But when Sandys moved for new commissioners the King lost his temper, accused the Commons of insincerity and berated them in violent terms. A deadlock ensued and Parliament concluded nothing, to the King's great annoyance.[37]

In August 1607, after the English Commons had been prorogued, the Scottish Parliament passed an Act which followed in most respects the proposals of the commissioners of 1604. This Act, however, was made conditional upon the passage of similar legislation in England and hence most of it fell to the ground.[38]

Rebuffed by the English Commons, James fell back upon the law. He knew that the judges believed that the Scottish post-nati were naturalized in England by common law; and he resolved to obtain a formal ruling on this important point. The ground was carefully prepared by the Council and by the King's legal advisers, with the assistance of Lord Kinloss, the Scot whom James had made Master of the Rolls.[39] A collusive suit involving an infant, Robert Colvill, born in Edinburgh in 1605, was made to turn upon whether the child was an alien or a citizen of England. The judges declared that Colvill was a natural subject of the English King.

'I found the case to be rare,' wrote Lord Chancellor Ellesmere, 'and the matter of great import and consequence, as being a special and principal part of the blessed and happy union of Great Britain.'[40] The decision was indeed a royal victory; but it meant that James could hardly hope to carry the cause of union any further through parliamentary action. He had defied the Commons after the session of 1604 and now he had defied them again. He had hastened, as Bacon feared,[41] to a mixture of both kingdoms faster than policy would conveniently bear. He had permitted his reckless generosity to his Scottish favourites to poison the first contact of the two peoples at the English Court. Henceforth for many years progress towards closer union came less from the actions of the King than from the natural consequences of the union of the Crowns. Scotland ceased after 1603 to have a foreign policy of her own, for the foreign policy of Great Britain was now determined in London. It was possible at last to begin a true pacification of the Border. King James did not solve the problem; but he subjected the Border to a long period of severe and salutary discipline. The union of the Crowns also increased his power in Scotland, and to that country he gave a strong and vigorous administration, dictated, I believe, in part by a desire to make Scotland an equal partner with England in some union of the future. The future was James's justification. Most of his dreams faded away into nothingness, but his dream of the union of his kingdoms was in time to be fulfilled.

[1] D. H. Willson, *King James VI and I*, London, 1956, 13, 138, 449, 452.

[2] *Cal. S. P. Scottish, 1581–3*, 523.

[3] D. H. Willson, *King James VI and I*, 249–50.

[4] C. H. McIlwain (ed.), *The Political Works of James I*, Cambridge, Mass., 1918 [Oxford, 1918], 271–3. A proclamation concerning the royal style, October 20th, 1604, printed in J. R. Tanner (ed.), *Constitutional Documents of the Reign of James I*, Cambridge, England, 1930, 32.

[5] *Commons Journals*, I, 171.

[6] McIlwain, *Political Works of James I*, 298.

[7] T. Rymer and R. Sanderson (eds.), *Foedera, Conventiones, Literae ...*, London, 1704–32. 20 vols., XVI, 605–06.

[8] S. P. Domestic, 14/10A: 16; 14/7: 85.

[9] *Letters to King James the Sixth from the Queen, Prince Henry, Prince Charles ...*, Maitland Club, No. 35, Edinburgh, 1835, lv.

[10] Speech of King James to the House of Commons, July 7th, 1604, S. P. Domestic, 14/8: 93.

[11] *Letters to King James the Sixth ...*, Maitland Club, No. 35, lv.

[12] *C. J.*, I, 180.

[13] D. H. Willson, *King James VI and I*, 74, 79–80.

[14] Proclamation for Concord between Englishmen and Scots, July 8th, 1603, Rymer, *Foedera*, XVI, 526.

[15] John Crane to Cecil, January 10th, 1604, *Cal. Hatfield House MSS.*, XVI, 4.

[16] The Denmilne MSS. in the National Library of Scotland contain a large collection of John Murray's correspondence. In 1624 he became the Earl of Annandale.

[17] E. Sawyer (ed.), Sir Ralph Winwood, *Memorials of Affairs of State ...*, London, 1725. 3 vols., II, 57.

[18] S. P., 38/7 (Docquet Book, under dates of May 4th and June 10th, 1604).

[19] *Reg. P. C. Scotland, 1613–1616*, 408.

[20] James Spedding, *The Letters and Life of Francis Bacon*, London, 1861–74. 7 vols., III, 311.

[21] Proclamation for the Union of the Kingdoms of England and Scotland, May 19th, 1603, Rymer, *Foedera*, XVI, 506–7.

[22] S. R. Gardiner, *History of England ...*, London, 1883–4. 10 vols., I, 177.

[23] *A Brief Discourse touching the Happy Union of the Kingdoms of England and Scotland*, Spedding, III, 90–9.

[24] Lord Balmerino, Secretary of Scotland, to Cecil, May 14th, 1604, *Cal. Hatfield House MSS.*, XVI, 98. McIlwain, *Political Works of James I*, 301. Thomas Thomson (ed.), David Calderwood, *History of the Kirk of Scotland*, Wodrow Soc., Edinburgh, 1842–9. 8 vols., VI, 247, 257.

[25] S. T. Bindoff, 'The Stuarts and their Style', *English Historical Review*, LX, 192–216.

[26] King James to Cecil, April 18th [?], 1604, S. P. Domestic, 14/7: 38. Cecil to Sir James Elphinstone, April 28th, 1604, S. P. Domestic, 14/7: 85.

[27] *C. J.*, I, 193–4.

[28] Speech of King James to the House of Commons, July 7th, 1604, S. P. Domestic, 14/8: 93.

[29] Lord Balmerino, Secretary of Scotland, to Cecil, May 14th, 1604, *Cal. Hatfield House MSS.*, XVI, 98.

[30] *Acts of the Parliaments of Scotland*, IV, 263–4.

[31] Heads proposed by the King to be debated by the commissioners for union, September 16th, 1604, S. P. Domestic, 14/9A: 35.

[32] King James to Cecil, November 22nd, 1604, *Cal. Hatfield House MSS.*, XVI, 363.

[33] Theodora Keith, *Commercial Relations of England and Scotland 1603–1707*, Cambridge, England, 1910, 4, 10–16, 22–4.

[34] The commissioners had left the question of justice along the Border to the consideration of the two Parliaments, but, after the English Parliament opened, the Government had come forward with specific recommendations.

[35] The Scots in reply prohibited the extradition of their countrymen for trial in England. *Acts of the Parliaments of Scotland*, IV, 368.

[36] *C. J.*, I, 364, 1035–6. D. H. Willson (ed.), *Parliamentary Diary of Robert Bowyer*, Minneapolis, 1931 [Oxford, 1931], 255–61.

[37] McIlwain, *Political Works of James I*, 290–9. *C. J.*, I, 366–8.

[38] *Acts of the Parliaments of Scotland*, IV, 366–71.

[39] The Case of the Post-Nati, *c.* October 1607. I wish to thank Mr D. McN. Lockie for his kindness in permitting me to examine this item in the page proof of a forthcoming volume of the Calendars of the Hatfield House MSS.

[40] Quoted in W. S. Holdsworth, *A History of English Law*, London, 1922–6. 9 vols., IX, 79.

[41] Spedding, III, 77.

The Procedure of the House of Commons against Patents and Monopolies, 1621–1624

★

Elizabeth Read Foster

IN 1621 and 1624 the House of Commons conducted an exhaustive examination of the King's grants of monopolies and patents.[1] It was Sir Edward Coke, 'Captain Coke' as James called him, 'the darling of the Parliament', who presided over the investigation and steered it through precarious legal shoals. His careful work as chairman of the Committee for Grievances in both 1621 and 1624 adds a revealing chapter to a tempestuous life;[2] and the investigation as a whole gives many interesting clues to the intricacies of the political situation. It shows also the way in which the House of Commons attacked grievances, evolving new ways of procedure or stretching older ones to meet the new situations which arose.

A monopoly, to follow Coke's definition, was 'an institution or allowance by the King by his grant, commission or otherwise, to any person or persons, bodies politic or corporate of or for the sole buying, selling, making, working or using of anything whereby any person or persons, bodies politic or corporate are sought to be restrained of any freedom or liberty that they had before, or hindered in their lawful trade'.[3] The Commons had complained of monopoly grants to Elizabeth. In 1603, in the famous case of *Darcy* v. *Allen*, the judges had declared them illegal, a statement which James reaffirmed in his Book of Bounty. This proclamation issued in 1610 as a measure of fiscal reform outlined James's proposed policy with regard to patents and monopolies. It listed two categories of grants which the King would not issue: (1) 'Things contrary to our Law', which were monopolies, and 'grants of the benefit of any penal laws, or of power to dispense with the law, or compound for the forfeiture'; and (2) grants which the King reserved to his own use.[4] But still the Crown issued grants in increasing numbers. They included not only monopoly grants for new inventions, for the introduction of new industry, or for the control of other industries like saltpetre and the printing of books long recognized as essential to the common welfare, but also grants of commercial privileges which involved dispensing with existing statutes, licences to perform functions belonging properly to the Government, and grants delegating to an individual the dispensing power of the Crown. In earlier times grants had been made by the Crown for the introduction of new industries, and the Crown itself had retained control of the industry. But by the end of the sixteenth century grants were made increasingly to private persons on their own application, and control had shifted from the Crown to the patentee, making possible grievous abuses.[5] The Privy Council had considered withdrawing some grants before Parliament met in 1621 to 'sweeten' the Commons for the subsidy. But nothing had come of this plan, largely through the influence of Buckingham.[6] Redress through the courts was slow and apt to be dangerous and unavailing if the grants were backed by King and favourite.[7] The quashing of an individual grant, as was clear from the case of *Darcy* v. *Allen,* would hardly stem the flood. It was increasingly evident that the only real hope for relief was in Parliament.

There were many men in the House of Commons, as there had been in the past, to complain of these grants. The country gentry had been particularly offended by Sir Giles Mompesson's grant of licensing inns.[8] The representatives of the outports had long been trying to break the monopoly of the London companies, and were glad to take advantage of prevailing winds to advance their own barks.[9] The common lawyers, who were so important in the House, were outraged at the grant of the right of dispensing with penal statutes.[10] Special interest groups in many trades lobbied for their own freedoms under the general head of 'grievances'. Personal animosities and the current distrust of the policies of the King and of his Ministers and favourites sharpened the complaints against Bacon, who had passed on the legality of many patents,[11] and perhaps against Buckingham, whose men held many of the grants and whose powerful backing had foiled earlier efforts at reform.[12]

There was much discontent, then, when the House assembled in 1621, and the Commons were ready to make the most of their historic position as 'representatives of the realm'. The decline of parliamentary government on the Continent, the precarious position of Protestantism, the failure of Court and Council to provide remedies, made them more than usually conscious of their own position and responsibilities.[13]

An awareness of public opinion runs through the debates of both sessions. In December 1621, although a message from the King about their privileges left the House dumbfounded, the House ordered Sir Edward Coke to give his report from the Committee of Grievances, 'that the Town may take notice, that we are again proceeding with Businesses'.[14] It was with their eyes on the 'country' that the Commons fought for their privileges. As William Mallory remarked: 'We are entrusted for our country. If we lose our privileges, we betray it; if we give way to this, we lose our privileges ... Let us not look upon ourselves only, but upon our posterity also ...'[15] Sir Henry Withrington reminded his colleagues of the imprisonment of Sir Edwin Sandys: 'I have heard this business hath been questioned three times before my coming up ... They told me in the country you are as like to speak as any man, take heed, you see what is become of Sir Edwin Sandys; you are brave fellows whilst you are together, but what becomes of you when you are parted ...'[16]

The debate on the subsidy shows a similar concern for the 'country'. In 1621 there was a good deal of discussion as to whether redress of grievances, Bills and subsidy should go together. Sir George More and Sir Edward Coke, both old Parliament men, agreed that grievances and supply were their chief business. 'Grievances and supply like twins, as Jacob and Esau, should go hand in hand.' 'It will be a good encouragement to us to enable us to give a good account of our doings to our country for whom we are entrusted.' When time grew short and it was apparent that Parliament would be adjourned before the grievances could all be prepared, Wentworth still fought for some Bills to go up to the King with the subsidy; for, 'He that thinks country men have no understanding or that they will be fed with words shall find himself much deceived ...'[17] Part of these debates followed what the Members loved to call the 'old parliamentary way' of bargaining subsidy for redress of grievances, a policy which they condemned roundly, but none the less astutely pursued just as they had under Elizabeth and in earlier times.[18] The Members of the Commons knew that the eyes of the country were upon them, that copies of their speeches circulated in manuscript or in printed form, that in ale-houses and in country seats talk was of Parliament matters.[19]

Both King and Commons felt tha ta Member of the House of Commons should inform the sovereign of affairs in his own shire and borough. In 1624 each Member was asked to report on recusants in his particular district.[20] As Glanville and Coke put it, the Commons represented not themselves, as did the Lords, but their counties and boroughs. To the Commons, the King, 'who would not have his subjects overburdened', referred the matter of subsidy 'because we know the countries best'.[21] Not only should a Member represent his 'country' to the King, but carry news of State back home as well. A petition concerning a collection for the Queen of Bohemia was read in the House of Commons in 1624, so that it could be generally known.[22]

But the Members of the House of Commons believed that they represented more than their own 'countries'. They stood, too, for the nation. 'Every man that sits have three powers, one of himself, and the country, and the whole realm after his coming.'[23] The whole of the House of Commons was greater than the sum of all its parts. It was more than an aggregation of local representatives, more than a body of informers, more than a group of messengers for the sovereign. It was the representative body of the realm. Because it was the representative body of the realm its privileges were important. Because it was the representative body of the realm it had its own peculiar function, as the Lords had theirs, and its own peculiar power.

From this concept, the Commons believed, proceeded not only their right but also their duty to inform the sovereign of grievances which afflicted his people. Grievances were no great matter to the Lords. 'The great ones are not acquainted with the caterpillars that annoy us.' Grievances, like the initiation of money bills, were the peculiar and important business of the Commons.[24] James himself recognized this ancient function of the Lower House in his opening speech in 1621, but he cautioned Members to consider only those grievances they brought with them from the country, not those which they found in town. The Speaker's conventional request for privileges on February 3rd included the plea that 'they may have Liberty to prefer their grievances to his Majesty and expect Reformation from his Justice'.[25] Coke elaborated this idea by maintaining that Parliaments should be summoned frequently to perform properly these essential duties. Members questioned his precedents but he defended his position with characteristic vigour.[26]

The Commons's function, they thought, was not only to consider and petition for redress of grievances and to present the griefs of their countries, but also to hear those griefs which men dared not present elsewhere. Parliament need fear neither prestige nor place. On April 26th, 1621 Sir John Jephson, Privy Councillor for Ireland, pictured the sorry state of Ireland to the House of Commons. Sir Edward Coke spoke in favour of an investigating committee, justifying first the Commons's jurisdiction over Irish affairs and secondly their consideration of such grievances. 'None of these main grievances durst any man complain of out of Parliament that are here now.' 'All grievances are not complained of out of Parliament. Who durst have spoken against those great ones we have talked of freely?' Who, indeed, especially since the Irish complaints were suspected to be a hit at Buckingham?[27] Much the same point arose in 1624 in connection with the Earl Marshal's court, when the abuses of the Heralds were discussed. 'Those things', commented Sir Edward Coke, who had reason to know, 'that have great authority are safest to be dealt withal by the Parliament.'[28]

Parliament, too, was the place where men turned increasingly for redress of grievances which could find no relief elsewhere. If the King and the Privy Council would not withdraw monopolies, if the processes of law were pitiful means to fight the increasing swarm of parasites that plagued the land, then the Commons would and could. By 1621 discontent was widespread and protests against the patentees came in from many parts of the country. By 1621, also, the Commons had developed a committee system and a parliamentary procedure capable of handling a complicated investigation and of seizing the initiative from King and Councillors who would rather have steered them rapidly to supply and away from grievances. In 1621 and 1624 the House of Commons had on its benches able men like Coke, Alford, Sandys, Wentworth, Pym, Glanville and Noy, articulate, bold, learned and experienced in the affairs of Parliament and law, who could take the leadership left vacant by the death of Salisbury and the negligence of a short-sighted King.[29]

On February 5th, 1621 Parliament's first day of actual business, the Members of the House of Commons fell to discussing the agenda for the session, and quickly divided their business into four main parts to be further debated at a committee of the whole House that afternoon: (1) the recurrent question of liberties and privileges, (2) the desirability of petitioning the King to execute the laws against recusants, (3) supply, and (4) grievances. The committee of the whole pursued these points in order, and it was not until February 19th that the matter of grievances engaged its full attention.[30]

Noy opened the discussion. Monopolies and the grant of powers to dispense with penal laws were, he said, the chief grounds of all grievances. Coke followed with a long speech, declaring all monopolies, all grants of dispensation from penal laws directly void in law.[31] These two speeches, introducing the Commons's investigation, might well have served also as conclusion and summary, for they state effectively and fully the attitude towards grievances which the House was to follow during both the sessions of 1621 and 1624. There was throughout an emphasis on patents, on monopoly grants, on grants of dispensations from penal laws, as the major grievances and the basic cause of many other evils. There was, too, always the effort to show that such grants were illegal, that the King had been misinformed in allowing them. If the King's counsel had misled him it was the Commons's task to show him where the error lay, to make known their findings, and in the light of them to appeal from the King ill-informed to the King better-informed.

There was no lack of material for them to consider. Complaints against the patents and monopolies poured into the House from all sides, for the streams of discontent found many channels. Privy Councillors and Government officials who sat in the House as elected Members, brought grievances to the floor.[32] Other Members of the House of Commons, true to their character as informers and 'general inquisitors', were eager with complaints. Some of them reflected local conditions, which the Members knew at first hand; some of them were 'notorious and known grievances', like the patent of inns and ale-houses, which would inevitably occur to the representative body of the realm. Sir Edward Coke spoke on February 22nd, 1621 of receiving 'complaints out of his own country' against the patent of ale-house recognizances. Savage, Mallett and Mallory brought in examples of Sir John Townsend's execution of the patent of concealments; and William Salisbury, who represented Merioneth, raised the question of concealed subsidies in Wales. Some Members had probably compiled lists of patents to be considered beforehand. Noy had prepared his opening speech well. Sir Edward Coke had taken part in the committee of judges which considered withdrawal of some grants before Parliament met, and Hakewill remarked on March 22nd that there were 'some Patents not yet named of greater consequence than any yet named'.[33]

On February 21st Sir Edward Sackville moved that the House send for Mr Sadler, Secretary to the Lord Privy Seal, who 'hath a note of all the Monopolies and suchlike grants, whereof he is collector and receiveth all the Benefit which comes to his Majesty'. He could therefore inform the House what monopolies there were, and what the King got from them. The House agreed and Sadler later appeared, bringing his book. Crew moved on May 17th, 1621 that all grievances collected in the last Parliament be considered and presented to the King together with those of the present session. In 1624 a similar motion was made: that the Committee of Grievances should consider patents condemned or questioned by the last Parliament. Rich extended the motion to include the grievances of 1610, and it was so ordered.[34] Such wholesale methods brought a great many patents and monopolies to the floor. Individual Members added particular grievances from day to day.[35]

How often these Members of Parliament were moved by their own initiative to present grievances, and how often they spoke as the representatives of special interests, it is difficult to say. Plenty of men outside the House of Commons, for one reason or another, were anxious to bring special patents to the floor and sought Members of the House to do this for them.[36] In some instances the process is quite clear. Thus, on April 17th, 1621, Mallory presented a petition from the company of Armourers against the patent of arms.[37] In other cases there is no mention of the method by which the petition was presented, and it probably in many instances came directly into the House or the Committee of Grievances without the special sponsorship of a Member of the House.

The interests of many petitioners are quite apparent from the petition itself. Thus the grant of privileges for making starch to Vaughan and his associates put other starch-makers out of business, and subjected them to the oppressions of the patentees who seized their stock, and fined them. Lobbyists for the Shrewsbury Drapers, hoping for a share of the export trade, repeatedly attempted to bring the exclusive patent of the French Company under attack.[38] But whether private gentlemen spoke for others or spoke for themselves only further research can reveal. John Lambe's statement, though obviously biased since he had been called into question by the Committee on Courts and was writing to the King, is interesting in this connection. 'The Complainants are underhand set on and countenanced by greater persons in this county that, through me, aim at your Majesty's Ecclesiastical jurisdiction ... '[39] Possibly there was more behind the petitions and the complaints of Members of the House against grievances of patents and monopolies than met the eye.

Privy Councillors, Government officials, Members of Parliament, private gentlemen, and 'lobbying' interests, eagerly supplied the House with grievances. General debate on seemingly unrelated subjects brought forth still more. On February 6th, 1621, in the debate on 'want of coin', Glanville analysed the causes of the scarcity. His reasons were various, but among them appeared the patent of the East India Company to transport silver. Spencer added the patent of gold lace, and Alford moved that a select committee examine 'all patents of that nature'. On February 26th the same question was raised again. Herrick mentioned as one of the causes of the decay of money, the patent of gold wire. Sandys, Coke, Phelips and others, questioned the patent of tobacco. The consideration of the depression in the cloth trade likewise involved grants, and brought the patent of Staplers, and the patent of dyestuffs under discussion.[40]

Bills also brought patents and monopoly grants to the agenda. Some, like the Bill presented by the grocers against the apothecaries, the Act against the patent of Welsh butter, the Bill to ratify the charter of the Goldsmiths' Company, may be regarded as another method of petitioning the House. The Bill for sea-marks, reported on March 9th, 1621, led to the order that the Committee of Grievances consider patents of the lighthouses of Dungeness and Winterton Ness.[41]

Some Bills, on the other hand, were more general in scope, and raised a larger issue where individual patents emerged indirectly. Thus, the debates in 1624 on the Bill of Monopolies bred a host of proposed exceptions, among them the question of the subpoena office. This point was debated on April 19th, and Coke finally moved and the House resolved that all patents mentioned in the Bill be 'seen and considered of, before anything be done'.[42] On April 28th, 1624 Noy's report of the Bill for Continuance and Repeal of Statutes had a similar effect. 'For either the law or the dispensation naught. And so to have it presented to the King.' Patents of dispensation were consequently ordered in to the Committee of Grievances.[43]

The examination of patents and monopolies in 1621 and 1624 came to be fairly stereotyped. A complaint, as we have seen, was presented either to the House or to one of its standing committees —in the case of patents and monopoly grants usually either to the Committee of Grievances, of which Sir Edward Coke was chairman, or to the Committee of Trade with Cranfield, who was also a Privy Councillor, as its chairman. Once the complaint came on to the agenda and had been accepted as worthy its consideration and proper to its work,[44] the committee (or the sub-committee as the case may be) warned the patentees to appear for a hearing and summoned witnesses on both sides. Either, with permission, might appear with or by counsel;[45] and this practice became so well established that several attorneys made it their special business to plead cases before the House.[46] The patent in question was called in, and any relevant documents necessary to a full investigation: the books and memoranda of the patentees, court records, or the accounts of Government officials. Often special groups or individuals interested in the recall of the patent supplied written affidavits of its ill effects.

The House was, then, exercising two distinct powers: that of summoning individuals to appear before it, and that of ordering in documents. Who could be and was summoned? By far the largest group were the patentees and men involved in some way in the complaints or petitions presented to the House.[47] Among them came officers of the Crown, such as the Lieutenant of the Tower, and Gibbs of the Bedchamber. Officers of the Crown were likewise called as witnesses, as Sadler, Secretary to the Lord Privy Seal.[48] The Commons attempted to summon witnesses and parties on both sides, and in cases involving the royal interest, arranged to hear the King's counsel.[49] In some cases the House actually 'sequestered' persons during the time of their examination.[50] It regarded refusal to obey a summons as 'contempt', and dispatched the Serjeant to fetch offenders guilty of repeated refusal.[51]

Patentees were usually ordered to bring their patents with them and any proclamations or commissions issued in support of the patent. This practice the King protested at the end of the session of 1624. 'You have a custom', he said, '(which I'll know whether it be agreeable to ancient usage or not) presently upon any complaint to send for the patent and to keep it with you ... When once ye have a patent, ye take it upon you to keep it from my patentees. You have nothing to do but to read it and see that it agree with the patent and then deliver it back to the patentees. And if you do not so, I must take a course it be done.'[52] 'No court', replied Sir Edward Coke, the next day in the House of Commons, 'doth judge on copies but on records, and therefore it is reason we should have the patents here brought to us.'[53] There was more than the inevitable lawyer's defence in Coke's statement, and there was more than idle protest in the King's remark. The two together may show much of the significance of the Commons's procedure and of the investigation as a whole. But the point for the moment is that James's statement was quite accurate as to fact. The Commons did call in patents, and did keep them while they were under consideration, which, with the amount of business before the Committee of Grievances, usually meant that they kept them a long time. In fact, the orders for the return of patents at the end of the session of 1624 seem to indicate that for that session, at least, they kept them during the whole session and did not ever return those which were condemned.[54] The calling in of the actual patent and its supporting proclamations and commissions was in effect, if the law be strictly read, a stay in the execution of the grant during the period of its consideration, for the patentees were not in possession of the legal authorization for their acts. The House also issued specific orders that patents should not be executed while they were under consideration, and that suits pending on them should be stayed.[55]

Account books and other documents relative to the patents and their execution, warrants, certificates and memoranda, were likewise ordered in, and in some cases these papers were seized.[56] In 1621 the King, possibly prompted by the company itself, attempted to withhold the books of the Merchant Adventurers from the Committee of Trade which had called for them. The House, partly at the instigation of the Cinque Ports, who held a brief against the company, raised the cry of breach of their liberties; but the question was pushed no further till 1624, when James compromised by allowing a committee of six to examine the books 'and pick out what was material to the business'.[57] To make its knowledge more complete the House, when necessary, searched court records and on occasion had them brought into the House.[58] Assuming, then, a sincere desire for a full investigation, the Commons had the necessary information at hand.

The Commons were not only quite conscious of the type of investigation they were thus able to conduct, but also explicit as to its nature. They insisted first that all valid complaints should be fully examined, and that both sides to a dispute should be heard. Where there were complainers, there were also defenders; and both were entitled to a hearing.[59] Defendants were not allowed written copies of the charges, but on one occasion at least (though it was not the case of a patent) provision was made that the charges should be specific, for 'no man is bound by the Law to answer to a general charge ... And therefore the honour and justice of the House to have the particulars set down.'[60] The King complained that the very name of patent had become odious to the Commons; patentees charged that the cards were stacked against them, and that they were not fully heard; but whatever the political motives that played into the matter, the constitutional and legal framework for an impartial examination was adequate.[61]

Actual procedure varied, of course, with the individual patent. In general, however, it was fairly uniform. A date was assigned for the hearing on each patent, and announced in advance, that the parties might be warned to appear and their counsel be prepared. The chairman of the committee probably led the questioning, though members were free to make remarks or interject questions of their own.[62] There was much discussion in both 1621 and 1624 of the power of the House to administer an oath and to examine upon oath, but it did not do so.[63] There were other means at hand for enforcing truthful statements; for as we have already seen the House heard both parties to a dispute, it searched records and examined corroborative evidence both oral and written. It punished witnesses for untrue statements, and delinquents only added contempt of the House to their other sins if caught in a falsehood.[64]

The examination may, for the sake of clarity, be divided into two parts: the first concerned the nature of the grant itself, the type of grant and its provisions, to what alleged purpose granted, and to whom; the second concerned the consequences of the grant, how executed, and the actual effect of its execution. The nature of the grant was often discovered by a reading of the patent itself, and by questioning the patentees.[65] Their counsel, their opponents' counsel, and Members of the House, like Noy, Coke or the Solicitor, who were trained in the law, interpreted the provisions. The patentees and their counsel were likewise asked to whom the patent had been granted, who procured it and who shared in it.[66] Sources of information on the consequences of the grant, its execution and its effect, were wider. Again the provisions, proclamations and commissions of the patent itself were consulted; again the patentees and their counsel were questioned. But their answers were weighed with the great body of evidence brought in by their opponents. It was against the execution that complaints were most readily lodged. Painters and bookbinders, for example, testified that the patent of gold foliate had raised its price and that far from conserving bullion, as it had promised, had actually spent it. Fishmongers claimed that Wigmore's patent raised the price of fish, and they were enjoined by the committee to set down the price of fish before the patent, and the quantity of fish brought in before and since.[67]

Such testimony came, as we have suggested, from various sources. The committee had plenty of material to work on. Those who attacked grants and those who defended them both strove to make a strong case, and presented their evidence in many ways. Oral testimony came from patentees and their counsel, complainers, petitioners and their counsel, and witnesses presented or called on both sides.[68] Written testimony was admitted in petitions and certificates.[69] Collateral and corroborative evidence appeared in the patents themselves, in proclamations and commissions issued for their execution, in memoranda of patentees, in State documents and court records.[70]

Members of the House of Commons, though sometimes called as formal witnesses, also testified voluntarily and informally.[71] Many had their own special interests to serve in so doing, such as Sandys of the Virginia Company who attacked the patent of tobacco.[72] Others spoke from more general concern or class interest, such as the country gentlemen who pointed out that

Mompesson's patent threatened the authority of justices of the peace. With the same Members of the House who sat as an investigating committee actively participating in gathering the case against the patentees, the King's charge of partiality was from the legal point of view quite justified.[73] Men like Sandys acted at once as witnesses and judges in their own case. Perhaps the House of Commons as a whole did much the same thing. Certainly though it acted within a framework of just procedure, it was also a political body, and the temper of that body was all too clear.

The political element in the investigation stands out perhaps most sharply in the proposed attack on the referees. The King had provided that all proposed grants be referred to certain of his Privy Councillors to be certified as legal and as 'convenient' to his subjects.[74] The House of Commons in examining patents and monopoly grants called for the names of these referees.[75] It was natural, of course, that a fact-finding body should pursue this policy; but the House had other motives as well. The whole attack on the royal grants was carefully couched in terms of respect for the King and the prerogative. Naming the referee shifted responsibility for grievous grants from the King, as James, his Councillors and the Commons all vigorously insisted.[76] Referees were also convenient scapegoats for patentees themselves. Some professed to know very little about the certification of the grants they held, but others sought refuge from the Commons's attack in the fact that the King's counsel had approved their projects. Thus, winds blew upon the referees from both sides. It was suggested in the House that they be called to account for their misdeeds, and punished. Their names were brought out in nearly every patent examination, but nothing ever came of the plans for dealing with them.[77]

Stronger currents may have been blowing. The complete omission of the referees' names in the conference with the Lords on Mompesson's patents, despite instruction from the Commons to the contrary, seems suspicious. Members of the Commons's committee were directly charged with having faltered from fear.[78] Perhaps there was more at stake than individual patentees or individual grants. The Lord Chancellor's name appears again and again as referee, and the Lord Chancellor's impeachment came in 1621. Buckingham's name, though rarely mentioned in the House, could easily have been spelled out as one of the greatest of all 'procurers'; and the drive against Buckingham was gathering force even now.

The attack on referees involved other issues as well. On March 21st, 1621 Coke reported Flood's patent of engrossing wills from the Committee of Grievances. In the debate that followed Noy criticized the patent vigorously, declaring it to be against the law and liberty of the people. He brushed aside Flood's defence that it had been certified by two great men (Bacon and Yelverton): 'I say if the certificates of two men shall make a law, we need not a Parliament. In some records I find that certain men made ordinance (5 E.2 New Ordinances) of which many might be good, but they were questioned at the Parliament at York where it was declared that they were made against the royalty and liberty of the realm. (15 E.2 *Revocatio novarum Ordinationum.*) For laws cannot be made but by a general consent which cannot be had but in a Parliament.' [79] Noy here posed the question which James himself had raised and was to raise again in 1624. It was a question implied in the whole attack on the referees, for the attack on referees, however much personalities played into it and political issues, was an attack on the legality of the King's grants.

How far, actually, did the Commons go, and to what purpose had been all their investigation, their calling of witnesses, their search of records and their examination of patentees and their papers? The committees acted as fact-finding bodies, but they did not rest content with this role. Throughout the examinations there was discussion. Lawyers and laymen alike commented on the facts discovered, laymen expounding the inconveniences which followed from the grants in question, the dangers to the commonweal, and lawyers interpreting those inconveniences in legal terms. Having investigated and debated, the committee summed up its findings in a 'judgment' of the patent, voting it to be 'inconvenient' or a 'grievance in creation', or a 'grievance in execution', or both. The decision of the committee was reported back to the House, usually by its chairman, who also carried the chief responsibility of defending its stand in the debate which followed. In every case of which we have record the House confirmed the report of its committee, and the patent then stood officially 'condemned'.

The legal reasons which the House of Commons and its committees found for condemning patents and grants they had examined were various and drawn from many sources. One of the simplest cases against a royal grant was that it was a monopoly. Monopolies were in general conceded to be illegal. They were held to run counter to the ruling principle at common law, which, as interpreted in the early seventeenth century, guaranteed freedom of enterprise.[80] Exceptions were made in two instances: when the monopoly was for a new invention, or when it was necessary for the good of the State. The term 'invention' included both originator and importer. It did not necessarily include improver.[81] The second exception admitted the power of the King or Parliament to restrict freedom of enterprise and the liberties of the subject for the good of the State.[82]

Mansell's patent for the sole manufacture and sale of glass was a monopoly involving both these exceptions. It had been granted as a privilege for what purported to be a new process of glass-making, which was also to be of benefit to the commonwealth by using less wood for fuel than the old process. To upset such a grant legally it was necessary to refute both these claims, and it was precisely this which the Commons undertook to do in 1621. The making of glass was not, they determined from the evidence they had heard, a new invention. Far from promoting the general welfare, the patent was detrimental to it. It did not conserve wood; and it created the three conditions which the judges in 1603 had found to be incident to a monopoly:[83] it raised prices, lowered quality and displaced workmen from their lawful trades. The Commons thus established their case, to their own satisfaction, and voted the patent a grievance in creation.[84]

A second ground against a royal grant was that it authorized a subject to dispense with a penal law. Such transference of prerogative power to an individual was, according to common law precedent, illegal. Blundell's patent of pedlars was found, according to the evidence accepted by the House of Commons, to grant the patentee power to dispense with the Statute of 39 Eliz. concerning rogues and vagabonds; and it was consequently judged to be against the law and a grievance in creation.[85] Mompesson's patent for the licensing of inns was found to empower the patentees to dispense with the Statutes of 13 Rich. II and 4 H. IV, and was judged to be against the law and a grievance in creation.[86]

The execution of patents was likewise condemned on the ground either that the provision for execution was in itself illegal or that illegal acts were committed in carrying out the provisions. The difficulty arose because the patentees were entrusted with the enforcement of their own grants, and, in some instances, empowered by a commission or proclamation to seize the goods of offenders, to compound with them or to fine and imprison.[87] Petitioners maintained that the patentees of gold foliate threatened those who complained about the quality of the product, sued one who made better foliate than they, imprisoned him and seized his goods, only releasing him on condition that he would work for them.[88] The Commons heartily condemned such means of enforcement. 'No proclamation ought to go out for any private cause',[89] Coke said. Imprisonment and seizure of goods by virtue of a patent were unlawful. Hence, patents executed in this way were illegal, and a grievance in execution.

The line between the execution of a patent and the patent itself was not always clearly drawn, nor were the Commons wholly consistent in making this distinction. But the essential point is that they considered both execution and patent in legal terms and condemned them on legal grounds. Patents were condemned in creation because the grant itself had been issued contrary to the King's intentions,[90] because it ran counter to precedent,[91] because it was contrary to various aspects of the common law. They were condemned in execution if illegal acts were committed in their enforcement, or if the provision for enforcement was in itself illegal and tended to the subversion of justice.[92]

In declaring it to be illegal the Commons made their strongest case against a patent. But when they could not clearly do this they might judge it 'inconvenient', either in creation or execution, or both. They defined as 'inconvenient' a grant which, though clearly obnoxious or injurious to the commonwealth, could not be proved definitely illegal. The distinction was not, however, always clear; and the Commons themselves were only too eager to blur the line between grants which were inconvenient and those which were illegal. 'Inconvenience' might mean various things. The King had a right to make certain grants; but if these infringed the right and inheritance of the subject they could be condemned. The question, then, whether a patent was illegal or inconvenient was the question whether the actual rights of the subject had been infringed, or merely the best interests of the commonwealth impaired.[93] The Commons, in considering these matters of inconvenience and illegality, were essentially concerned with defining the rights of the subject, and their definition obviously tended to be quite broad. The King protested the procedure in 1621 and again in 1624. 'I am sure you will not take upon you to be judge of my seal. It is not enough for me if some of your doctors of law stand up and say this patent is against the law. I must for the law rely upon my learned counsel and upon my judges, whether the patent be in itself good by law or not. But if there fall out any inconvenience in the execution of it, you may complain of it ...'[94]

The Commons had, in fact, evolved out of the old private Bill procedure a method of investigation and of passing judgment very like a court procedure.[95] There is some evidence that patentees feared the House of Commons.[96] By answering its summons and pleading their cases before it they tacitly acknowledged its jurisdiction. In some instances they even surrendered their patents;[97] and the House attempted to enforce its judgment by punishing 'projectors'[98] and cancelling patents.[99]

The House of Commons claimed and was generally recognized to be a court with jurisdiction over its own Members, over its privileges and over offences against the House.[100] It claimed sole jurisdiction in these areas, though it had still to gain its point with the King as the arrest of Members bore witness. But it was also reaching out for wider powers, as is clear from its handling of impeachment cases and the famous Floyd affair.[101] In the impeachment of Mompesson and Michell the Commons insisted that the charges they sent up to the Lords be fully proved, and that the judgment be based upon the charges presented. They were raising their role from mere informers to partakers in the act of judicature itself.[102]

In the consideration of patents and monopolies they took an even clearer stand. They investigated facts, pronounced a judgment and made some efforts to execute that judgment. Patents and monopolies could not be construed as offences against the House. For their jurisdiction in this field the Commons relied on the idea that grievances were the special province of the representatives of the realm.[103]

Rightly or wrongly the Commons laid claim to power to investigate and condemn the King's patents. But, as in Floyd's case, they did not insist on all the logical implications of their claims. Sir Edward Coke protested the King's criticism of the procedure of condemning patents. Coke asserted the Commons's right to call in and examine the original patents. But even Coke recommended in 1624 that the condemned patents be turned over to the King's Council 'with a request that they may be proceeded against'.[104]

Neither he nor the other Members of the House were willing to leave the patents to the Commons's condemnation alone. When, then, by vote of the House a patent stood officially condemned as an 'inconvenience' or 'grievance' in the explicit and legal sense of the word,[105] the House of Commons proceeded in several ways. In some cases it drew up a special Bill to deal with a special patent, like the Bill to regulate lighthouses,[106] thus remedying the situation in the conventional parliamentary way.

The larger group of patents was included in a general petition of grievances presented to the King at the end of the session of 1624 by the House of Commons without the assistance of the House of Lords. This, too, was the old parliamentary way, but the petition had been drawn up with special care. It included only those 'grievances' investigated by the Commons and shown to be 'grievances' in the technical sense of the word—'grievances' because they were against the law and infringed the rights of the subject.[107] The Commons were consistent throughout. They had based their condemnation of patents on common law precedent. They petitioned the King on the same basis. Their petition of grievances in 1624 was far more than a petition of grace. It was more nearly the kind of petition they were to use in 1628. It was more nearly a petition of right.[108]

As the King protested the Commons's procedure against his grants, so, too, could he protest and with justice the great Statute of Monopolies which emerged from the sessions of 1624 as Parliament's third method of dealing with the King's grants. The Statute of Monopolies was, as Dr McIlwain has sagely pointed out, the first statutory invasion of the prerogative.[109] But it is significant of the House of Commons's political thought, of its medieval inheritance and of its legal personnel, that it was framed as a declaratory Act. The purpose of the Statute was not to introduce new law but simply to fix what the Commons regarded as the proper interpretation of the common law in its application to patents and monopolies. It declared what the law was in general, as they had declared it in the particular instances raised by the patents they condemned.[110] As a declaratory Act the Statute, though certainly it limited the prerogative, cannot accurately be described as an attack upon it. It affected the prerogative because it gave a statutory definition to the subject's interest in royal grants, and thus set a statutory limit to the area in which the prerogative operated.

The preparation of the Bill of Monopolies in 1621 and 1624 was regarded by the Commons as not only important but, like a money Bill, their own particular province. They felt slighted in 1621 when the Lords rejected their Bill and proposed a conference to draw a new one. 'The Lords have no inconvenience by monopolies, but the poor cedars and shrubs have danger of it.'[111] Parliament was adjourned before the two Houses could agree. In 1624 the Commons tried again and this time sent their Bill to the Lords with special recommendation and a large delegation of Members, 'for the Speaker saith a good Bill in Queen Elizabeth's time miscarried in the Upper House, because they supposed it was not much favoured below, having no more attendance'.[112] The Lords, after conference with the Commons, raised seventeen exceptions. In addition, Coke reported, they 'will not consent to have the Bill to touch or concern all, but only those that are hereafter to be granted, not those patents which are in present execution, but to reserve them for their time only and to make sure against any in future ...' The Commons were disappointed, but, as Coke advised, willing to compromise to save the Bill.[113] Thus altered, it finally passed both Houses, and, accepted by the King at the end of the session, became law.[114]

To summarize, then, the House of Commons in 1621 and 1624 undertook the investigation of patents and monopolies because there was no adequate remedy elsewhere. Less and less, men turned to the Privy Council for redress of grievances, partly because the very men who sat there had obtained or passed the grants and partly because the Privy Council seemed less and less to represent the public interest. Progress in the courts was slow. Thus circumstances added stature to the House of Commons's traditional role as petitioners for redress of grievances. The development of their procedure, the evolution of the committee system, the emergence of sound leadership, equipped the Commons to meet their new responsibilities effectively. Out of the old private Bill procedure and the methods used in the Committee of Elections, they evolved an interesting technique of investigation and judgment. They even made some attempt to execute their judgments. But at the same time they realized that their action could not stand alone, that only the King, the Council or the courts could finally void a royal grant.

To this end they prepared their petition of grievances. In the petition they included only those grants which had been investigated and condemned. Sir Edward Coke felt that a patent so condemned in Parliament could not be asked for again. This was the significance of the Commons's procedure against it. This was the significance of their petition to the King.[115] It was, they hoped, a compelling statement, for it came from the representative body of the realm. Grievances were, they thought, their special business. The petition assumed added importance when the Lords so amended the Bill of Monopolies that it would not void past grants. Thus all the methods which the Commons had used against patents and monopolies had their place: investigation and condemnation, the passing of Bills to void individual grants, petition (to withdraw condemned patents), and the passing of the Statute of Monopolies which prohibited such grants in the future and provided that they should be tried in the common law courts.

The Privy Council withdrew a large number of grants after Parliament adjourned.[116] The great Statute of Monopolies had been passed. So far the efforts of the House of Commons were successful. They had, moreover, evolved a technique of investigation of royal administration which would prove valuable in years to come. The revival of impeachment, which stemmed directly from the monopoly investigation, was to be used again with telling effect; and the 'country' could not be unaware that when other remedies had failed the Commons had forced redress of grievances.

---

[1] The sources for the Parliament of 1624 parallel those of 1621. The most valuable of these are the manuscript accounts, which I have used through the courtesy of Wallace Notestein and Hartley Simpson. This collection consists of ten accounts of 1624: (1) the diary of Edward Nicholas, hereafter referred to as *Nicholas*; (2) the diary of John Pym, hereafter called *Pym*; (3) an anonymous diary (hereafter called *Gurney*) found among the Gurney papers at Keswick Hall, Norfolk, but since purchased by Harvard University; (4) the diary of Sir Walter Erle, hereafter called *Erle*; (5) the

diary of Sir Thomas Holland, hereafter called *Holland*; (6) the diary of John Holles, hereafter called *Holles*; (7) D'Ewes's *Journal*, hereafter called *Harl. 159*; (8) an account of two meetings of the Committee of Courts of Justice in the *Book of Committees* (May 7th and May 10th, Lords MSS., this is part of the same manuscript published in *Commons Debates 1621*, VOL. VI); (9) the 'Braye Manuscript' in the possession of Lord Braye at Stanford Hall (*Historical Manuscripts Commission*, Tenth Report, Appendix VI), a journal drawn up by John Brown who became Clerk of Parliament in 1640, almost identical with the *Commons Journal* with some few corrections and additions; (10) Rawlinson D723, a collection of 'separates', February 19th–February 24th, with some account of February 23rd. In direct quotations I have modernized spelling.

² David Harris Willson, *The Privy Councillors in the House of Commons, 1604–1629*, Minneapolis, 1940 [Oxford, 1940], 153. *S. P. Venetian, 1621–1623*, XVII, 271. Patents and monopolies were investigated by other committees, such as the Committee on Trade; but the procedure followed was the same throughout.

³ Sir Edward Coke, *The Third Part of the Institutes of the Laws of England*, London, 1660, Chapter LXXXV, 181.

⁴ *Commons Debates 1621*, VII, Appendix B, 491–6.

⁵ W. S. Holdsworth, *A History of English Law*, Boston, 1924 [London, 1934], IV, 346–53. E. Wyndham Hulme, 'The History of the Patent System under the Prerogative and at Common Law', *Law Quarterly Review*, XII, 141–54.

⁶ James Spedding, ed., *The Letters and Life of Francis Bacon*, London, 1861–74, VII, 152. Willson, 43–5.

⁷ Little came of Elizabeth's promise to leave the patents to common law, and one case at least was stayed. *Holdsworth*, IV, 348. Glanville remarked in 1624 'that heretofore when a man would speak against a patent of monopoly, it must be before a council table and there have a perpetual emparlance and could not have the trial of it by the common law, and this was the cause of the preferring of this Bill [the Bill of Monopolies]'. *Nicholas*, f. 25v. (Folio references are to Nicholas's 1624 diary.) There were a number of complaints in 1621 that the proclamations accompanying patents took protests against the execution of the patent to the Star Chamber. Wallace Notestein, Frances Helen Relf, Hartley Simpson, eds., *Commons Debates 1621*, New Haven, 1935.

⁸ *Commons Debates 1621*, II, 109–10; V, 483–4. In 1624 Wentworth 'desired course might be taken to prevent an abusive clause now usual in patents to command the justices to aid and assist them. They are to execute the laws of the kingdom and ought not to be made subject to every paltry patentee, which is a slavery makes men weary of the office of a justice of peace'. *Pym*, ff. 81v.–82.

⁹ The Commons were partial to the outports and often applied the term 'monopoly' to companies. Astrid Friis, *Alderman Cockayne's Project and the Cloth Trade*, London, 1927, 153ff., 163–4. *Commons Debates 1621*, II, 217, and note 27. T. C. Mendenhall, *The Shrewsbury Drapers and the Welsh Wool Trade in the XVI and XVII Centuries*, London, 1953, Chapter VI.

¹⁰ For the decision of the judges in 1605 in the case of the grant of the power of dispensing with penal statutes, see Sir Edward Coke, *The Seventh Part of the Reports of Sir Edward Coke*, London, 1727, 36–7. The Book of Bounty, 1610, also declared such grants illegal. *Commons Debates 1621*, VII, Appendix B, 492. For protests in 1621 and 1624 see Edward Nicholas, *Proceedings of the House of Commons in 1620 and 1621*, Oxford, 1766, I, 63–5, 146–7; *Commons Debates 1621*, VI, 249; V, 35–6, 41–2, 258; IV, 79, 147–8. In 1624 the debate on the continuance and repeal of statutes again raised the question in connection with the Earl of Nottingham's patent. See the debate on May 22nd, 1624, *Erle* ff. 189v.–190; *Nicholas*, ff. 216–216v.; *Gurney*, 235. Paul Birdsall, ' "Non Obstante" — A Study of the Dispensing Power of English Kings' in *Essays in History and Political Theory in Honour of Charles Howard McIlwain*, Cambridge, Mass., 1936 [Oxford, 1936], is valuable. The protest at this time was not against the dispensing power which was generally conceded to be a prerogative right, but against its grant to others. A speech of Sandys's makes this especially clear: *Nicholas*, I, 200.

¹¹ S. R. Gardiner, *History of England from the Accession of James I to the Outbreak of the Civil War, 1603–1642*, London, 1908, IV, 40, 46–50. *Nicholas*, I, 222–3.

¹² For grants promoted or procured by Buckingham, see *Commons Debates 1621*, VII, 312, 367, 379, 391–2, 415–17, 461, 469–70; *Nicholas*, f. 31. For his procuring of the

enrolment of grants, see *Commons Debates 1621*, VII, 311, 332, 340, 345, 348–9, 370, 379, 386–7, 390, 416–17, 429, 443, 458, 470. John Hacket, *Scrinia Reserata: A Memorial offer'd to the Great Deservings of John Williams D.D.*, London, 1692, 49, comments on both Bacon's and Buckingham's part in monopoly grants. For the significance of the attack on patents in relation to Buckingham see Gardiner, IV, 45, 51–4, 85. *Cabala, sive Scrinia Sacra ...*, London, 1691, I, 2. *S. P. Venetian*, XVI, 767, 774, 789; XVII, 2, 40, 56, 84. Tillières to Puysieux, Paris Transcripts, *P.R.O.*, 3/54–5. See also the letters of Salvetti, the English representative of the Grand Duke of Tuscany, March 19th, March 26th, April 16th, April 23rd, May 21st, 1621. *Salvetti MSS.* 27962 A, I and II, *Salvetti MSS.* 27962 B. Willson, 43, 148, 292.

[13] *S. P. Venetian*, XVI, 608, 631, 644.

[14] *Nicholas*, II, 361.

[15] *Commons Debates 1621*, II, 484. See also the debate on December 11th, 1621, *Commons Debates 1621*, VI, 232. Pollard feels that in the early seventeenth century, Parliament insisted on its privileges for its own sake and only later translated privileges into terms of responsibility to the constituencies. A. F. Pollard, *The Evolution of Parliament*, London, 1920, 178–9. While this may have been true for the eighteenth century (Pollard, 179–81), the evidence indicates that it is not for the early seventeenth. The House of Commons was conscious of public opinion and the fight for privileges was connected with the concept of themselves as 'the representative body of the realm'.

[16] *Commons Debates 1621*, II, 485.

[17] *Ibid.*, 21–3; 163.

[18] The link between subsidies and grievances is clear throughout the debates in 1621. In 1624 subsidies were promptly voted in a wave of enthusiasm for the proposed change in foreign policy, the break with Spain and the possibility of war with the old enemy. The bitterness of the debate on May 27th, 1624 reflected the Commons's regret at having acted so impetuously: '... if we had not agreed at the beginning of Parliament to give subsidies we should not in the end of it been put to these extremities by their Lordships. It were good we would find out and fall again into the old way of Parliament, which is now passed by ... It is our own faults, that we are thus used by them.' *Nicholas*, ff. 231v.–232. For some interesting reflections on this point see Margaret Judson, *The Crisis of the Constitution*, New Brunswick, N.J., 1949, 72–5.

[19] *Commons Debates for 1629*, ed. Wallace Notestein and Frances Relf, Minneapolis, 1921, v–lxiii. Wallace Notestein, *Winning of the Initiative*, London, 1924, 42–3. J. E. Neale, *Elizabeth I and her Parliaments 1559–1581*, New York, 1952 [London, 1953], points out the propaganda possibilities of the subsidy preamble, pp. 124, 161.

[20] *Commons Journal*, 754, 776.

[21] *Holles*, f. 97, *Gurney*, 136–7 (1624).

[22] *Nicholas*, f. 118; *Gurney*, 181–2.

[23] *Holles*. ff. 29–29v. *Holland*, 2v. Coke has some interesting comments: Sir Edward Coke, *The Fourth Part of the Institutes of the Laws of England*, London, 1658, 2, 12, 14, 49.

[24] Sir Edward Coke said in 1624: 'The House, as they invited none, so neither could they refuse any that complained. The Members of the House were inquisitors of the realm, as coming from every part of it and being more sensible of grievances than the Lords in the Upper House were because they were once liable unto them.' *Harl. 159*, f. 60v.; see also *Holles*, f. 29v.; *Holland*, f. 2v.

[25] *Commons Debates 1621*, V, 431.

[26] *Nicholas*, I, 134; *Commons Journal*, 551; *Commons Debates 1621*, V, 36.

[27] *Commons Journal*, 551; *Commons Debates 1621*, III, 91; V, 102; VI, 396.

[28] *Holland*, II, f. 57v.; see also *Pym*, f. 81v. In 1624 the House suspected that petitioners were being kept from Parliament. A committee was appointed 'to inquire, who those men were that were deterred from complaining to this House; and who did deter them'. *Commons Journal*, 759–60; see also *Harl. 159*, ff. 101v.ff.

[29] Notestein, *Winning of the Initiative, passim*. Willson, 236ff.

[30] *Commons Debates 1621*, II, 24; VI, 249, note 1.

[31] *Nicholas*, I, 63; *Commons Journal*, 551; *Commons Debates 1621*, IV, 78; VI, 249–51.

[32] *Commons Debates 1621*, VI, 251, 265; II, 123, 134. Willson, 248.

[33] *Commons Debates 1621*, IV, 78, 183; VI, 249, 265. *Nicholas*, I, 63, 218–19.

[34] *Nicholas*, I, 73. *Commons Debates 1621*, II, 114; V, 303, note 8; III, 280. *Nicholas*, II, 87. *Commons Journal*, 718. *Nicholas*, f. 62. *Erle*, f. 66v.

[35] *Nicholas*, I, 81. *Commons Journal*, 563, 575, 623, 718. *Commons Debates 1621*, V, 309; IV, 183, 196, 200; VI, 81; II, 122, 378. *Nicholas*, f. 21; *Holles*, f. 93v.

[36] The Venetian Ambassador, for instance, was interested in opening up the trade in glass, raisins and muscatels, which had been closed by the grants to Mansell and to the Levant Company. He evidently encouraged opposition to both these grants. *S. P. Venetian*, XVII, 26; XVII, 59.

[37] *Commons Debates 1621*, V. 330. *Commons Journal*, 578. *Nicholas*, I, 260–1.

[38] *Commons Debates 1621*, VII, Appendix B, 513–15. Appendix B also contains other revealing petitions. *Mendenhall*, 180–7.

[39] *Commons Debates 1621*, VII, Appendix C, 606–9. See also Hacket, 191; Willson, 181–2.

[40] *Commons Debates 1621*, II, 29–30, 140, note 20, 204, 214–15; IV, 19, 95–8; V, 159, 262–3, 469, 486–8, 524–9; VI, 10, 16, 456. *Nicholas*, II, 86–8. *Commons Journal*, 549.

[41] *Nicholas*, f. 46, *Gurney*, p. 74, *Pym*, f. 17v.; Holland, ff. 78ff. *Commons Journal*, 564. *Commons Debates 1621*, IV, 110; II, 204; VI, 456.

[42] April 19th, 1624. *Commons Journal*, 771; *Pym*, ff. 71v.ff.

[43] April 28th, 1624. *Commons Journal*, 693, 778. *Pym*, f. 82.

[44] Sub-committees were appointed to receive petitions and sort them. (*Nicholas*, I, 115, 220, 278. *Commons Debates 1621*, IV, 146; II, 208, 274, note 3; V, 328–9. *Commons Journal*, 550, 572, 582.) Possibly they rejected some. (*Commons Debates 1621*, IV, 146. *Commons Journal*, 550.) Sub-committees also prepared the committee's work by investigating particular petitions. They acted as a fact-finding body which heard witnesses and complainants, and examined relevant documents, reporting their findings to the grand committee in cases where the committee did not undertake the investigation itself. (*Commons Debates 1621*, V, 319; II, 291, note 2; III, 195; VI, 217, and in many other places.) The sub-committee to consider the Merchant Adventurers' patent was granted the power of summons and the power to call in documents. (*Commons Journal*, 598–9; *Commons Debates 1621*, III, 111.) There was a strong feeling in the House that all petitions should be answered and those rejected so marked and returned. (*Commons Debates 1621*, II, 207–8; III, 22. *Nicholas* I, 279. *Commons Journal*, 582.)

[45] For 1621, see *Commons Debates 1621*, I, Index, 180. For 1624 the examples are equally numerous: *Erle*, ff. 81, 86v.–87v.; *Holland*, f. 82; *Pym*, ff. 49v.ff; *Nicholas*, ff. 221–221v., and elsewhere.

[46] *Commons Debates 1621*, II, 50, note 23.

[47] See, for example, *Commons Debates 1621*, V, 469, 476–7, 296, 245; VI, 451, 266, 271, 456–7, 79, 462–3; II, 112–13, 365; III, 441; IV, 92, 339. VI, 1624: *Pym*, f. 22v.; *Nicholas*, ff. 79–79v.; *Erle*, f. 92; *Nicholas*, f. 172v.

[48] *Commons Debates 1621*, II, 114, 291, note 2; VI, 62, 278; IV, 192–3; *Nicholas*, I, 156; *Commons Journal*, 554, 574. Belasyse notes in his diary: 'Blundell [patentee of pedlars] and Mompesson were called in person to answer, though they were the King's servants.' *Commons Debates 1621*, V, 35. Mompesson was, of course, an M.P., but he doubtless would have been summoned, as others were, even without this special claim to jurisdiction.

[49] *Commons Debates 1621*, III, 197. *Gurney*, 216; *Holland*, II, ff. 18v.–19, *Harl. 159*, ff. 109v., 111.

[50] *Commons Debates 1621*, II, 112–13; VI, 271. *Commons Journal*, 535–6.

[51] *Commons Debates 1621*, III, 146; IV, 335. *Commons Journal*, 780.

[52] *Harl. 159*, f. 35.

[53] May 29th, 1624. *Nicholas*, ff. 244–6 for Coke's speech and the debate in the House.

[54] *Commons Debates 1621*, V, 142–3. There was an interesting debate at the end of the session in 1624 on what to do with the patents in the House. Those which had not been 'censured' were ordered to be given back to the patentees. Various suggestions were made about those which had been 'condemned as grievances'. Wentworth thought that they should be endorsed 'condemned', or turned over to the King's Council, with the request that a *scire facias* be brought against them. Coke supported this last plan. The Chancellor of the Duchy was for marking them 'condemned', and leaving them in the House, with the order that if the King's Council should send for them that they be delivered. *Nicholas*, ff. 244–6. Digges was against having an order in the matter; and Wentworth, according to another account, was of the same mind,

moving that the Clerk should simply do as had been done before. It was finally resolved that there should be no order. *Erle*, ff. 199–199*v*.

⁵⁵ For specific orders staying the execution of specific patents, see *Commons Debates 1621*, II, 133; VI, 8, 459–60; IV, 193; V, 321, 330. *Commons Journal*, 563, 565, 573–4, 578, 637. *Nicholas*, I, 88, 90, 261. For the debate on the stay of the execution of the patent of surveying sea coals in Newcastle, and the King's attempt to intervene, in 1624, see *Commons Journal*, 736; *Holles*, f. 100*v*.; *Erle*, ff. 82*v*.–83; *Holland*, ff. 52ff.; *Erle*, ff. 192–192*v*.; *Gurney*, 241. For general orders on the stay of all patents condemned or under consideration, see *Commons Debates 1621*, VI, 464, 479. In both 1621 and 1624 there were breaches of the House's orders. *Commons Debates 1621*, IV, 335. *Nicholas*, II, 251, 306–7. *Commons Journal*, 652. *Nicholas*, II, 306–7. In 1624 there were even more cases; for in the three years since Parliament had last met many of the patents condemned in 1621 had been put in execution again in defiance of the Commons's order of June 2nd, 1621. *Commons Debates 1621*, VI, 479. The offending patentees were ordered to bring these patents in and attend the House for censure. *Holles*, f. 83; *Gurney*, 39–40; *Erle*, ff. 61–61*v*.

⁵⁶ See, for example, *Commons Debates 1621*, VI, 456–7; V, 323; III, 2–3. *Commons Journal*, 573. In Michell's case a warrant was granted to search his study. *Commons Journal*, 540. *Commons Debates 1621*, II, 170; V, 28, 274. For a description of the type of papers the House of Commons had in this case see *Commons Journal*, 551.

⁵⁷ *Commons Debates 1621*, III, 157–8, 246ff.; IV, 339. Friis, 88, note 1. *Commons Journal*, 758. *Holles*, f. 125. For the report on the committee's search of the Book see *Erle*, ff. 139–139*v*.; *Holland*, II, ff. 22ff.; *Pym*, ff. 64*v*–65.

⁵⁸ *Commons Debates 1621*, II, 481; VI, 480. *Nicholas*, II, 159.

⁵⁹ There must be an examination: *Commons Debates 1621*, VI, 253; II, 214–15; *Commons Journal*, 540–1, 771, 773; *Pym*, ff. 77*v*.–78; *Nicholas*, ff. 168–9; *Holland*, II, f. 44; *Harl. 159*, f. 106*v*. Both sides must be heard: *Commons Debates 1621*, V, 88 and note 9; II, 278; *Commons Journal*, 575; *Harl. 159*, ff. 109*v*., 111. For records of examinations, indicating that both sides were heard, see *Commons Debates 1621*, V, 319, 123. *Nicholas*, f. 175*v*. There were some complaints that patentees had not been fully heard: *Commons Debates 1621*, II, 321; John Rushworth, *Historical Collections*, London, 1659, I, 147. Michell maintained that Coke's questioning of him had been sarcastic and had prejudiced the House: *Commons Debates 1621*, VII, 505–2; VI, 264, note 6; II, 125, note 39; 129, note 11; 167, note 25. The King maintained that the examination was cursory: 'Your judgment is too quick in those matters.' *Harl. 159* f. 126.

⁶⁰ *Nicholas* I, 147, 163; II, 82–3. *Commons Debates 1621*, VI, 359; III, 383; V, 171, 194.

⁶¹ Noy's speech on February 19th, 1621 set the tone of the whole attack on patents as an *investigation*: 'Let these and all other in the like case who have done this against the King's mind [i.e. procured grants against the Book of Bounty] be called to give an "account of their husbandry", to be rewarded if they have done well, "if ill, to be punished".' *Commons Debates 1621*, IV, 78–9. The King protested that the Commons should not call in patents until they knew them to be grievous. *Commons Debates 1621*, VI, 388–9; Rushworth, *Collections*, I, 47. This, of course, invalidated an investigation such as Noy outlined before it had begun. However, since most of the grants called were condemned, the King's statement that the very name of a patent was objectionable to the House (*Harl. 159*, f. 35) may have been a good deal more realistic than Noy's. James was probably right that calling in a patent would lead to its condemnation, and therefore became in itself a brand of condemnation on it.

⁶² *Commons Debates 1621*, VI, 352; IV, 33.

⁶³ The power to use an oath was flatly denied (*Commons Debates 1621*, II, 3; 283; III, 24; *Harl. 159*, f. 67) and as flatly asserted (*Commons Debates 1621*, III, 167, 181–2; VI, 400ff.; IV, 312). There was some discussion of settling the point by Bill (*Commons Debates 1621*, II, 160 and note 15) or by the petition to the King on privileges (*Commons Debates 1621*, VI, 342). Procedure without oath was justified on the grounds that the House was the representative body of the realm 'and therefore not to be presumed to be ignorant of the country'. (Glanville: *Commons Debates 1621*, V, 46. Coke said: 'We are judges here and have notice of all things in the commonwealth.' *Commons Journal*, 557.) The power to administer an oath involved the whole question of the jurisdiction of the House, and much of the debate centred on this point, which was raised in the Floyd case and the procedure against Mompesson and Bennet. The question was

raised in 1624 during the debate on the Subsidy Bill. Sandys said: '... heretofore it hath been debated on and inclined to be the opinion of this House that in such cases as this House hath power to give a final judgment in and end this House may administer an oath, but in such cases as this House doth not finally determine but transmit it over to the Lords the House did seem to doubt whether we had power or not to administer an oath, but did resolve nothing in it but made claim to have right and power to do it.' *Nicholas*, f. 205; see also f. 225*v*., and Coke's statement, *Holland*, II, f. 87*v*.)

[64] *Commons Debates 1621*, IV, 187; VI, 82; III, 249–54, 338. *Commons Journal*, 639.

[65] For typical examples see *Commons Debates 1621*, V, 89–90, 478–9; IV, 200, 352–3; III, 63, 82–4; 195. *Nicholas*, I, 75–7, 115–17, 222, 295–6, 303, 320–4; *Nicholas*, II, 38–9. *Commons Journal*, 538. *Erle*, ff. 61*v*., 80*v*.

[66] *Commons Journal*, 541. *Commons Debates 1621*, IV, 129; II, 172–3; V, 31–2; 275ff.; VI, 34–5.

[67] *Nicholas*, I, 294–5, 339–40. *Commons Debates 1621*, V, 88, 105–6.

[68] *Commons Journal*, 543. *Commons Debates 1621*, V, 278; VI, 26; IV, 121–2; II, 195–7, 255ff. *Nicholas*, I, 339–40, 360–3. *Nicholas*, II, 39–40.

[69] *Nicholas* I, 156, 360–3. *Commons Debates 1621*, VI, 83 and note 4; VII, 508–11; II, 261; IV, 288. *Commons Journal*, 602. *Erle*, ff. 183*v*.–184.

[70] *Commons Debates 1621*, II, 166–7; IV, 140, 192–3; VI, 456–7; V, 311.

[71] *Commons Debates 1621*, VI, 259–62; IV, 108; III, 82–3, 193–4. *Nicholas*, I, 218–19, 295–6; 321–4, 360–3. *Nicholas*, II, 36–8. *Erle*, ff. 61*v*.–62. *Nicholas*, ff. 81*v*.–82*v*.

[72] *Commons Debates 1621*, V, 262, 524–9.

[73] *Harl. 159*, f. 35.

[74] William Hyde Price, *The English Patents of Monopolies*, Boston, 1906, 25–6. *Commons Debates 1621*, VII, 491–2.

[75] *Commons Debates 1621*, VI, 259–62, 7, 269, 27–2, 57; II, 234–44, 250–1; V, 323, 311, 59; III, 42–3, 63, 102–4, 195. *Nicholas*, I, 146–7, 294–5, 305. *Commons Journal*, 541.

[76] *Commons Debates 1621*, IV, 19, 78, 99, 158; II, 84–90, 108, 150; V, 480. *Nicholas*, I, 17, 63–4, 89. *Commons Journal*, 583–9, 555. The King saved himself from blame by placing responsibility on the referees. F. H. Relf, ed., *Notes of the Debates in the House of Lords, 1621, 1625, 1628*, Camden Society, London, 1929, 12–15. In 1624 he spoke of 'my judges and Council without whom I have done nothing, and if there be in any patent any clause or thing that is not fit, they are on fault for it and not I'. *Nicholas*, ff. 243–243*v*.

[77] *Commons Debates 1621*, VI, 269; IV, 99, 188; VII, 501; II, 161, 252–3, 147; V, 291, 25; III, 68. *Nicholas*, I, 196, 147–8, 309–10. 1624: *Holles*, f. 100*v*.; *Erle*, ff. 82*v*.–83; *Holland*, ff. 52ff.; *Nicholas*, ff. 79*v*.–80; *Gurney*, 115. This was the debate on the patent of surveying sea coals in Newcastle. Sir John Saville accused Coke of being 'too tender to men of his coat' and 'he would have the referees questioned'. *Holles*, f. 100*v*.

[78] *Commons Journal*, 540–1, 546. Norman Egbert McClure, *The Letters of John Chamberlain*, Philadelphia, 1929, II, 351–2.

[79] *Commons Debates 1621*, II, 254.

[80] Sir Edward Coke, *The Second Part of the Institutes of the Laws of England*, London, 1642, commentary on Magna Carta, c. 29. Sir Edward Coke, *The Eleventh Part of the Reports of Sir Edward Coke*, London, 1727, 86–8. D. O. Wagner, 'Coke and the Rise of Economic Liberalism', *Economic History Review*, VI, 30–44. Eli F. Heckscher, *Mercantilism*, London, 1935, I, 269ff. Edward S. Mason, 'Monopoly in Law and Economics', *Yale Law Journal*, XLVII, 34–9. Friis, 459. *Commons Debates 1621*, V, 105–6. *Nicholas*, f. 132*v*. It was, however, generally conceded that both King and Parliament had the right to restrict this freedom for the good of the Commonwealth. The exceptions in the law which were consistently made for chartered companies might be explained in these terms.

[81] E. W. Hulme, 'The History of the Patent System under the Prerogative and at Common Law', *Law Quarterly Review*, XII, 141–54; XVL, 44–56. 'On the History of Patent Law in the Seventeenth and Eighteenth Centuries', *Law Quarterly Review*, XVIII, 280–8.

[82] *Wagner*, 31.

[83] Coke, *Reports*, XI, 86–7. The existence of these incidents was not necessary to establish the fact of monopoly, though their presence could, according to Coke's

statements in the House of Commons in 1621 and 1624, void it. *Commons Debates 1621*, v, 105–6, 121–2; III, 195. *Holles*, f. 118.

[84] *Nicholas*, II, 73.

[85] *Nicholas*, I, 146–7. *Commons Debates 1621*, v, 35–6; IV, 147–8; II, 250.

[86] *Commons Debates 1621*, II, 180–3.

[87] For examples see *Commons Debates 1621*, v, 586–8; IV, 95–6; II, 134, 176; VII, 513–14, 442–3.

[88] *Nicholas*, I, 339–40.

[89] *Commons Debates 1621*, II, 112–13. See also *ibid.*, II, 118–21, 193, 413–14; IV, 66, 71, 90; v, 48, 483–4; VI, 284. *Nicholas*, f. 114.

[90] The Commons argued in good English fashion that the King, having declared in the Book of Bounty that he would not issue certain types of grants, would not issue them contrary to his own declaration. When such grants were found to exist it was clear that the procurers had misinformed the King as to their nature. (See, for example, *Commons Debates 1621*, II, 145, 250, 253–4.) This doctrine was applied by the Commons in 1621 and 1624 not only to the King's intentions as expressed in the Book of Bounty, but also to his intentions as expressed in the particular grant under consideration. The same point had been made by the Judges in the decision in the case of *Darcy* v. *Allen*: 'The Queen was deceived in her grant; for the Queen as by the preamble appears, intended it to be for the weal public, and it will be employed for the private gain of the patentees, and for the prejudice of the weal public...' Coke, *Reports*, XI, 87. It was common practice for procurers of patents to promise benefit to the commonwealth. Sir Edward Coke said: 'Projectors like watermen, look one way and row another; they pretend public profit, intend private.' *Commons Debates 1621*, v, 76. For other examples of this point, and for patents thus condemned, see *Commons Debates 1621*, II, 78, 193; IV, 288–99; v, 41, 483–4.

[91] Monopolies were, for instance, shown to be illegal by common law precedent. *Commons Debates 1621*, VI, 249–51; IV, 79–81, 258; II, 228–9; III, 2; v, 74. *Commons Journal*, 697. This point was so well established that in some instances it sufficed to say that a grant was a monopoly, its illegality followed. *Harl. 159*, ff. 97*v.*–98, 106.

[92] Noy and Coke classified the grounds on which patents were condemned by the House, *Nicholas*, I, 63–6; *Commons Debates 1621*, IV, 78–81; VI, 249–51; v, 258; III, 44, 280.

[93] *Commons Debates 1621*, v, 32, 277; IV, 189.

[94] *Harl. 159*, f. 35.

[95] Hearings were also held on private Bills, parties appeared by counsel, and witnesses were examined. This procedure has long been recognized as judicial or semi-judicial in character. Charles Howard McIlwain, *The High Court of Parliament*, New Haven, 1910 [Oxford, 1934], 125, 219–23; Pollard, *The Evolution of Parliament*, 118.

[96] *Commons Debates 1621*, IV, 92, 203–4; II, 272; v, 292; VI, 26; VII, 312. *Commons Journal*, 577.

[97] *Commons Debates 1621*, v, 521, 267; VI, 271–2.

[98] There was some debate on how to punish patentees. *Commons Debates 1621*, II, 113–14, 131; VI, 265. *Commons Journal*, 651. *Nicholas*, f. 212*v*. Those 'projectors' actually punished were Members of the House and were 'sequestered' from the House or expelled. *Commons Journal*, 536, 566–7. *Commons Debates 1621*, v, 315; II, 255; VI, 460–1; III, 130; IV, 289; VI, 125. *Nicholas*, II, 3, 182. *Gurney*, 170; *Holland*, ff. 78ff.

[99] *Commons Debates 1621*, v, 263, 308; III, 2–3. The remark of a Member of the House of Commons during the debate on monopolies in 1601 is interesting in this connection: 'Let us do generously and bravely, like Parliament men, and ourselves send for them and their patents, and cancel them before their faces, arraign them as in times past, at the Bar, and send them to the Tower.' Quoted in Edward P. Cheyney, *A History of England from the Defeat of the Armada to the Death of Elizabeth*, New York, 1926 [London, 1926], II, 299–300. The Long Parliament 'called in' and 'cancelled' a large number of monopoly patents. Price, 46.

[100] The King conceded this in 1621: *Commons Debates 1621*, III, 134; VII, 626; *Nicholas*, II, 294. The Lords likewise conceded it: *Commons Debates 1621*, III, 183; VI, 401; IV, 313.

[101] *Commons Debates 1621*, III, 122–8, 134–52, 163–8, 173–84, 191–2, 205, 208–9, 231, 237–9, 272; VI, 128; v, 134; 364, IV, 296.

[102] *Commons Debates 1621 passim* for the debates on the Mompesson case and those of Sir John Bennet, Lambe and Craddock. Mompesson's patents were the chief complaint against him. These were examined by the House of Commons and declared to be grievances. In 1624 Phelips made an important speech, protesting that the Lords had not censured Cranfield 'upon every particular of their charge'. *Harl. 159,* f. 116v.; *Erle,* ff. 183–183v. See also *Erle,* ff. 186v.–187 for a similar protest in another case. McIlwain, *The High Court of Parliament,* 190–4, discusses the struggle of the Commons to take part in the actual judgment.

[103] *Commons Debates 1621,* III, 140, 167; IV, 77, 292, 405. The King in his message about Floyd asked whether the House of Commons 'hath a power of judicature in such matters as do not concern our own [the Commons's] privileges and Members or a public grievance of the kingdom.' *Commons Debates 1621,* IV, 290.

[104] *Nicholas,* ff. 244–6; *Erle,* ff. 199–199v.

[105] The term 'grievance' was used in 1621 and 1624 in two distinct ways. It was loosely applied to actions or grants whether they were investigated or not in the sense of complaint. *Commons Debates 1621,* V, 475: the patent of inns is a 'grievance fit to be examined and redressed'. It was also used in a second more technical sense; and in this sense it was only appropriate after a grant had been investigated and discovered for certain definite legal reasons to be a *grievance* in a certain, definite legal way: in creation, in execution or in both. In this second sense it was used in contradistinction to 'inconvenient' and acquired the specific meaning of illegal.

[106] *Commons Debates 1621,* III, 7; VII, 218ff. For similar Bills see *Commons Debates 1621,* IV, 253; V, 95; *Holland,* f. 82; *Pym,* ff. 49v.ff.; *Nicholas,* ff. 217–217v.; *Harl. 159,* f. 120. Bills were also drawn up which affected or voided patents not previously condemned: *Commons Debates 1621,* V, 469; VII, 77–80, 108ff.; V, 270; III, 148; VII, 259.

[107] I am speaking here only of that part of the petition which concerned patents and monopolies. For the petition see *Harl. 159,* ff. 35v.ff. and *S. P. Domestic, 1623–1625,* CLXV/53. A committee of thirty took the petition to the King, and the Solicitor spoke. *Commons Journal,* 714. *Erle,* ff. 198–198v. For the King's remarks on this occasion see *Harl. 159,* f. 35; *Nicholas,* ff. 243–243v. Charles answered the petition in 1625.

[108] Coke: 'A petition of right is when we petition that grievances may be suppressed ...' *Commons Debates 1621,* III, 367. '... there is a petition of grace (as to have insufficient justices put out) and a petition of right (to have grievances suppressed).' *Commons Debates 1621,* II, 413–14. Coke also made the point that a petition of right required an answer. *Commons Debates 1621,* II, 495–6.

[109] Charles Howard McIlwain, *Constitutionalism, Ancient and Modern,* Ithaca, New York [Oxford, 1940], 1940, 138.

[110] There were other general Bills drawn to void patents or to make certain types of grants illegal in the future—for instance, the Bill of Concealments, *Commons Journal,* 533; *Nicholas,* I, 135–6. For others see: *Commons Journal,* 569; *Commons Debates 1621,* IV, 183, 231; III, 18; V, 113.

[111] *Commons Journal,* 661, 663, 664; *Nicholas,* II, 302–3; *Commons Debates 1621,* II, 508–9, 521–2; VI, 230, 237.

[112] *Gurney,* 114; *Nicholas,* f. 77v.; *Holles,* f. 100; *Pym,* f. 28v.

[113] *Gurney,* 238. *Commons Journal,* 696; *Nicholas,* f. 188v.; *Holland,* II, f. 69v.; *Pym,* f. 86.

[114] *Commons Journal,* 793–4.

[115] The petition was also a device for saving time. In 1621, towards the end of the session, Coke moved 'that since there are so many Grievances here in the House complained of ... as that we cannot make Laws against them all, that we should have a Petition made to the King, beseeching his Majesty to be pleased by a Proclamation or otherwise to decry or make void the same ...' *Nicholas,* II, 248.

[116] Many of the patents condemned by the House of Commons in 1621 were revoked by proclamation on July 10th, 1621. For this proclamation, its preparation by the Privy Council and the Privy Council's consideration of the Commons's action against grants, see *Commons Debates 1621,* III, 416, note 25, and the references there cited. For some further examples of the Privy Council's consideration of grants condemned by the Commons see *Commons Debates 1621,* Appendix B; *Acts of the Privy Council, 1621–1623,* London, 1932, 408; *Acts of the Privy Council, 1623–1625,* London, 1933, 238, 247, 256, 491.

Charles I and the Constitution

★

Harold Hulme

This essay interprets and summarizes a subject which is found scattered in the few existing lives of Charles I and in the histories of the period. It is not based on new material but on the standard works dealing with the first half of the seventeenth century. They are: S. R. Gardiner, *History of England, 1603–1642*, 10 vols., London, 1904–9 (hereafter referred to as Gardiner, *History*); S. R. Gardiner, *History of the Great Civil War, 1642–1649*, 4 vols., London, 1910–11 (hereafter referred to as Gardiner, *Civil War*); John Rushworth, *Historical Collections*, 8 vols., London, 1659 (hereafter referred to as Rushworth); Margaret A. Judson, *The Crisis of the Constitution*, New Brunswick, 1949; Frederick C. Dietz, *English Public Finance, 1558–1641*, New York, 1932 [London, 1933]; William H. Price, *The English Patents of Monopoly*, Cambridge, Mass., 1913 [Oxford, 1906]; J. W. Allen, *English Political Thought, 1603–1644*, London, 1938; W. H. Holdsworth, *A History of English Law*, London, 1924, Vol. VI, 4–141; Harold Hulme, *The Life of Sir John Eliot, 1592–1632*, New York, 1957 [London, 1957]; and several other works cited in the notes at the end of the essay. Not all the above titles are to be found there as the notes are used primarily to identify quotations.

FROM one century to another the English constitution has undergone many changes. Such changes were made to meet the demands of king and people as voiced in Councils, Parliaments, and courts of law. In the seventeenth century a violent change took place. The demands of the King and of many people were sharply opposed to each other. Some have asserted that Charles I was responsible for this change. Others have insisted that forces alien to the interests of the Crown were directing the constitution into a totally different mould. In order to discover where the responsibility for these changes lay it is necessary first to examine the constitutional pattern of the time. Such a pattern existed during the Tudor period and was being altered slightly in the reign of James I. It was twisted completely out of shape during the rule of his son Charles. The purpose of this essay is to discover the role played by Charles I in the constitutional changes of his reign.

The phrase 'Tudor absolutism' has a familiar ring. What does it mean? It did not mean that the King was above the law. Henry VIII admitted that he was under the law, statute law. He, like the other Tudors, also accepted the dominance of natural and common law. But the royal prerogative was supreme where the law had not insinuated itself. Parliaments were convened and dissolved at the will of the King. Prerogative courts were established as long as they did not conflict or interfere with existing courts of law. Officials high and low were appointed and dismissed at the pleasure of the Crown. The declaration of war and the establishment of peace, the headship of the Church after the breach with Rome, the regulation of trade, commerce and manufacture, all fell under royal control. In short, policy and administration were the special preserve of the Tudor monarchs. In addition the sovereign could imprison men and women for days or years without showing cause and without trial. Except for the doubtful benefit of trial by jury the common law had hardly begun to protect the person of an Englishman. To be sure it had long been defending his property rights, out of which all personal rights were to grow.

Those property rights were also protected by Parliament whose control over taxation at this time was unquestioned. That the King should live of his own, even during the inflationary days of Queen Elizabeth, was a principle accepted by contemporaries. Tonnage and poundage was granted by Parliament at the beginning of every reign. Impositions were used for the first time and only on rare occasions in the reign of Elizabeth to regulate the foreign wine trade. Benevolences, though requested at the beginning of the Tudor period, were never solicited by Queen Elizabeth. A general forced loan was attempted by Wolsey in 1525 but proved to be such a dismal failure that it was never tried again during the century. To be sure, Privy Seal loans from individual wealthy subjects, which were forced in many instances though usually repaid, were commonly employed by all Tudor sovereigns.

As we have seen, these monarchs admitted that taxes could only be obtained from Parliament. They also admitted that the highest law of the land, statute law, could be made only by Parliament. Throughout the sixteenth century King, Lords and Commons together were the unquestioned authors of this law.

The making of law, the raising of taxes, the formulation of policy and the direction of administration, are not the only elements which fit into the constitutional pattern. That pattern must also include the art, though not necessarily the science, of governing. In this field the Tudors, especially Henry VII, Henry VIII and Elizabeth, displayed their greatest abilities. They ruled with their people. They—particularly Elizabeth—had their finger on the pulse of the nation. Whether by proclamation, in Parliament or on progress Elizabeth knew how to handle her subjects. Tudor public relations were excellent.

In spite of all this seeming perfection in government, signs of unrest and indications of coming trouble had made their appearance before the death of the great Queen. Ever since Henry VIII had taken the House of Commons into partnership, first to coerce the papacy into granting him a separation from his wife and then to break with Rome, that assembly had become a place of importance. In succeeding decades more and more of the gentry, wise in the government of their counties and in the ways of the world, crowded into the Lower Chamber of Parliament. The Commons began to ask for rights and privileges, soon they were taking them without asking, finally they were claiming powers no constitutional precedents could justify. This spirit, growing more fearless from reign to reign, fostered the loyal Puritan opposition in the Elizabethan House of Commons and gave the Queen no end of trouble in Parliament after Parliament. If it was not Puritanism that caused opposition in the Lower House, it was the desire of the Commons that the Queen should marry and that she should announce her successor. No wonder Elizabeth declared that the Commons were trespassing on ground hallowed by prerogative royal. By employing her charm, a show of force, her superlative tact or the thunder of an angered sovereign, she was able to dominate and control these obstreperous but loving Commons. At the same time the Members of the Lower House were becoming conscious of their growing strength. By the end of the reign when they believed the property rights of Englishmen were being endangered by the indiscriminate granting of mono- polies of manufacture, they dared to question the Crown's right to make such grants; they dared to lock horns with an acknowledged power of their sovereign. Elizabeth bowed to the storm and recalled those monopolies most bitterly denounced. Such fearless spirit as was being displayed in the Parliament of 1601 was bound to give trouble to the best possible successor to the ageing queen.

Furthermore, during the last two decades of the sixteenth century Magna Carta and the writ of habeas corpus began their careers in defence of English liberty. The former was cited by lawyers defending Puritans before the Court of High Commission. The latter was issued to question the legality of imprisonment by the Privy Council. By the death of Elizabeth liberty, freedom, property rights and privileges were familiar words to many Englishmen.

Such in part was the heritage of James VI of Scotland on becoming James I of England. This monarch, imbued with the Roman law principle that all power emanates from the King, imbued with an overweening vanity, with great loquacity, little tact and less common sense, was a grave hazard to the Tudor constitution. This threat to the constitution implicit in the nature of James was all the more serious because of the spirit of inde- pendence which had developed in the Elizabethan House of

Commons and was very much alive among the Stuart Commons. James had barely ascended the throne when a clash occurred. The King declared that the Commons's privileges were granted by him, to which the Commons replied that their privileges were ancient inherited rights. The struggle over privileges, particularly freedom of speech, stirred the feelings of both King and Commons time and again until in 1621 it reached a climax when James, to show his absolute power and authority, tore with his own hands the Great Protestation from the Journals of the Lower House. But in the next Parliament the tables were turned when the ageing, ailing King begged the Commons to discuss all those subjects they had been forbidden to mention in 1621. Almost through a fluke the Commons, shortly before the death of the first Stuart, had secured freedom of speech in practice though not in theory.

But other subjects besides privileges made harmony between King and Commons impossible in the majority of the Parliaments of the reign. For one there was impositions. In spite of the Bate case decision of 1606 which favoured the Crown's right to levy these duties, the Commons soon saw that the basis of this decision, that they could be levied as part of the royal prerogative to regulate foreign trade, was being used by the Government as a blind to hide what amounted to taxation without the consent of Parliament. As a result there arose on all sides the cry that impositions endangered the property rights of Englishmen. Because no agreement could be reached between King and Parliament, James and his son continued to levy these duties in spite of the bitter complaints of the Commons in most of the Parliaments of the two reigns.

Subsequent to the initial attack on impositions, monopolies felt the heavy hand of the Commons. Twenty years after their violent denunciation in Elizabeth's last Parliament the Commons assailed both evil monopolies and evil monopolists. Once again the Crown was forced to retract and dull the point of the prerogative by recalling a number of monopolies. Worse, in the next Parliament the prerogative of granting monopolies was brought under statutory control by the Monopoly Act of 1624.

While these conflicts over privileges, impositions and monopolies were in progress the first Stuart King had his troubles with the Puritans. Fearing without real cause the rise of Presbyterianism in England, James at the beginning of his reign turned on the Puritans with the threat to harry them out of the land. The Puritans, growing stronger in and out of the House of Commons, remained in opposition, but not with the same degree of loyalty they had displayed under Elizabeth. James's flirtation with the Catholics during the latter half of his reign, the influence of the Spanish ambassador Gondomar over the impressionable King, the proposed marriage of Prince Charles to the Spanish Infanta and the decision that Charles should marry the French Catholic princess Henrietta Maria, all helped to arouse opposition among the Puritans as well as among many Anglicans. Moreover, religion threatened the constitution directly when many Puritans wanted Parliament to control the Church and thereby endangered the headship of the King.

If Puritanism threatened the Elizabethan organization of the Church of England, James I threatened the position of common law in the nation. When Sir Edward Coke told the King that he was under no man but under God and the law, and that the law protected the King, James was furious. He believed himself to be the source and fountain of the law. Only grudgingly would he consent to the principle that statute law was made by King, Lords and Commons. In Peacham's case and in the case of *in commendams* James tried to interfere with common law. And in his famous speech in Star Chamber in 1616 he declared that his absolute prerogative, as opposed to his private prerogative, was above the law. But he never had an opportunity to put this claim into practice. There is no question but that James was a threat to the dominance of the common law. But he was never strong enough or able enough to implement this threat. At least Sir Edward Coke, either from the Bench or in the House of Commons, always managed to defend it from any serious royal encroachment.

As we have seen, the Tudor constitution had received a severe buffeting during the first quarter of the seventeenth century. Both King and Commons were kneading and pommelling it. In this struggle the King gained a little actual ground. But he defined his position in no uncertain terms, terms which the far wiser Elizabeth had left to the imagination. Whether he called it divine right and non-resistance or the absolute prerogative, nobody could be in ignorance of the position in the State claimed by James. At the same time Parliament, particularly the Commons, was gaining strength. Those extremely articulate members of the Lower House were beginning to define their own terms, define their powers and even define their place in the constitution. Frequently those definitions were not upheld by precedents, certainly not Tudor precedents. It was necessary to fall back on totally un-historical medieval precedents to find support for claims the Commons were beginning to make before the death of James I.

That King, however, through the medium of policy and administration let us call it, left a legacy to his son which was to have profound effect on the constitution. In spite of some rather generous parliamentary grants of supply, in spite of tonnage and poundage, impositions, three benevolences, frequent Privy Seal loans not always repaid and many other sources of revenue, James, because of the strong inflationary tendencies of the times and because of his unbridled extravagance, left a debt of close to a million pounds at his death. He left the credit of the Crown lower than it had been during most of the Tudor period, so low that the State was close to bankruptcy. Those two able Lord Treasurers, Salisbury and Middlesex, came too soon or too late to be able to do more than thrust their fingers into the holes in the dike. But this was only part of James's legacy to Charles.

The other part was fully as disastrous. It was the Duke of Buckingham. On the accession of Charles I, the domineering, all-powerful favourite of the father was ready to rule the country of the son. Like a gambler he played for the highest stakes with only a chip or two with which to begin his game. Or to use a simile commonly employed in his day, Buckingham turned England into the tail of a comet of which he was the head. He could see its rise and ignored its inevitable fall. Had there been no Buckingham it is conceivable that there might have been no 'country' party. Without a 'country' party there would have been no Roundheads. Had there been no Roundheads Oliver Cromwell would have died as an inconspicuous country gentleman. And good King Charles would have been remembered for his peaceful, innocuous reign. Such speculation sounds fantastic, but it contains more than a grain of the possible.

Turning from speculation to facts and from the background to the subject before us, we must remember that on his accession Charles I was popular. Little was known about him and that was only good: he had refused to marry the Spanish Infanta and had advocated war with Spain. The implications of the French marriage had not penetrated the minds of most Englishmen. The early Protestantism of Henry IV, not completely forgotten by men across the Channel, might come to life again in his daughter, Henrietta Maria. Though there was no truth in such a thought, as the new Queen of England was a devout, indeed a rabid papist, Englishmen in general believed that a French Catholic was not nearly as bad as one of the Spanish variety.

But Charles's popularity quickly came to an end. Puritans and Anglicans alike began to suspect the Government had promised France more lenient treatment of English Catholics. Buckingham's unpopularity rapidly eclipsed the glory of a king. In the Parliament which assembled on June 18th, 1625, but not until the second session at Oxford in August, the Commons initiated an attack on the Government which culminated in a denunciation of the favourite. Remembering that they had spoken freely in the last Parliament of King James, the Commons on August 10th and 11th replied to a request for supply to equip a fleet for an attack on the enemy (supposedly Spain) by denouncing the past policies in the cold war which was being conducted to recover the Palatinate for Frederick and Elizabeth. For such policies they finally blamed the Duke of Buckingham and forgot that supply had been requested. The only reply Charles could make was to dissolve Parliament.

A new spirit permeated the Commons in this Parliament. By comparison with that found in the Elizabethan and most of the Jacobean Commons it was revolutionary. It had no place in the constitution. Yet Charles had nothing to say. That was the trouble. Neither gifted in speech nor in intelligence, totally untrained in the art of government, he could do nothing with his obstreperous Commons. Policy in these early years he left to Buckingham. One gets the impression, however, that when the King addressed the Commons the words were his own. For example, on August 10th he sent a message to the Lower House in which he spoke of the serious threat of the plague and went on to say, with Sir Richard Weston delivering his words, 'therefore [that he] desires a present Answer about Supply; if not, he will take more care of the Commons than they will of themselves, and will make as good a shift for himself, as he can ...'[1] Such language must have originated with the King and can hardly be called tactful.

With the failure of the expedition to Cadiz, with Buckingham's inability to pawn the crown jewels in Amsterdam and with the promise to pay Christian IV of Denmark thirty thousand pounds a month for his military support against the Catholic League, another Parliament had to be summoned early in 1626. As with practically all previous Parliaments this one was assembled for the sole purpose of raising money for the Crown through taxation. But the Commons soon developed other plans. Under the guidance of Sir John Eliot and Sir Dudley Digges these plans turned into a violent attack on Government policies and eventually evolved into a masterly denunciation of the Duke of Buckingham. Charles scolded and repeatedly demanded supply. But the Commons made it clear that money would be granted only if the King dismissed his favourite. Gardiner's comment is:

> To ask the King to abandon his minister on the ground that the Commons could not trust him, though the acts at which they took umbrage had been done, always nominally and often really, by the authority of Charles, was to ask him to surrender himself as well as Buckingham. Neither Elizabeth nor even his father had allowed anyone to dictate the choice of counsellors. If the advisers of the Crown and the officers of State were to be accepted or dismissed at the will of the House of Commons, the supremacy of the House would soon be undisputed.[2]

In the light of the existing constitution, Tudor or Jacobean, this was revolution. So, too, in a sense, were the charges made by the Commons in the impeachment proceedings against the Duke. In an impeachment the Commons must bring criminal charges against the defendant which they can prove before the Lords. Most of the charges against Buckingham were political, and those with a criminal flavour had no standing in a court of law without proof. That proof was common fame, which meant rumour, hearsay or public opinion. Never before had there been an attempt to fit such an impeachment into the law of the land. No wonder the Lords ignored the charges. Politically the Duke was too strong in the Upper House.

In these circumstances it is no wonder that Charles was becoming more and more exasperated with the Commons. There is little doubt that he was warranted in looking for evidence of treason against Eliot and Digges. But he would have been wise to admit publicly that he had failed to find what he had been seeking. Foolishly he got himself involved with the Commons's privilege of freedom of speech when he gave reasons for the arrest and short imprisonment of these two men. In the end Buckingham was not dismissed and the King received no money from Parliament.

Constitutionally Charles I was standing on firm ground during his first and particularly his second Parliament. Politically his support of Buckingham and his policies was inadvisable, to say the least. Politically the Commons were absolutely right in attacking the Duke. But their words and actions can in no sense be fitted into the constitution of the early seventeenth century.

Frequently on addressing the Commons Charles was far from politically prudent, as when on March 28th, 1626 he said: 'Remember that Parliaments are altogether in my power for their calling, sitting and dissolution; therefore, as I find the fruits of them good or evil, they are to continue or not to be.'[3] How right he was constitutionally. Again on June 30th, 1626 Charles stated his position in a Declaration where he gave 'the Grounds and Causes' for dissolving the first two Parliaments of his reign. This document declared:

> ... he well knoweth that the Calling, Adjourning, Proroguing and Dissolving of Parliaments, ... do peculiarly belong unto himself by an undoubted Prerogative inseparably united to his Imperial Crown; of which, as of his other Regal actions, he is not bound to give an Account to any but to God only, whose immediate Lieutenant and Vicegerent he is in these his Realms and Dominions by the Divine providence committed to his charge and government.'[4]

This time the cloak of divine right was cast over the shoulders of the King to make his power over Parliament even more impressive.

Now that Parliament was dissolved and no money in the treasury the King's financial status was becoming desperate. Money must be found somewhere, somehow. England was at war with Spain and rapidly drifting into war with France. When during the summer of 1626 a benevolence or free gift had proved a failure, it was decided in September to try a general loan. Privy Seal loans, all of them more or less forced, had been a common practice. Since the accession of Elizabeth ten or so had been levied, most of them repaid, on about ten thousand of the richer inhabitants of the country. Now it was proposed that all who were on the subsidy books should lend at the rate of five subsidies. Like Privy Seal loans this general loan was to be forced, but unlike such loans the rate of the general loan was to be much higher than ever before. Instead of a few thousand many tens of thousands would be asked to lend—nay, told to do so. Legally there was little if any difference between this general loan and the Privy Seal loans. Politically the difference was great. Now that Parliament had refused to grant four subsidies and three-fifteenths, the King was ordering all his tax-paying subjects to lend at the rate of five subsidies. Furthermore, many people now knew that the Government was in such financial straits that there was little chance this loan would ever be repaid. In other words, this was taxation without consent of Parliament. So thought the judges when they refused to acknowledge that the loan was legal; and the dismissal of Chief Justice Sir Randal Crew made no difference. Though Charles, looking at the law through a telescope, saw nothing illegal about the loan, many of the more intelligent Englishmen agreed with the judges and therefore refused to lend. Some, to the number of seventy-six, were imprisoned for their refusal, so that they would be turned into examples for the rest of their countrymen. There were many, of course, who refused to pay and were not imprisoned. And yet the refusers were a distinct minority. Five subsidies should have produced about three hundred thousand pounds. The loan raised between two hundred and forty and two hundred and fifty thousand pounds. In other words the vast majority of English taxpayers, some out of fear and most with grumbles and protests, loaned their King rather large sums of money. As so often happened during this period attention has centred on the actions and opinions of a minority, while those of the majority have been ignored. This was bound to be the case because the minority was vociferous in its protests, while the majority was inarticulate and lacked enthusiasm in the support it gave the King. On the basis of precedents, narrow though they might be, Charles was acting as a constitutional king, although the judges and many of the gentry and nobility expressed the opinion of the day that the forced general loan was illegal.

When five of the knights who had been imprisoned for their refusal to lend sued out writs of habeas corpus in November 1627 they sought to discover from the Court of King's Bench why they had been imprisoned and if it was possible for them to be released on bail. The result was one of the greatest constitutional cases in English history. The case hinged on the right of the King to imprison without showing cause. In other words it raised the question whether prerogative arrest was legal or not. In spite of the argument presented by the defence that Magna Carta asserted that no man 'shall be ... imprisoned ... except by lawful judgment of his peers or by the law of the land',[5] in spite of supporting statutes from the reign of Edward III, and in spite of precedents where persons imprisoned by the Privy Council had been bailed before trial, the judges decided in favour of the Crown. They based their decision on numerous Tudor precedents where men had been imprisoned for varying lengths of time without any cause being shown to the Court of King's Bench. These judges can hardly be called subservient when it is remembered that three of them just a year earlier had refused to declare the general loan legal. Their decision in the five knights' case based, as it was, on the weight of precedents was undoubtedly correct. The argument presented by the defence, that the loan was illegal therefore it was entirely wrong for the King to imprison men who had refused to lend, had nothing to do with the issue before the court. It was: Can a man be imprisoned by the Privy Council—that is, the King—without cause being shown? The answer was yes. That being the case, must such a man be released on bail? The answer was no.

Whether or not the forced general loan was legal and prerogative arrest was allowable in law, it was extremely bad politics for Charles I to permit these issues to be brought before the public. His initial mistake was to ask for a general loan. He did not understand how to govern. It might logically be argued that by the end of 1627 Englishmen should have lost faith in their King and should have turned any love they had for him into hatred. But that was not the case. The vast majority in the land still venerated their sovereign, still respected him. Rightly or wrongly they placed the blame for all the errors in government on the despised Duke of Buckingham. Something must be done to prevent the Duke and his kind from continuing to make such errors, from bringing ruin on the kingdom and from breaking the law.

When the funds provided by the general loan proved inadequate to meet the pressing needs of the Government, Buckingham and other Ministers saw that the only recourse was to a Parliament. But Charles had had his fill of that brood of cawing rooks who inhabited the House of Commons. He feared that they would again peck at the eyes of his favourite. In the end an agreement was reached with the leaders of the 'country' party that if a Parliament was assembled the Duke would be unmolested. Had Charles and Buckingham understood the feelings of Englishmen in the early months of 1628 they would have realized that in order to obtain sufficient money to meet their needs they would have to make concessions little to their liking.

In January 1628 the arrested gentry were released. Parliament assembled on March 17th. In this well-known gathering the Commons under the leadership of Sir Thomas Wentworth soon had fitted their grievances into a Bill of Rights. But when the King made it clear beyond a shadow of a doubt that he would not sign such a Bill, the Commons under the direction of old Sir Edward Coke turned their Bill of Rights into a matter of record, a petition of right. The great Petition of Right passed by both Lords and Commons and reluctantly accepted by Charles I in order to obtain the five subsidies promised by the Commons curbed the power of the King to a greater extent than any document since Magna Carta. The Commons believed that the law of the land based on Magna Carta and supporting statutes had been broken when Englishmen were forced to pay a tax, benevolence or loan without consent of Parliament; it had been broken when men were imprisoned without cause shown; it had been broken when soldiers were billeted against the will of the inhabitants; and it had been broken when martial law was declared in time of peace. Now that the King had accepted the Petition of Right the Commons believed that the law could not be broken again in these four vital respects. The first two were particularly important, as the power to levy taxes of all kinds was now more than ever under the control of Parliament, and the person of every Englishman was now protected from arbitrary arrest. In the eyes of the Commons the legal power of the Crown was no more restricted by the Petition of Right than it had been by existing law before the passage of this document. They believed that the Petition would prevent the Ministers of the Crown from breaking the law as they had done in the past.

In the eyes of Charles his powers were clearly restricted by the Petition of Right. If he was to remain a constitutional king he must never ask for a benevolence or forced loan of any kind. He could never imprison any of his subjects without giving a reason. His father and Queen Elizabeth had been able to do all these things without anybody questioning their right to do so. The prerogative of the Crown had unquestionably been limited. Charles should have blamed the Duke of Buckingham and his financial troubles, originating with his father, for his misfortune. But England's king did not have the political insight or the desire to place the blame where it was due. To him the Commons were alone responsible.

Before dissolving this Parliament Charles must attempt to obtain one more service from these Commons. A tonnage and poundage Bill must be passed. In the first Parliament of the reign the Commons, instead of voting these Customs duties for the entire reign as had been the practice since the fifteenth century, voted them for only one year. The reasons for this limited grant do not concern our story. But the Lords for some unknown cause neglected to pass the one-year tonnage and poundage Bill. The King, however, could not afford to forgo over one hundred and fifty thousand pounds a year from these duties because of a parliamentary slip. He continued to collect tonnage and poundage not only for the first year of his reign but for the first four years without a Bill being passed by Parliament. In both the second and third Parliaments the tonnage and poundage Bill got no further than the second reading before it was pushed aside for more pressing business. Now at what appeared to be the end of his third Parliament Charles hoped that this Bill would finally be passed through both Houses. Instead the men of the Lower House suddenly decided that tonnage and poundage should be included under the term 'tax' in the Petition of Right. There never had been a hint of this when the Petition was being debated in the House. Now it was proposed that a resolution should be passed which stated that tonnage and poundage was one of those taxes which the King could not levy without the assent of Parliament. In desperation Charles prorogued Parliament to prevent the passage of this resolution. He dared not dissolve it because that would mean the passage of a tonnage and poundage Bill would be postponed, possibly for years. A fundamental principle with Charles I was that he would not break the law if it was in any manner possible to avoid it.

To secure the passage of a tonnage and poundage Bill he summoned the second session of his third Parliament to meet in January 1629. Though Buckingham was dead Charles knew that he must have this Bill passed. In fact, the death of his favourite may have made Charles more law-abiding than he had been while the Duke was alive. When the King addressed the Lords and Commons on January 23rd, four days after the opening of the session, he declared 'that he had no intention to claim that the levying of tonnage and poundage was his by right. His actions stemmed from necessity ... Now he was most anxious that they pass the Bill for tonnage and poundage, so that "my by-past actions will be included, and my future proceedings authorized".'[6] Charles publicly admitted that he had broken the law. He virtually apologized for his actions and begged the Lords and Commons to enable him to collect these duties legally. Of course, he also implied that should this Bill fail to pass he would have to continue collecting tonnage and poundage through necessity, which would mean illegally.

Poor Charles had bad luck with this most desired Bill. Again it was pushed aside when the Commons became greatly excited over the privilege of a Member whose goods had been seized because of his refusal to pay tonnage and poundage. In addition religion so excited the Commons that in the end, on that famous second of March, instead of presenting the King with a tonnage and poundage Bill the Commons passed three memorable resolutions, two of which declared that

> Whosoever shall counsel or advise the taking and levying of the subsidies of Tonnage and Poundage, not being granted by Parliament, or shall be an actor or instrument therein, shall be likewise reputed an innovator in the Government, and a capital enemy to the Kingdom and Commonwealth.
>
> If any merchant or person whatsoever shall voluntarily yield, or pay the said subsidies of Tonnage and Poundage, not being granted by Parliament, he shall likewise be reputed

a betrayer of the liberties of England, and an enemy to the same.[7]

The blame for the failure to pass the Bill lies squarely with the Commons, who unconsciously were moving slowly towards revolution.

Now the King was placed in a difficult position. He must either stop collecting his Customs duties and forgo a large percentage of his annual revenue, or he must continue to collect them and become a self-confessed breaker of the law. With royal finances in bad shape he was forced to take the latter alternative. In continuing to collect tonnage and poundage for the next dozen years Charles for the first time was acting as an unconstitutional king in the narrow legal sense. Though many of his subjects denounced his actions, this practice did not raise as great a storm of protest as did a number of policies which were inaugurated during the next ten years of his reign and which Charles believed to be within the law.

Before considering these policies let us examine the role of religion in the development of the constitution. Soon after his accession Charles began to show favour to those clergy of the Church of England who supported the teachings of Launcelot Andrews, Bishop of Winchester, which can be summarized under the headings authority, ceremony and free-will. This movement within the Church, called by contemporaries 'Arminianism' but better described by the term 'Anglo-Catholicism', fell under the direction of Richard Neile, Bishop of Durham, and particularly William Laud, who was advanced to the see of London in 1628. To the Puritans, and also to many Anglicans, Anglo-Catholicism was believed to be only a short step from Roman Catholicism. Moreover, to the delight of Charles the Anglo-Catholic clergy exalted the royal prerogative and placed great emphasis on non-resistance in defining divine right. Pushing Anglo-Catholicism into the crevices of the Church of England at every opportunity, Charles and Laud ignored George Abbot, the Calvanistic Archbishop of Canterbury. In all he did as regards the Church the King was acting in the pattern of the Elizabethan settlement. He was working within the constitution of the Church as established by law.

The Puritans, and many Anglicans too, did not understand that the King and his Bishop of London, soon to be Archbishop, had no intention whatsoever of returning to Rome. These opponents were sure that popery was just around the corner. The attack which had been smouldering in previous Parliaments burst into flame in the session of 1629. Anglo-Catholicism was denounced on all sides. As may be seen from Sir John Eliot's speech of January 29th[8] and from the resolutions on religion prepared by a sub-committee on February 23rd but never presented to the House,[9] the proposal that Parliament take control of the Church of England was very much in the air. The end result was the first of the three resolutions of March 2nd which declared:

> Whosoever shall bring in innovation of religion, or by favour or countenance seem to extend or introduce Popery or Arminianism, or other opinion disagreeing from the true and orthodox Church, shall be reputed a capital enemy to this Kingdom and Commonwealth.[10]

Arminianism was the Anglicanism of Charles I. Though they did not blame the King but his Ministers and bishops for this form of Anglicanism, the Commons were condemning the Church established and upheld by the Crown. By 'true and orthodox Church' they could have meant only one approved by Parliament, specifically the Commons. How the Puritan Commons of Elizabeth's reign would have envied these actions taken by the Puritan Commons of Charles's reign. I am sure that Elizabeth would have been in complete sympathy with the Anglo-Catholicism of Andrews, Neile and Laud. That she would have approved the means and practices of enforcement soon to be employed by Laud is another matter. But that she would have taken forceful action after the passage of the resolutions on March 2nd is certain. It would be much more correct to say that Elizabeth would never have permitted the situation to deteriorate to such an extent as to give the Commons the opportunity to introduce the three resolutions. As was so often the case Charles was a complete failure when it came to the art of government. And as has already been said, the art of government is a facet of the constitution which cannot be ignored in the Tudor and Stuart periods.

That facet played a leading role in a series of events which began on March 3rd when Sir John Eliot and eight of his colleagues in the House were arrested. If only the Elizabethan tactics of a few weeks or months of imprisonment, followed by the release of the prisoners accompanied by a gracious message from the King, could have been imitated. But the circumstances produced by the Commons themselves, by the Petition of Right and by the nature of Charles made that impossible. On March 2nd the Commons were on the verge of revolution without realizing it. And then, according to the great Petition, an imprisonment must be followed by a charge. That charge was seditious conduct. That the words and actions of the nine Members on March 2nd and during the preliminary meetings could be labelled seditious conduct is indeed questionable. It depends entirely on one's point of view, whether living in the seventeenth or twentieth century. But certainly the trickery employed by Charles to prevent seven of the nine from being released on bail was hardly good public relations. If the criminal charge of seditious conduct is acceptable the trial of Sir John Eliot, Benjamin Valentine and William Strode in the court of King's Bench was perfectly legal. Privilege of Parliament did not protect these Members against such a charge. That Charles, who hated Eliot more than any other Member of the House of Commons because of his violent attacks on the Duke of Buckingham and other Ministers, should refuse to release Sir John from the Tower even temporarily to regain his health is understandable. But once again this refusal from the national point of view was bad policy, especially as Eliot died in the Tower of his disease. Charles never cared about the national point of view. In the long run, of course, Eliot's death was the King's loss and the Commons's gain.

Let us look back for a moment and survey the changing position of the Commons to March 2nd, 1629. By that time a situation had arisen in the House of Commons which might have led to a much happier ending of the reign had Charles been able to seize his opportunities. In the last half-dozen Parliaments of Elizabeth's reign the Commons had developed, as we have seen, an independence and initiative never witnessed before.[11] With this new spirit there was always associated an intense loyalty to and love for the Queen. In James's first Long Parliament both independence and initiative asserted themselves on a number of occasions. Though loyalty remained the same, love between the new King and his subjects could not be kindled. And then by 1610 a new loyalty to the rights of Englishmen began ever so slightly to

threaten or compete with loyalty to the Crown. This was definitely
true in the great debates on impositions in the Parliament of 1614.
But in the first session of 1621 a good deal of the old harmony
between King and Commons seemed to be re-established only to
be shattered in the second session over freedom of speech. In the
last Parliament loyalty and harmony between the Commons and
the Government, though not necessarily James, over hostility to
Spain blossomed out as never before during the reign. But
throughout the four Parliaments one senses that independence
and initiative were growing stronger from session to session. By
luck in 1624 it was channelled into co-operation with the Crown.

In 1625 Sir John Eliot in his *Negotium Posterorum*[12] tells us about
the activities of the 'country' party in the House of Commons.
That party had its roots in the temper of the Commons dating
from the reign of Elizabeth. It gained more of the feeling for
opposition in various episodes of the first three Parliaments of the
reign of James. But from 1625 on, the 'country' party was
essentially the anti-Buckingham party. In the eyes of Charles it
showed itself first in the Parliament of 1625 and then dominated
the Commons in that of 1626. In 1628 this party instead of using
denunciation took the initiative to tie the hands of Buckingham
with the Petition of Right. That document plus the murder of
the Duke almost spelled the end of the 'country' party. But in the
House of Commons initiative voicing itself essentially through
opposition could not subside so easily. In the session of 1629 a
vociferous minority, though of course no longer anti-Buckingham,
was still anti-ministerial, as can be seen from Eliot's denunciation
of Sir Richard Weston on March 2nd.[13] In its opposition this
group, not now a party in the earlier sense, found itself at times
treading very close to the toes of the King. Revolution was in the
offing. A majority of the Commons, certainly by March 2nd,
sensed it and did not like it. Had the three resolutions of that day
been put to a division instead of being orally acclaimed, it is my
opinion that however loud the 'Ayes' sounded they would have
been defeated.[14] Loyalty to the Crown, though devoid of the old
Elizabethan love, was strong in both the Lords and Commons
when Charles dissolved his Third Parliament on March 10th,
1629.

At that time he had the opportunity to gain the support of the
nation. His initial steps were most correct. In the Proclamation of

Dissolution, in his speech to the Lords at the time of the dissolution, and in the Declaration where he explained in detail what had happened since the opening of the Parliament and why he had taken certain steps, Charles put the blame for his troubles not on the whole House of Commons, not on a majority, but only on a small minority whom he called 'vipers'. For example, he said to the Lords:

Let me tell you, that it is so far from me to adjudge all the House alike guilty that I knew that there are many there as dutiful Subjects as any in the world, it being but some few Vipers among them that did cast this mist of undutifulness over most of their eyes; yet to say truth, there was a good number there, that could not be infected with this contagion; insomuch that some did express their duties in speaking, which was the general fault of the House the last day.[15]

As Gardiner says: 'The Declaration set forth by the King to justify the dissolution was an able statement of his case against the House of Commons. In his own mind at least Charles took his stand upon the law.'[16] He promised to obey the Petition of Right and to prevent any innovations in religion. Rightly he protested that he had permitted the Commons in defending their liberties and those of Englishmen to encroach upon his prerogative far beyond anything done under his predecessors.

There was the trouble. Both James and Charles had allowed the Commons to get out of hand. Now instead of trying to adjust himself to the new situation and bring about as much harmony as possible between King, Parliament and people, Charles decided to rule without Parliament. He cared nothing about the country— that is, the articulate part of the country. At the same time he remained isolated from his subjects, both high and low. He believed that he alone knew what was good for his people. With a total lack of imagination, stubborn and at the same time irresolute, and with a lack of intelligence shocking when contrasted with that of Elizabeth or even James I, Charles destroyed all the goodwill, which early in 1629 was ready to back him, by insisting on his absolute sovereignty in Church and State, in Scotland as well as in England. With it all he tried to stay within the law as he understood it. But frequently his understanding of both the law of the land and of moral law differed from that of his subjects, so that he readily could be accused of breaking both on occasion. That Charles ruled for eleven years without summoning a Parliament was not unconstitutional or illegal, except that many Englishmen were beginning to feel that the frequent meeting of that body was a vital and necessary part of their Government. It is true, however, that the King and his subjects could have worked and lived together in harmony without a Parliament. Because harmony failed to develop Charles was censured for not summoning a Parliament. Because the necessity of raising money was the key to his rule, and because he raised it without the help of Parliament, he aroused intense opposition. In the eyes of many he was violating the fundamental principle of no taxation without the consent of Parliament.

For the next decade Charles and his Ministers were forced to devote much of their time to finance. Expenses must be cut and new revenues raised. So thought the Lord Treasurer, Sir Richard Weston, already a peer by the spring of 1628 and created Earl of Portland in February 1633. By April 1629 peace had been made with France, and in November 1630 also between England and Spain. The drain of war on the treasury had been stopped.

In the meantime the Government, continuing to collect tonnage and poundage of necessity, antagonized many men of principle engaged in trade. Eventually they swallowed their principles and paid with only a mental protest. And then, as we have seen, feeling was being aroused by the treatment of the gentlemen who had been imprisoned for seditious conduct in the session of 1629. The condemnation of three of them in the Court of King's Bench in 1630 and the martyrdom of Sir John Eliot in 1632 added fuel to the fire of discontent.

That discontent among articulate middle-class Englishmen was further provoked between 1630 and 1635 when compositions for knighthood were forced on them to the tune of one hundred and sixty-five thousand pounds. These fines were legal without a doubt. But they were bitterly resented by the men who were forced to pay them. These men also resented another scheme to raise money which presumably was born in the fertile brain of Attorney-General William Noy. That was forest fines.

By July 1634 the policy of the dying Attorney-General was being executed by Sir John Finch, soon to be made Chief Justice of the Common Pleas. In the Forest Court of the Earl of Holland,

Chief Justice in Eyre, Finch, supported in his opinion by three judges, declared that the perambulation of the forests made by Edward I was illegal because it 'had distorted land newly attached to the forest in the reign of Henry II, which it was beyond its power to touch'.[17] Between 1634 and 1637 Holland held 'justice seats' in the Forest of Dean, Waltham Forest, New Forest and the Forest of Rockingham. In one instance the circumference of a forest was extended from six to sixty miles. The fines levied were extremely heavy, as for example twenty thousand pounds on the Earl of Salisbury. But through the bounty of the King and the actions of commissioners of compounding the fines were greatly reduced, with the result that barely twenty-four thousand pounds fell to the treasury over a period of three years. The annoyances caused and the indignation aroused among high and low were, however, far in excess of the monetary gain to the Crown.

What angered all classes, touched the pocket-book of the poor man even more than the rich, were the monopolies of manufacture granted by the Crown to corporations or companies in conformity with the Monopoly Act of 1624. Prices on one commodity after another were raised by these vultures, as the monopolists were called. Of course, Charles's profit was considerable, and legal profit it was too. The soap monopoly alone produced over thirty thousand pounds a year for the royal coffers. At the same time the Court of Star Chamber received much additional business when it protected the hated monopolists from interlopers and from men who believed in freedom and in the property rights of Englishmen. Little wonder that in the early years of the Long Parliament any Member who had been or was a monopolist or who was in any way connected with a monopoly was deprived of his seat in the House of Commons.

Whether it was tonnage and poundage, knighthood fines, forest fines or monopolies, they all produced great or small sums for the royal treasury. At the same time they all provoked the growing hostility of the nation to the Government of Charles I. Rightly Ministers were blamed, for Englishmen knew that men like Weston, Noy and others had the intelligence totally lacking in the King to concoct these various schemes to raise money. But Charles approved and sanctioned them, therefore the responsibility of initiating them rested squarely on his shoulders.

So, too, was the King responsible for that most.hated of all Stuart taxes, ship-money. It was obvious to all that English sea power was at an extremely low ebb. A war was raging on the Continent which at any moment might embroil England. Pirates, especially Dunkirk privateers, were swarming in the Channel. England was unable to collect from the Dutch fees which would license them to fish in the North Sea off the English coast and under English protection. Foreign ships in the Channel and off the Dutch and Flemish coasts would not dip their sails in recognition of England's sovereignty of the seas. Such by 1634 were universally acknowledged conditions.

At the same time Charles was contemplating a secret alliance with Spain against the Dutch. A few years later he was thinking seriously of allying with France. In both cases the object was the restoration of the Palatinate to his sister's son. In both instances a strong fleet might be most helpful. Of course, neither Spain nor France, the Dutch nor the Emperor trusted Charles or believed that he would ever dare to use his fleet in actual warfare. Consequently the proposed alliances never materialized; nobody was afraid of Charles I and England.

All these situations and conditions constituted the justification for ship-money, whether it was the first writ of 1634 or the sixth and last writ of 1639. England was in serious danger; so Charles, the sole judge of the status of the country, declared. Hence he could levy ship-money to build and maintain a fleet at sea to dispel the danger. That is what ten of the twelve judges announced in December 1635. That was the gist of the answer of the twelve judges to the queries of the King in February 1637. And that was the basis of the decision of seven of the twelve judges against John Hampden in the Exchequer Chamber early in 1638.

That the King was the sole judge as to when the country was in danger was firmly supported by precedents. But was the country between 1634 and 1640 in such imminent danger that the King could ask his subjects to pay him money to build and maintain a fleet to withstand that danger without summoning Parliament? Most ship-money writs were issued six to seven months before effective use could be made of their proceeds. There was plenty of time to summon a Parliament to meet any danger which might arise. But Charles was afraid of the Commons and dared not summon a Parliament. He must rule the country without Parliament if it was in any way possible.

Most Tudor precedents, particularly Elizabethan precedents, pointed to the levying of extraordinary revenue only through Parliament. The same was essentially true under James I. Charles had assented to the Petition of Right which said that the King might not levy a tax without the consent of Parliament. Ship-money was a tax being levied without the consent of Parliament and, since the nation was not in immediate danger, without any moral basis. But Charles believed that because the judges supported his right to declare at any time the nation to be in danger, he was acting legally. Though they paid him seven hundred and forty thousand pounds in ship-money over a period of six years his subjects believed that he was taxing them illegally. Many believed incorrectly that he was not using all this money to build ships and maintain them at sea, but was using it to run the Government without Parliament. Englishmen's property rights and freedom were being endangered by ship-money, so thousands thought. From an impartial point of view Charles I should not have levied ship-money without obtaining it from Parliament. Actually the ship-money fleets between 1635 and 1640 did nothing and prevented nothing. Had they never existed Charles's political position abroad would have been no different, while his political position at home might have been much stronger.

It might have been had not Charles I, head of the Church of England, and William Laud, Archbishop of Canterbury, stirred up a hornets' nest with religion. Anglo-Catholicism or Arminianism (on the rise since the opening of the reign) dominated the Church when Laud became Archbishop in 1633. The Anglican Church based on the Elizabethan settlement and Thomas Hooker's strong defence of it in his *Ecclesiastical Polity* needed Laudian 'beauty of holiness' to give it substance. Unfortunately the fourth decade of the seventeenth century was the worst possible time to introduce such practices. And Laud, applying 'thorough' to the Church in England as Wentworth was applying it to the State in Ireland, could not have employed a worse method to implement his measures. The fussy little red-faced man became a dictator of the worst sort, and Charles supported him to the hilt.

Puritans were outraged. To them 'beauty of holiness' was

popery. They believed the hated Archbishop was about to acknowledge papal supremacy at any moment. The King, dominated by a papist Queen and seemingly tolerant towards the followers of the Roman Church, appeared to the Puritans to be following in the footsteps of his Archbishops. In fact, neither Laud nor Charles had any intention of ever going back to Rome. To be sure there was a measure of tolerance in the King, but it did not cover those bigoted Puritans whom he believed were ready to destroy both his Church and State. Not understanding the people, Charles could only blindly approve the methods Laud employed to produce religious uniformity in England. 'Beauty of holiness' was forced down the throats of Englishmen by a small minority of the clergy supported by the King. No wonder thousands of Puritans fled to America and the whole body moved further to the left. No wonder most Anglicans, clergy as well as laity, hated Laud and either became Puritan sympathizers or remained conformists bearing a grudge. Seeing uniformity being established throughout the land and blind to the intense opposition of both Puritan and Anglican, Charles and Laud by 1635 decided to do for Scotland what seemingly had been accomplished for England.

On his visit to his northern kingdom in 1633, accompanied by Laud, Charles found the churches of Scotland drab and unkempt. The bishops in Scotland exercised little authority over clergy who preached a Calvinistic creed. There was growing hostility among the people towards the bishops as they fell more and more under the influence of Laud. To remedy these conditions Charles, with the help of Laud, prepared in 1635 (and issued in 1636) canons which gave the Scottish bishops more authority and the Church a uniformity modelled on that of the Church of England. Neither the Scottish clergy nor laity were consulted. To be sure, the opinion of a few Laudian bishops of Scotland was sought on the canons as well as on the Prayer Book to be used in the north. That book caused the real trouble in Scotland. Considered by the Scots to be both popish and English was more than enough to make it hated in the northern kingdom. In December 1636 it was ordered to be adopted in every parish in Scotland. There followed the well-known story of the riot in St Giles Cathedral in Edinburgh in the summer of 1637, the universal opposition of the Scots to the Prayer Book, and, because of the obstinacy of Charles in refusing to modify his policy in any way, the signing of the National Covenant by the people of Scotland in the early months of 1638. That document based religion in Scotland on the authority of the General Assembly of the Church and the Scottish Parliament. The King as head of the Scottish Church was ignored. Charles, though he might have been willing to set aside the Prayer Book, could never accept such a policy. Therefore he must wage war on his northern kingdom to re-establish his headship of the Church. During the spring and early summer of 1639 preparations by both sides for battle, without any bloodshed taking place, constituted the so-called first Bishops' War. With a demoralized army refusing to fight the Scots whose swords were itching to defend the Kirk and with insufficient funds with which to pay and feed his troops—the old story again—Charles was forced on June 18th to sign the Treaty of Berwick.[18] The wording of this document was so vague, and it left so much to a General Assembly and Scottish Parliament of the near future, that neither Charles nor the Scots appeared to benefit. Nothing was said about the King's headship of the Scottish Church. He took it for granted that he was to be accepted as such, while the Scots believed that a General Assembly without royal interference was to rule their Church. On learning this Charles must either submit or wage another war. But his finances were exhausted.

Instead of conducting a glorious war in the Channel with his ship-money fleet to restore the Palatinate to his nephew, he had participated in an inglorious war on the border of Scotland to lose his religious if not his political power in that land. The only positive result was an empty treasury and the inevitability of summoning an English Parliament again.

What was Charles's position in England by 1640? Was he still a constitutional King? During the past decade he had, with one exception, ruled according to the law. At least so it seemed to the King and the supporters of his prerogative. That exception was, of course, the levying of tonnage and poundage. Charles knew that the collection of these duties was illegal; he did not want to exact them, but circumstances forced him to do so. With ship-money Charles believed that he was acting legally because the judges had supported him on three occasions. Fear may have influenced some of the judges in their support of the Crown. More likely they upheld the prerogative as long as it did not infringe the property rights of Englishmen. And they placed the safety of the nation above the rights of the individual. By 1637 the great body of intelligent Englishmen considered ship-money illegal. Though contemporaries felt that the law and precedents supporting the other financial schemes of this decade were being stretched to their detriment, they could not accuse Charles's Government of ignoring or breaking the law.

The English constitution and English law, as is well known, are based essentially on precedents. When the struggle for power between Crown and Parliament began under James I and was continued at a hotter pace under Charles precedents played a major role. Debates in the House of Commons, arguments of lawyers in and out of court and decisions of judges all turned upon precedents. Today students of the early seventeenth century know that opponents of the Crown in and out of Parliament frequently abused the precedents they cited. The men of that day had no sense of history. They stretched and twisted precedents out of their historical context. They turned Magna Carta from a feudal charter into the Charter of Liberties of the English people. But they do not seem to have been conscious of their misinterpretations. Much the same was done with precedents by the supporters of the Crown, though they did not abuse history nearly as much as their opponents. Indeed, it has been the custom of many Whig historians of the nineteenth and twentieth centuries to condone the abuse of precedents by the Parliamentarians and to condemn the same practice by the Royalists. In all fairness to Charles I and his Government this is not good history. As I have tried to show, the King, his judges, lawyers and supporters in Parliament, when citing precedents, upheld the constitution and the law as they believed them to have existed for the past century or more. To be sure, at times their interpretation of precedents appeared to be extremely narrow. At times the common law appeared to be endangered. And at times the prerogative appeared to be encroaching upon the law. But when compared with the sixteenth century, were not many lawyers and even judges of the seventeenth trying to push and stretch the law in protecting the rights of Englishmen far beyond what anybody in the Tudor period had contemplated? If this was true, it was all to the good when looking back from the present. But those were not the thoughts of Charles I and his supporters who were looking back from their own day. They saw no reason why Tudor absolutism should not be followed by Stuart absolutism.

The great difference between the two absolutisms, as we have seen, was that the first worked because it had the support of the people, while the second failed because it was opposed by the people. Charles I could rule but he could not govern. He was hopeless as a politician, both as head of the Church and head of the State. Similarly the qualities of a statesman were completely lacking in Charles. He had no domestic policy except to rule the State and the Church as an absolute monarch with complete disregard of the feelings of the people. Therein lay his trouble. He was neither English nor Scottish. He never identified himself with the countries over which he ruled. He was interested in the power and position of the Crown as it affected him, not England or Scotland. In this respect, as in so many others, he was the complete opposite of Queen Elizabeth I. In addition Charles believed that he alone knew what was good for his subjects and that they should blindly accept his ministrations. It must be admitted that the King and his Privy Council during the late 1630s did much for the masses. For a few years the little fellow, who in no way counted politically, was more contented and better cared for than he had been for years. At the same time more and more of the men of the middle and upper classes were complaining at the exactions of the Government and at the follies of the Laudian Church of England.

Finally, from the point of view of a statesman, Charles I had no foreign policy. He had one aim. That was to restore the Palatinate to his nephew. But how that object should be attained was at the mercy of the royal whim of the moment. He disregarded the interests of England as well as of other European countries in attempting to reach his goal. And because he had no policy he never reached it. The simple fact is that Charles Stuart did not know how to be a king. He had little intelligence, character or personality. But he was not stupid. 'He was a shrewd critic of other men's mistakes', Gardiner says, 'and usually succeeded in hitting the weak point of an opponent's argument.'[19] Though Charles could criticize he lacked completely any constructive power.

As a ruler he was totally incompetent, but he was not as evil as he has been pictured. Modern historians in describing the activities of Charles I have frequently emphasized the latter adjective. Gardiner in particular, guided by nineteenth-century nonconformist morality, has blackened him by declaring that he was incapable of telling the truth, could not be trusted by his subjects and wriggled out of promises whenever possible. These practices, to a greater or lesser degree, were indulged in by many capable sovereigns during the age of absolutism in western Europe. Best remembered, similar actions were part of the behaviour pattern of the ablest of them all, Queen Elizabeth I. She twisted, she dissembled, she lied whenever it was to her advantage. Her Commons, her Ministers, ambassadors and rulers were all treated at times to the same immoral tactics. Yet Elizabeth has been praised by historians for these performances by gilding them with such terms as cleverness, astuteness and feminine guile. Of course, Elizabeth was one of the greatest and most successful rulers England has ever known and one who loved her people and her country. Charles, on the other hand, was one of the weakest and most unsuccessful kings, who took little interest in England and its people. With the former the good submerged the bad. With the latter incompetence magnified the evil. Today we should try to be fair to Charles I. If he is to be remembered for his weaknesses, his failure to understand his people and country as well as his irresolution and similar traits should stand far above his duplicity.

In his day this king needed a lot of sound advice which he had to be willing to follow if his reign were to be even partially successful. In December 1639 Thomas Wentworth, to be made Earl of Strafford in the next month, advised Charles to summon a Parliament as an experiment. Such advice, which Charles and his Privy Council accepted, had a dangerous implication. It was that should the Commons fail to vote supply the King would be justified in using any means at his disposal to raise the funds he needed. At the time the Crown was in serious danger in Scotland. The men of the North in interpreting the treaty of Berwick were virtually denying that the King was the head of the Church of Scotland. At the same time they appeared to be depriving him more and more of his political power in his northern kingdom. The only means Charles and Strafford could think of to regain the King's former position there was to make war on Scotland, to force the people under the power of the Crown in Church and

State. In order to be able to do this an English Parliament must be summoned. If no funds were forthcoming the King would be justified in taxing his subjects without the consent of Parliament. That was the situation. And that was the argument of Strafford.

When Parliament met in April 1640 there were so many grievances to be considered and redressed that it was little wonder the Commons would not think of voting twelve subsidies in exchange for giving up only ship-money, a tax they considered illegal. Instead of conferring with the Commons, as any politician would have done, Charles abruptly dissolved Parliament.

During the summer of 1640 preparations for war against Scotland were being pushed on all fronts. Various ways of raising money were employed, and none of them produced enough. In the eyes of most Englishmen they were all illegal and were in direct violation of the Petition of Right. Ship-money was levied; loans from the rich and from the city of London, which refused, were demanded; a benevolence was received from the clergy; and coat-and-conduct money, the counterpart of ship-money to be used to equip the army, was exacted. As the last practice was being considered by more and more people to be illegal, Charles, who always wanted to stay within the law if it was in any way possible, was delighted when his legal advisers found that Parliament in the reign of Henry IV had declared that the King might issue Commissions of Array when an invasion was impending. These commissions would not only provide armed men from each county but also money to pay for arms and equipment from those who could not fight. Commissions of Array would produce the same results as coat-and-conduct money, and in the eyes of Charles were undoubtedly legal. But most Englishmen felt that the Government had produced another obscure precedent which was to be used to oppress them.

The Second Bishops' War in the late summer of 1640, more unpopular in England than the first, was also a greater disaster for Charles and his Government. In October both the terms of the treaty of Ripon and the advice of the Great Council at York made the summoning of an English Parliament obligatory.[20] Though Strafford could be blamed for the misgovernment and misfortunes of the summer and autumn of 1640, Charles's role as king was becoming weaker with the passage of every month. The Crown's absolute sovereignty was about to receive a frontal attack, and it was hardly in a position to withstand it.

Soon after the opening of the Long Parliament revolution in the Government of England began with the impeachment and ultimate attainder of the Earl of Strafford. The Commons initiated that revolution when they attempted to define a new type of treason with which they charged the Earl. That was treason against the fundamental laws of the land. Actually intimidation by a London mob of both the Lords and the King secured the final passage of the Bill of Attainder. Constitutional procedure was scarcely maintained. In the midst of confusion and fear, produced by rumours and reports of an army plot, of the landing of Dutch and French troops and of the threat of an Irish army which the King would not disband, it is remarkable that bloodshed did not ensue. England desperately needed a strong man to bring order out of chaos, to restore the constitution or to smite the enemy with the sword. One strong man, Strafford, lay helpless in the Tower. The other strong man, John Pym, was hampered by the conflicting views of the Commons. Only Charles was free to act, and he was too weak to do so. On May 10th, 1641 he signed the Bill of Attainder out of fear that harm would come to his beloved wife at the hands of the mob. We cannot blame him. On the same day he signed the Bill which said that this Parliament could not be dissolved or prorogued without its own consent. Why did he do it? Out of fear of the mob? Surely the mob would have been satisfied with the attainder of 'Black Tom Strafford'. The King's action was that of a weak man who would not and could not think under stress. Undoubtedly Charles was advised to sign this Bill, but it was extremely bad advice given by men who were as scared as their King. Charles was now at the mercy of a Parliament which had tasted blood. A revolution had begun which the Commons would not and could not stop. And the King had no legal way to stop the Commons.

Had Charles had an ounce of strength in his character, instead of the weakness of indecision, he would have refused to disband his army in the north after a settlement had been reached with the Scots that summer. He would have marched that army and the Irish army on London and re-established his power. Certainly he had a far greater chance of success at that time than a year later. Instead he devoted the summer of 1641 to signing Bills passed by both Houses which deprived him of much of his prerogative. These powers could be restored to him only by an act of God or by the force of arms. Charles's weak nature made him an optimistic gambler. He always hoped that circumstances would arise in the future which would restore to him all he had lost. He believed that his enemies would quarrel and destroy each other.

The ink of his signature on the Bill declaring ship-money illegal was hardly dry when in August 1641 he departed for Scotland. Though barely a year ago the Scots had shown only contempt for his authority, he now believed that they would help him to regain his lost powers in England. During his absence religion proved to be more and more of a divisive force in the House of Commons. The struggle between 'root and branchers' and moderate reformers soon began to be merged with a political revolution, growing ever more radical. That revolution had completed a stage when on November 22nd the Grand Remonstrance passed the Commons by a majority of eleven. The radicals had won. That document would have established a parliamentary monarchy in which the King would have had little more than nominal power. Not only was the State virtually controlled by Parliament, but also a Presbyterian Church directed by Parliament was to replace the Church of England. Fortunately for Charles the Grand Remonstrance went much too far for many Members of both Houses of Parliament and for thousands of his subjects. A royalist party of considerable strength was now in the making.

Charles, returning without any gains whatsoever from his Scottish junket three days after the passage of the Grand Remonstrance, was in a strong position *vis-à-vis* the Commons. Restraint, dignity and common sense might have done much for him against his hot-headed opponents. Early in January 1642 he destroyed any gains he might have made by ordering his Attorney-General to impeach five Members of the House of Commons and one peer. He had taken an unconstitutional step. An impeachment must originate with the Commons. He antagonized the Lords by ordering the studies of the five Members sealed and their persons arrested. That was the function of the Lords in an impeachment. And then on the next day, January 4th, possibly goaded by Henrietta Maria, Charles lost all sense of proportion and propriety by going to the House of Commons in person to arrest the five Members. They had been warned and had fled to the city. The die was cast. Charles was as hot-headed as the Commons. War was inevitable.

Both sides prepared for the crisis during the following months. Both sides aimed to gain control of the militia and obtain possession of the magazines. Charles procrastinated while the Commons tried to secure the passage of a militia Bill which would permit Parliament to appoint the militia officers. Having failed with the Bill, the Commons passed the militia ordinance which they hoped would enable them to achieve their objective without the consent of the King. To justify their ordinance the Commons on June 6th backed it with the principle of the sovereignty of Parliament; behind it, they implied, lay the sovereignty of the people. But four days earlier the sovereignty of Parliament had been far more clearly pronounced in the Nineteen Propositions to the King. These propositions placed all power in the hands of Parliament and left the King a figurehead. If Charles could not accept the Grand Remonstrance, it was even less possible for him to accept the Nineteen Propositions.

On June 21st the King sent to the Commons an Answer to the Propositions. It had been composed by Sir John Colepeper, Chancellor of the Exchequer, and Viscount Falkland, Secretary of State. In this document there is a description of mixed government, sometimes called the classical theory of the English constitution,[21] which reads as follows:

> There being three kinds of government amongst men, absolute monarchy, aristocracy, and democracy, and all these having their particular conveniences and inconveniences, the experience and wisdom of your ancestors hath so moulded this [government] out of a mixture of these, as to give to this kingdom ... the conveniences of all three, without the inconveniences of any one, as long as the balance hangs even between the three estates, and they run jointly on in their proper channels ...

It then proceeds to enumerate briefly the 'ill' and 'good' of each of the three and continues: 'In this kingdom the laws are jointly made by a king, by a house of peers, and by a House of Commons chosen by the people, all having free votes and particular privileges.' It then lists the usual powers of the King, such as the making of peace and war, the choosing of officers, Councillors and judges, etc. But there is no mention of the King's power to summon and dissolve Parliament. These powers of a 'regulated monarchy' the Answer goes on to say, are necessary to maintain the authority of the King whereby he is enabled to enforce the law and preserve the liberties and proprieties of the subjects. Such a monarchy must also have authority in order to retain the respect of 'the great ones' and prevent feuds and factions from developing among them as well as to secure from the people 'a fear and reverence' to hinder 'tumults, violence and licentiousness' from arising.

The Answer thereupon shows the relation of the King to the Commons, the role of the Commons and the functions of the Lords as follows:

> Again, that the prince may not make use of this high and perpetual power to the hurt of those for whose good he hath it, and make use of the name of public necessity for the gain of his private favourites and followers, to the detriment of his people, the House of Commons (an excellent conserver of liberty, but never intended for any share in government, or the choosing of them that should govern) is solely entrusted with the first propositions concerning the levies of moneys ... and the impeaching of those, who for their own ends, though countenanced by any surreptitiously gotten command of the King, have violated that law which he is bound (when he knows it) to protect, and to the protection of which they were bound to advise him, at least not to serve him in the contrary. And the lords being trusted with a judicatory power, are an excellent screen and bank between the prince and people, to assist each against any encroachments of the other, and by just judgments to preserve that law, which ought to be the rule of every one of the three ...

This little discourse on government in England is a refreshing interlude[22] in the midst of a long denunciatory, cumbersome Answer given to the Nineteen Propositions. For the most part Charles discloses the evils of the Commons's proposals and shows why he cannot possibly accept them. Towards the end he concedes some minor points which deal primarily with religion.

Our concern with this segment of the Answer to the Nineteen Propositions is whether Charles believed in a mixed government, in a balance between King, Lords and Commons. Did Colepeper present a new conception which the King would have difficulty in accepting?

As we have seen, the Tudors believed in a government composed of King and Parliament—that is, Lords and Commons. They recognized that taxes could not be levied or laws made without the consent of Parliament. James was forced to accept the same procedure, though he attempted with little success to raise sufficient revenue without going to Parliament for it. On his accession Charles followed in the footsteps of his father and the Tudors, but he became so disgusted with the Commons that he ruled without Parliament for eleven years. Charles, as we have seen, tried during the 1630s to abide by the law as he understood it. In his eyes he was maintaining a constitutional absolutism. Had he had the ability, and had opinion in the nation made it possible, he would have continued indefinitely to rule without Parliament. Technically he would have been within the letter of the constitution but not within its spirit as it had been developing since 1581. By 1629 the Commons had made the frequent summoning of Parliament a part of that spirit of the constitution. Charles's failure to rule as a constitutional absolutist forced him to accept the practice of his predecessors and of the early years of his reign. By 1640-2 the government of England was again by King, Lords and Commons. They made the laws. They voted taxes.

Just as in the 1630s one of the three, the King, had stepped out of balance with the other two and was forced back into place with the summoning of the Short and Long Parliaments, so now in the Long Parliament the Commons had stepped out of balance and must be brought into position again. The Commons were beginning to dominate the Lords (having forced the bishops out of the upper House) and the King, and in the Grand Remonstrance and the Nineteen Propositions they showed how far they hoped to go. There no longer was that balance which had existed during the period of Tudor harmony. Just as Charles in the minds of many of his subjects had produced during the 1630s an imbalance, so by June 1642 the Commons had produced for all to see an even worse imbalance. No wonder Charles accepted—

though he must have hated to do it—Colepeper's little treatise on the mixed-balanced government of England.

In his description of the working of a mixed government Colepeper lists the powers of the King as well as those of the Lords and Commons. As might be expected the King's powers are far greater and broader that those of the Commons. Because of the immediate situation the limitations on the Commons are far more stringent than they are on the King. The Commons were to participate in enacting laws and were to initiate money Bills as they had been doing for centuries. The Commons could also impeach a Minister who had violated the law. This was Tudor theory and Jacobean fact. But it is strange that Charles should have agreed to the inclusion of this power. The cases of the Earl of Strafford and the Duke of Buckingham must still have rankled with the King. But he must have supported wholeheartedly the statement that the Commons were 'never intended for any share in government, or the choosing of them that should govern'. That was the essence of the greater part of the rest of the Answer. Finally Charles is coupled with the Lords and Commons in his favourite function—the preservation of the law.

One gets the impression that the King approved the paragraphs of the Answer which describe the mixed government of England without having examined them too closely and also because he had no alternative. Charles would have been willing to rule according to Colepeper's description of the Government if the Commons could have been made to adhere strictly to the role assigned to them. Under the best conditions at that time the Commons would not have been willing to do that. And by June 1642 Charles was only too well aware of it. Had he been able to establish a Government which fitted his thought and desires of that date he would have ruled without Parliament but in strict and narrow obedience to existing law, his old constitutional absolutism. But the feelings of too many people made that impossible. Civil war was the only solution.

After the war had commenced Charles regarded the Parliamentarians as rebels. As such he felt he need not treat them as gentlemen. He made promises which he failed to keep. And yet Charles had a sense of honour which prevented him from openly breaking his word, even to rebels. The result was that whenever he made a public statement or negotiated for peace he used language which did not commit him to anything or which enabled him to circumvent the words he had employed. Gardiner explains this quality as follows:

> Charles could explain away a promise which he had formerly made, or could couch a promise which he was making in words which he intended to explain away at some future time; but nothing would induce him deliberately to use binding words with the express intention of disregarding them on the plea that the form in which his promise was made did not officially and legally amount to a contract.[23]

In a sense, during the period of the civil war and his captivity Charles never made a real promise to his enemies.

During the war Charles was anxious to make peace, but only on his own terms. In his conduct of the war he insisted on his supremacy as he had insisted on it during peacetime in his conduct of the State. Consequently he never gave his entire confidence to anybody, just as he had failed to give it to Laud and Strafford. The Duke of Buckingham and Queen Henrietta Maria were the only exceptions to this rule throughout his reign. Charles's indecision, which drove his wife to distraction, and his duplicity, which drove the Commons to distraction, lost him the war as well as his life. As we shall see his obstinacy at the very end may also have been a cause of his death. From the letters captured in the King's cabinet after the battle of Naseby it could be seen that Charles refused to acknowledge Parliament as lawful, that he had negotiated for the landing of an Irish army in England, that he was ready to abolish laws against English papists and that he had attempted to introduce the soldiers of the Duke of Lorraine into England. He completely disregarded the feelings of the English people in using any means at his disposal to gain his objective. He was fighting the spirit of the nation when he attempted to bring to his support Welshmen, Irishmen, Scots, Frenchmen, Lorrainers and Dutch. Cromwell and Fairfax were leading Englishmen against their King, were appealing to a new spirit in the nation.

As a prisoner Charles was 'always trying to outwit his gaolers, and always trying in vain'.[24] His attitude seemed to be: 'You cannot do without me! You will fall to ruin if I do not sustain you.'[25] Though Charles may have been willing to give up his power temporarily, even during his own lifetime, he believed that his son must have the same authority his father, James I, had passed on to him. Until the end Charles insisted that the King of England should retain the prerogative of the Tudors. He would not compromise, while England was ready for a government of compromise. As he had said at Oxford in November 1644: 'I will not part with the Church, my crown and my friends.'[26] By his crown he meant his power as it had existed before the opening of the Long Parliament, possibly even before his approval of the Petition of Right. Of the three, the Church of England was closest to Charles. He believed that it was God's Church and that he had been appointed by God to maintain it on earth. The strongest trait in Charles's character was his absolute devotion to the Church of England. Of his support of his friends little need be said when considering Charles and the constitution. Yet we must not forget the dilemma he was placed in when confronted with Strafford's Bill of Attainder. His friend had to be sacrificed to the safety of his wife, so Charles believed. But he could never forgive himself for this act, or forget the friend from whom he was forced to part.

Through all the strife and struggle Charles adhered to his ideal in government, constitutional absolutism, in which to be sure he would accept the services of a subservient Parliament. But the King must always retain the power to veto. When there was any disagreement between King and Parliament the decision must be left to him. As Gardiner says: 'When he [Charles] spoke of monarchy he meant the monarchy of Henry VIII and Elizabeth, not the monarchy of William III and Victoria. He was hankering after the restoration of the system which Laud had praised and which Strafford had supported.'[27]

But monarchy was about to be destroyed by a revolution. The defeat and capture of Charles were in reality of no great value to Cromwell and the Independents. As their prisoner Charles was actually a danger to them when he persisted in his intrigues and in his stubborn dependence on the past. When on December 27th, 1648 Charles I refused to relinquish his negative voice in government, Cromwell was finally convinced and joined the Council of Officers in demanding the death of the King. The court which was constituted to try him had, of course, no legal right of existence. It would have been more fitting to the temper of the times, to the revolution, had the court been composed only of officers of the army, had it resembled a court martial rather than a civil court. Force alone had overthrown Charles, and the agents of force should have condemned him. It was ridiculous to say that the court sat 'in the name of the Commons in Parliament assembled, and all the good people of England'.[28]

The charge declared that Charles Stuart 'having been "trusted with a limited power to govern by and according to the laws of the land, and not otherwise, had attempted to erect an unlimited and tyrannical power to rule according to his will, and ... had levied war against the present Parliament, and the people therein represented"'.[29] In the end the charge was high treason, which could only have been against the fundamental law of the land and against the people of England.

In his trial Charles I assumed the stature of greatness. He refused to acknowledge the jurisdiction of the court and to plead to the charges brought against him. Sir John Eliot had done the same in 1630. But here there was a difference. Charles refused to answer except to lawful authority, and no court in England created to try its king had any lawful authority.

> 'It is not', he said, 'my case alone; it is the freedom and liberty of the people of England; and do you pretend what you will, I stand more for their liberties; for, if power without law may make law, may alter the fundamental laws of this kingdom, I do not know what subject he is in England that can be sure of his life, or anything that he calls his own.'[30]

Thus spoke a king who based his power on the law. In the past that law had at times been filtered through the narrowest possible channels. But now Charles stood firmly on the broad stream of English liberties supported by the law of the land. When he met his death on January 30th, 1649, like a true king, Charles I became a martyr to Tudor absolutism because he failed to understand Tudor harmony. He was also a martyr to the Church of England with its 'beauty of holiness' which William Laud, because of his nature and personality and because of the religious feeling of the nation, had failed to make the people of England understand.

[1] Rushworth, I, 190.

[2] *History*, VI, 119–20.

[3] Hulme, *Eliot*, 122, Rushworth, I, 225.

[4] *Ibid.*, I, 406.

[5] W. S. McKechnie, *Magna Carta*, Glasgow, 1914, 375.

[6] Hulme, *Eliot*, 288.

[7] S. R. Gardiner, *The Constitutional Documents of the Puritan Revolution, 1625–1660*, Oxford, 1906, 83.

[8] Hulme, *Eliot*, 280–2.

[9] Wallace Notestein and Frances H. Relf, *Commons Debates for 1629*, Minneapolis, 1921 [London, 1935], 95–101, 101, note *a*. Gardiner, *Constitutional Documents*, 77–82.

[10] *Ibid.*, 82–3.

[11] This may be seen throughout the second volume of Sir John Neale's *Elizabeth I and her Parliaments, 1584–1601*, London, 1956.

[12] Edited by A. B. Grosart, 2 vols., P.P., 1881.

[13] Lord Treasurer. Hulme, *Eliot*, 312.

[14] Notestein and Relf, *Commons Debates for 1629*, 105. See also p. 106 where in 'Independent Account of March 2nd' it says: 'and (as some say) this protestation or proposition was agreed on by some in the House.' None of the other accounts in this work says anything about the House acclaiming the resolutions.

[15] Rushworth, I, 662. For the Proclamation see *ibid.*, 660–1, and for the Declaration see also *ibid.*, Appendix, 1–11.

[16] *History*, VII, 78.

[17] *Ibid.*, 363 note.

[18] Dietz, *English Public Finance*, 286–7, claims that Charles was well able to finance both Bishops' Wars. Gardiner, *History*, VII, 39–40, declares that the lack of funds was one of the reasons why Charles signed the Treaty of Berwick. C. V. Wedgwood, *The King's Peace*, London, 1955, 249–51, 274–5, shows how difficult it was to raise sufficient funds for the first Bishops' War. Why should Wentworth have advised Charles in November 1639 to summon a Parliament as an experiment for the purpose of raising money, why should Charles have asked the Short Parliament for the huge sum of twelve subsidies, if the King was as well off as Dietz implies he was in 1639 and 1640?

[19] *History*, VIII, 299.

[20] At the meeting of the Great Council the Earl of Bristol, the acknowledged leader of the peers, spoke frankly to the King when he said: 'You see, Sir, how you have lost your kingdom's heart by your taxes and impositions, and that till you be united to them by giving them just satisfaction in all their grievances, you are no great king; for without the love and hearts of his people what can a king do; and whosoever advises you otherwise he is against your honour and greatness.' *Historical Manuscripts Commission, Report on the Manuscripts of the Duke of Rutland*, I, 524 as quoted in C. H. Firth, *The House of Lords During the Civil War*, London, 1910, 71.

[21] See Corinne Comstock Weston, 'Beginnings of the Classical Theory of the English Constitution' in *Proceedings of the American Philosophical Society*, Philadelphia, April 1956, VOL. C, No. 2, 133–44. I have taken my extracts from the Answer as given by Miss Weston in the Appendix to her article. There she gives only that part of the Answer which deals with the exposition of mixed government in England. For the entire Answer see Rushworth, IV, 725–35.

[22] Those paragraphs as printed in Rushworth, IV, 731, describing mixed government in England seem to stand apart from the rest of the Answer. Suddenly the royal first person plural is changed to 'the prince'. You get the impression that Colepeper (responsible for this description, Weston, *op. cit.*, 135) may have added the account of mixed government to the Answer after he, Falkland, and possibly the King had laboured over the whole document. Though Sir Edward Hyde approved the publication of the Answer (*ibid.*), he believed that the bishops should take the place of the King as one of the three estates. To Hyde the King was not an estate but was head of them all and bound them together. B. H. G. Wormold, *Clarendon, Politics, History and Religion 1640–1660*, Cambridge, England, 1951, 12. Clarendon in his *History of the Rebellion*, Macray, Oxford, 1888, V, 326–32, summarizes the Answer—that is, gives its

'substance' but fails to mention anything about the paragraphs dealing with the mixed government in England.

[23] *Civil War*, III, 74–5.
[24] *Ibid.*, II, 288.
[25] *Ibid.*, III, 341.
[26] *Ibid.*, II, 86.
[27] *Ibid.*, III, 190.
[28] *Ibid.*, IV, 297.
[29] *Ibid.*, 299.
[30] *Ibid.*, 301.

'There are No Remedies for Many Things but by a Parliament'

Some Opposition Committees, 1640

★

Mary Frear Keeler

A QUESTION that recurs regarding the period when conflict between Charles I and his subjects was moving towards open war is that of who and what propelled the critics of the King to rebellion. Into the debate regarding motivation for the English revolution, economic or otherwise, this paper will not venture. Its intent will be, rather, by examination of certain aspects of the leadership of the early weeks of the Long Parliament, to demonstrate some of the means by which men of the opposition went about correcting the wrongs of the era of Wentworth and Laud.[1] Its time-span will be the months of November and December 1640 and the early part of January, before Strafford was brought to trial, and before the debates on 'root and branch' began to split the ranks of the reformers.

Recent studies of the membership of this Parliament have increased our knowledge not only of the individual Members but of the forces at work in the elections, of local conditions and patronage which might be expected to influence the Parliament's temper and decisions.[2] The published diaries of Sir Simonds D'Ewes, the antiquarian, have let us see the Commons at work, both in general debate and in committee.[3] In *The Reign of King Pym* J. H. Hexter has delineated forcefully the patterns of the groups with which that astute politician John Pym worked in 1642 and 1643 when he was at the height of his power.[4] Each new study has led to some revision of the interpretations by Gardiner, although his masterpiece has borne modern scrutiny remarkably well. With Gardiner's views on the early leadership of the 1640 Commons this paper proposes to deal.

Writing of Pym's position in the Parliament newly assembled in November of 1640, Gardiner describes him as 'the directing influence of a knot of men who constituted the inspiring force of the Parliamentary Opposition', but not arrived at the peak of his leadership.[5] Yet but a few pages later, reviewing the way in which the Commons busied itself with one grievance after another, he writes as follows.

Every member who spoke had some particular grievance to recount, and some particular remedy to demand. There was no party organization and no recognized leadership. It was hard to fix the attention of the House even to the most necessary subject, and a debate once begun was apt to wander away in all sorts of directions.[6]

With the concluding sentence none will disagree. But the second may well be called into question. Both within and beyond the 'knot of men' to which Gardiner's earlier remark refers at least a shadow of party organization seems to lie.

More recent students of the period have pointed to the evidence that an opposition of some kind had been in the making well before 1640, as far back as the Parliaments of James I.[7] At least a nucleus of parliamentary opposition was well established before the 1629 dissolution, a nucleus which embraced some of those who were to return as M.P.s in 1640.[8] As the subjects of Charles I joined in resisting the forced loans or the payment of ship-money, or defended Puritan lecturers against interference by the agents of Laud, they strengthened by political action the bonds of kinship, acquaintance and common interest by which many were already linked in great county and area groups.[9]

But when 1640 came, how strong were such ties and by what means could leadership best be identified and effectively exercised within a Parliament? The answer to this question must be sought in a variety of places. We know who the orators were and a good deal about the debates, particularly in the Lower House. But committee membership also can provide interesting clues. A study of a number of the early committees of the session may throw some light, both on the bases for appointment to committees and on the leadership within the Commons.

Not all committees need be examined. Gardiner correctly pointed out the multiple interests by which the Long Parliament in its early weeks was distracted.[10] New committees were named daily, now for a private petition or on the grievance of an individual, again for a terrifying London rumour or a matter of court intrigue. Committees were spawned so rapidly, in fact, that it became difficult to schedule meetings, and even earnest members found it impossible to attend all of those to which they had been assigned. D'Ewes, who was an assiduous committee-goer as well as taker of notes, recorded on December 19th that the committee on ship-money had to be adjourned to a later date because the same meeting-place and a portion of the same members were then occupied with another committee that was investigating the Star Chamber abuses. Even the latter had to wait for half an hour on this occasion for eight members to be present so that proceedings might start.[11]

The very circumstance of a crowded committee calendar, however, provides a useful key for selecting committees for study. The Commons found it necessary by January of 1641 to draw the line between the committees needed for getting on with their work and those which could be set aside. A special Committee on Committees, chaired by the Yorkshireman Sir John Hotham, reported on January 12th with a select list of the committees that should be retained.[12] Besides the five grand committees the list included sixteen to which had been assigned special problems ranging from the charges against the Earl of Strafford, the Archbishop of Canterbury and other officials of the Crown, to the matters of ship-money, abuses of the Lords-Lieutenant, and other features or policies of the royal administration which it was the intent of the 'country' faction to revise. In this report we find streamlined the programme which the opposition considered to be of first importance. And in the membership lists of the committees named we may expect to find the key men of the opposition, and some clues as to how the critics of administration organized their attack.

A glance at the lists is sufficient to show that the same names keep recurring. Not all appear on every committee, it is true, and occasionally striking omissions occur. There are many variations. In several cases we find men who are clearly spokesmen for the opposition listed side by side with M.P.s who were to serve on but a single one of the selected committees. Men with military experience, for example, and men from the northern shires were appointed (November 21st) in greater numbers to the committee for studying the problems of the army in the northern counties and how it was to be paid.[13] Members who had been sheriffs or had served in earlier Parliaments appear in considerable numbers on the committees ordered to consider abuses in the levying of ship-money and the breaches of parliamentary privilege. As the committees continued their work the lists did not remain stable. Sweeping additions occurred in numerous cases after the date of Hotham's report, notably for the Star Chamber committee (January 29th and March 11th),[14] and that on parliamentary privilege (February 23rd).[15] And it was ordered on December 5th, when the committee on the levying of ship-money was appointed, that all who would come should have 'a voice' except those members who as sheriffs or other officials had been employed in the levy of the tax.[16] It is the lists as they are recorded in the *Journals* at the time the committees were appointed, however, which will best serve our purpose in seeking out the early opposition leadership.

As a further limit this study will be confined chiefly to the committees that were to deal with general problems rather than with individuals, and with civil rather than with religious issues. The Committee of Privileges, which dealt with contested elections, can be avoided because of the specialized nature of its work. We can omit also the committee on a Bill for annual Parliaments. Among the others the lines cannot always be drawn sharply. If, however, we eliminate the committees on the Archbishop of Canterbury,[17] Secretary Windebank and the recusants,[18] the Bishop of Bath and Wells[19] and the Bishop of Ely,[20] on which obviously the Puritans were well represented, we may be able to discern more clearly the nature of the approach towards secular issues. On the committees thus arbitrarily eliminated from this study appear the names of many of the same M.P.s who were at work also on the more general grievances of the country.

It becomes apparent quickly that the leaders of the opposition were more numerous than the 'knot of men' to which Gardiner referred. That term suits well the very small committee named on the third day of the Parliament (November 11th) to prepare in haste the charges against Strafford. This was a group of six (Sir John Clotworthy, George Lord Digby, Denzil Holles, John Pym, Oliver St John and William Strode, with Pym named first), which on the following day became eight (by the addition of Sir Walter Erle and John Hampden, and the substitution of Harbottle Grimston for Holles, who asked to be excused).[21] But the nine men named on this 'Close Committee', as it was sometimes styled, do not seem to have had continuity as a group. Each was named to others of the selected committees, but there were other men who were named as many times—more frequently than some of these—and were evidently considered as sharing in the leadership.

This fact may be illustrated by a group sometimes referred to as The Twenty-four, which was appointed on November 10th, earlier than the Strafford group, to draw up a declaration on the state of the kingdom.[22] This was the committee from whose labours emerged a year later the Grand Remonstrance.[23] It might be thought of as designed to shape the policy—platform it cannot yet be called—of the opposition. All of the Strafford committee except Holles and Strode were named to it, but not a man who can be identified as a spokesman for the Crown at this period (eight of its members eventually became Royalists, but all of them were in November advocates of reform).[24]

The significance of this committee on the state of the kingdom becomes more evident as it is compared with the others mentioned in Hotham's January report. Nine of its twenty-four members (Barrington, Crew, Colepeper, Grimston, Hampden, Kirton, Selden, Seymour and Strangways, as well as Holles of the Strafford Committee) appear in the list of nineteen that served under Hotham's leadership as the Committee on Committees.[25] Of the sixty-one who comprised the first list of the committee appointed on December 3rd to consider the abuses and jurisdiction of the courts of Star Chamber and High Commission nineteen were also of The Twenty-four (absent were Belasyse, Clotworthy, Pierrepont, Rudyard and Seymour).[26] Fifteen of The Twenty-four were named among the forty-nine for the question of the Lords-Lieutenant (December 14th),[27] and ten among the thirty-two to consider the High Constable and Earl Marshal's Court.[28] Eight of them were in the sixteen ordered to prepare the charges against the judges who had presided at the ship-money trials (December 7th),[29] several of their number, such as Hampden and St John apparently being considered at this time as ineligible to serve; and six were named to the committee on abuses in the levying of ship-money (December 5th).[30] Seven were appointed to the committee on the breach of parliamentary privileges; another seven were ineligible to serve because their own cases were to be considered (H. Belasyse, Crew, W. Erle, Hampden, P. Heyman, Pym and Selden).[31] In smaller numbers The Twenty-four are represented in the lists of committees charged with studying the less spectacular of the general grievances. Two exceptions are Rudyard and Clotworthy, the latter of whom was a newcomer to English Parliaments; neither was named to other committees in our select list.

Although most of the committees to prepare charges against particular Ministers of the King have been excluded from this study, it is of interest to note the relationship between The Twenty-four and the Committee on Archbishop Laud. Twenty-nine names were listed on December 16th for a committee to deal with the promoters of the new canons, particularly with the Archbishop of Canterbury; thirteen of them were of The Twenty-four.[32]

Since the latter was obviously a committee of importance its members should be studied with some care. Every member was, at the time the committee was named, a critic of Stuart policies, as most of them had been on earlier occasions. Digby, the first named, and seven others (Bagshaw, H. Belasyse, Capel, Colepeper, Kirton, F. Seymour and J. Strangways) were later to desert Parliament for the royalist cause, but the other two-thirds of the group are recognizable as staunch Parliamentarians (Barrington, Clotworthy, Crew, W. Erle, M. Fleetwood, Grimston the younger, Hampden, Harley, P. Heyman, Peard, Pierrepont, Pym, Rudyard, O. St John, Selden and T. Widdrington). Of the whole group eight were lawyers by profession (Bagshaw, Crew, Grimston, Peard, Rudyard, St John, Selden and Widdrington), and five either were in or had previously held administrative positions under the Crown (Fleetwood, Harley, Pym, Rudyard and Seymour). With the exception possibly of Selden, and of Peard, whose family was aligned with merchant and legal interests in Barnstaple, all stemmed from the gentry, and a considerable number had ample estates. All but Clotworthy had sat in earlier Parliaments, most of them having been fellow M.P.s in the 1620s.[33]

If this was indeed a committee for charting the course of the opposition, it was a fairly homogeneous group. There are, however, some interesting omissions. Edward Hyde was not here, nor Lord Falkland, although both of these men will be found on other committees in Hotham's list. Missing, too, are a number of men noted for their strong puritanical views, men such as Miles Corbet or Cromwell, Nathaniel Fiennes, Hesilrige, Heveningham, Rigby and the Wallops. Likewise missing are clear-cut Royalists such as the Ashburnhams and Arundels, the Fanshawes, the Hattons, a Killigrew or a Slanning. This was a committee, then, not greatly tinged with radicalism, with few extremists of either side, but made up of men determined to halt the encroachments on the liberties and properties of the King's subjects as they had experienced them in recent years.

The committee which had been assigned the task of choosing the committees that were to survive must also be considered as one of importance, Hotham's committee which made its report in January.[34] The pattern of its membership differs but slightly from that of The Twenty-four. In addition to the nine who were members of both committees (Barrington, Crew, Colepeper, Grimston, Hampden, Kirton, Selden, Seymour and Strangways), there were three men who were currently reformers but were later to become Royalists (Hotham, Hyde and G. Palmer), and five steady Parliamentarians (Barnham, Cage, D. Holles, Stapleton and White). The number of lawyers again is interesting (Cage, Crew, Grimston, Palmer, Selden and White), as is also the presence of but a single townsman, the elderly Cage of Ipswich, whom D'Ewes once described as a 'country gown man'[35] and who had a considerable knowledge of the law and of parliamentary precedent. With the exception of the puritan lawyer White, all were M.P.s of experience, although Colepeper, Grimston and Stapleton had sat for the first time in the Short Parliament. The presence of Cage, Stapleton and White may lend to this committee a stronger Puritan colour than was evident with The Twenty-four, but this difference may be offset in part by the presence of such members as Hyde and Geoffrey Palmer. Once more it should be noted that the hotter heads are missing. Since all of the members of this Committee on Committees with the exception of Barnham, a man in his sixties and not inclined to great activity in this Parliament, were named frequently to the other select committees, it appears that they should be counted, with the Strafford group and The Twenty-four, as among those who were close to Pym in the organizing of the Commons. With the inclusion of the Hotham committee the count of the opposition leadership rises to thirty-three.

In addition to the men named thus far, however, there are others, a score or more, whose names appear so frequently in the roster of the committees in our selected list that they seem to be luminaries also in the opposition forces. This will become clear as the committees are examined separately.

Of the committees appointed to work with particular grievances the one assigned for the prerogative courts of Star Chamber and High Commission may well be considered first. Not only was the clamour against those courts among the matters earliest to claim the attention of the Parliament, but the committee became one of the largest of the grievance committees. Designed apparently to replace a number of committees which had been appointed earlier for the cases of particular victims of Star Chamber justice, it was named as a general committee of sixty-one on December 3rd. Other names were added in January and March, those of January including specified members chiefly from the northern shires, with the general addition of the burgesses of Yorkshire, the knights from Northamptonshire and all the lawyers of the House.[36] For the purpose of this study only the list of December need be examined.

Once more the familiar names are there, with Holles leading the list. Nineteen of The Twenty-four, and all but five of Hotham's committee are listed (Barnham, Hyde, Palmer, Seymour, Stapleton; Hyde's later appointment to study Star Chamber sentences did not come until May). So we can account for twenty-three of the sixty-one names. But the remaining list of thirty-eight shows a wider diversity than was discernible in the committees previously studied. There is an additional group of reformers who were eventually to become Royalists, men such as Sir Henry Anderson, Sir Thomas Bowyer, the younger Digby, Lords Dungarvan and Russell (the Earl of Bedford's heir), and John Whistler. But there were also seven who must be thought of as defenders of the King's programme at the moment, men who were courtiers and royal officials, or sons of courtly families, and who ranged from Sir Thomas Jermyn, Comptroller of the Household and Privy Councillor, who had more than once participated in Star Chamber sessions, to one of the young Westons (Cornwallis, T. Coke, 'Mr Comptroller', B. Noel, E. Verney, 'Mr Weston', and Wilmot). The names of most of these Royalists do not occur in the rosters of the other general grievance committees. Noel and Wilmot, however, were named on that concerned with the army, Noel and Coke on that for the Lords-Lieutenant, and Noel on the one for Weymouth.[37] The appointment of supporters of the King to the large Star Chamber committee may represent a nod to the principle of impartiality, but the smallness of their group meant that they could have little influence upon decisions.

In contrast with these the ranks of the reformers were buttressed with men of stern stuff. Brereton of Cheshire was here this time, and Miles Corbet, Oliver Cromwell and Sir Arthur Hesilrige. There were other east country Puritan gentlemen such as D'Ewes, Masham and Moundeford, such west country Puritans as Nicoll and Upton, and Puritans from the south in the persons of Partridge, Rivers and Stapley, to mention only some of those noted for their religious views. A dozen or more of this committee who took the more extreme position on religious issues, including Cromwell, were named to none of the other general grievance committees in Hotham's list. Their presence on the Star Chamber and High Commission committee suggests that the religious rather than the civil issues relating to the courts interested them most, and that while they were helpful to the opposition as the denunciation of prerogative justice was being prepared they were not needed in such numbers for other decisions. It is perhaps of interest to note that more of the Puritan members of this committee were from the country than from the towns, and that even the town representatives, such as Cage of Ipswich, Corbet of Yarmouth, Ellis of Boston and Peard of Barnstaple, were men of the law rather than of trade. A possible exception is Broxholme of Lincoln.

From the Star Chamber committee list, by selecting the men whose names are to be found with some frequency on others of the key committees, we may add several to our growing list of opposition leaders—i.e. Anderson, Brereton, D'Ewes, N. Fiennes, G. Gerrard, Hesilrige, Irby and Whistler. With these additional names the number stands at forty-one.

To keep this study within the limits of committees whose assignments were in no sense regional, only three others of the general committees reported by Hotham will be considered. Two are concerned with ship-money. The larger of the two, named on December 5th to consider complaints against the manner in which the tax was levied, was directed particularly at sheriffs and their deputies who had collected too zealously, an order being added that 'all, that will come, are to have Voices at this Committee', except those who as sheriffs or other officers had been employed in levying ship-money.[38] Of the opportunity a number of members availed themselves, according to the records D'Ewes kept of the committee meetings.[39] The limitation on the sheriffs seems not to have been applied completely. Irby and Pierrepont, who had collected but had complained of the tax, were not named; D'Ewes, who had collected with difficulty and had complained, was appointed a member.[40]

The list of December 5th contains thirty-eight names. As usual there is a representation from The Twenty-four (Capel, Colepeper, Crew, Lord Digby, Heyman and Widdrington; speakers in committee sessions besides were E. Hungerford and F. Seymour, although their names are not on the December 5th list).[41] From our larger group of opposition leaders there were Hyde and Holles, but Grimston was replaced by his father and Strangways by his son. Once more the preponderance of the membership was on the side of reform, with only an occasional name, such as that of Leveson, to suggest that the King's side would be heard. Bellingham, Grenville and Sutton, future Royalists, were probably considered at this period as sympathetic with the opposition forces. Only the last of these three, Sutton, who was named to the committee on the Lords-Lieutenant, was a member, however, of any other of the general grievance committees. The ship-money levy list included Brereton, Sir Hugh Cholmley and Nathaniel Stephens, each of whom had declined to pay the tax, but not the most celebrated refuser, Hampden, nor St John, nor Pym. A goodly number of former sheriffs were named, twelve or thirteen,[42] their proportion to the whole committee list being somewhat larger than was true of sheriffs in the membership of the Commons. About a third of the committee, therefore, had had experience with the functions of the county office to which ship-money collecting had been assigned. No merchants were named to this committee, all of the members being county men.

A second committee that dealt with ship-money was the one appointed to get nearer to the source of the grievance. On November 27th the Commons established a committee of twenty men to consider the judgments in Exchequer concerning illegal taxes and the goods of subjects, and on December 7th it authorized a committee of sixteen to inquire about pressure on the judges who had made the decision in Hampden's case. The next day the two groups were combined and enlarged into a committee of forty-four. Further additions occurred on December 12th, in March and in May. The group named on December 8th, however, will suffice for the purpose of this study.[43]

Like the bits of coloured glass in a kaleidoscope the familiar names are present, arranged in different patterns but with the same identities. All but two (Clotworthy and Digby) of the select committee on Strafford are here. Seventeen of The Twenty-four are named, and of Hotham's Committee on Committees all but three (Barnham, Cage, Stapleton). The group includes Pym and Hampden, Falkland and Hyde, F. Seymour and St John, a veritable galaxy of the opposition leaders. Bulstrode Whitelocke, too, was a member, one of the four who were to be thanked particularly by the House on January 14th for their work in this business (Falkland, Hyde, St John and Whitelocke).[44] There was Hampden's good friend Arthur Goodwin, one of the knights from Buckinghamshire, and Barrington's kinsman Lytton, one of the Hertfordshire knights. There were numerous members who had protested the ship-money levy and other 'irregular' taxes, such as Ayscough, Hampden, Falkland, Palmes, Rolle and Seymour, and others. But officials of the Crown, too, were listed on this important committee, as in the case of the one for Star Chamber. While the December 7th committee on the judges contained the names of no officials except the Parliamentarians Fleetwood and Pym, the earlier list of November 27th, with which the judges' committee was combined, included 'Mr Solicitor' (Sir Edward Herbert), and on December 8th two Privy Councillors, Sir Thomas Roe and 'Mr Treasurer' Vane, were added. Of the lawyers of the House fourteen were named in the combined list; of the townsmen only Jane and Rolle. Of extremists on the popular side only one or two appear, but subjects who had suffered and legalists to argue the points of the law were there in abundance.

Some eight of the opposition men named for service on one or both of the ship-money committees were named to other grievance committees so frequently as to indicate that they should be added to the 'organization' list, i.e. Ayscough, Cholmley, Falkland, A. Goodwin, Lytton, Palmes, J. Rolle and probably Whitelocke.

With the committee appointed on December 18th to deal with

breaches of parliamentary privilege, and specifically with the violations that occurred in connection with the Short Parliament and that of 1628,[45] this survey of the grievance committees will end. By its nature it was somewhat different from the preceding ones. Particularly it was to examine the cases of fourteen men, all but two of whom (Eliot and Hobart) were Members of this Parliament (W. Long became a Member late in 1641).[46] None of those so named was appointed to this committee. The absence of seven of The Twenty-four (Belasyse, Crew, Erle, Hampden, Heyman, Pym and Selden), and of three others whom we have established as leaders (Holles, Hotham and Strode), indicates that those whose cases were to be discussed were excluded from serving on the committee. But a large enough number of their close associates were named to ensure that the record of their sufferings would be heard with sympathy.

Twenty-nine men were listed originally for the committee. With the twenty-four additions of February 23rd[47] we need not be concerned. Although seven of The Twenty-four were ineligible, seven of their fellows were in the December list, with four others from the Hotham committee. The remaining eighteen members, with the single exception of 'Mr Ashburnham', presumably John, the courtier, were of the reform element in Parliament. And most of this committee were men who stayed with Parliament in 1642, when the battle-lines were drawn. Only Kirton, Mallory, Palmer and Seymour turned eventually from reform to the Royalist side.

The make-up of this committee indicates that due regard was paid to parliamentary experience. Two of those named in the list were newcomers to the House, Palmer and White, but since both were lawyers the matter of experience as M.P.s was perhaps less important. All of the others had been Members before, nine of them new in the Short Parliament (Fiennes, Glyn, Grimston, Kirkby, Maynard, Peard, Rigby, St John and Stapleton), and the rest veterans of 1628 and earlier sessions. To be noted in the list were such stalwarts of the 1620s as Sir Francis Seymour and his friend or agent Kirton, and Sir Oliver Luke, who had sat in all but two of the Parliaments since 1597 and had been one of Eliot's intimate friends. Cage of Ipswich, Sir Edward Hungerford and Sir John Strangways, M.P.s since 1614 and spokesmen against Buckingham in his day, were named, as were Sir Arthur Ingram, who had sat eight times previously, and Sir Christopher Wray, who had served five times before. William Mallory of Yorkshire, whose imprisonment after the 1621 session did not disqualify him, apparently, from investigating the cases of later years, was in this list, although he was not named early to the other grievance committees. Neither Hyde nor Falkland was named at this time, although both were added in February. Nine of the number, chiefly those with less experience in Parliament, were lawyers; two (Ingram and Rolle) were merchants. Of Privy Councillors there were none. Nor were there other royal officials of significance. Here, indeed, was a committee in whose hands the question of parliamentary privilege would be safe.

From the committee on the breaches of privilege several names may be added to our organization roster—Glyn, Hungerford, Ingram, Luke, Maynard and C. Wray—for each of these appears elsewhere in the lists of the Hotham committees. Others of the committees whose membership lists have been checked for duplicate names are the one on the army in the northern counties (November 21st), on the High Constable and Earl Marshal's Court (November 23rd), on the Lords-Lieutenant and Deputy Lieutenants (December 14th), and on the petition from Weymouth concerning duties on salt, soap and leather (December 21st).[48] In each instance, besides the men who were selected because of the special interest in or experience with the matter to be considered, there are repetitions of the names that occur in the other committee lists. A tally of such names helps to round out the roster of members whom we may count as the active core of the opposition. Appointed to serve on more than two committees are the following not heretofore mentioned: Sir Ralph Hopton, a reformer at this period but later a Royalist, and the Parliamentarians, T. Bowyer, J. Broxholme, the Lords Fairfax and Wenman, and Samuel Owfield, wealthy Puritan son of a London fishmonger, who had become a landowner in Lincoln and Surrey.

If the assumption that repeated committee memberships is significant, what conclusions can be drawn from the comparisons just made of the key committees of the 1640 opposition? From the committees appointed to deal with secular grievances there has emerged a list of fifty-five men who were named to three or more of the committees, a figure which should probably be increased by ten to include others who were named but twice, but whose work seemed to be valued particularly, as in the case of a Clotworthy or a Whitelocke. Another half-dozen might be added, drawn from the Hotham committees that were excluded earlier from this study, bringing our number of an active opposition to approximately seventy. The heaviest responsibilities of leadership within such a group may not always, of course, be revealed by the number of committees to which men were appointed, and it must be recalled that at times outstanding men were excluded because their own cases were to be discussed. Nevertheless it is safe to conclude that appointment to more than five early committees is at least significant.

By this criterion we find at the top of the list, with eight appointments each, Colepeper and Strangways; with seven each, Barrington, Capel, Heyman, Holles, Kirton, St John and Seymour; and with six each, Erle, Grimston, Hampden, Palmer, Pym, Selden and C. Wray. In this group of sixteen, which may be thought of as the hierarchy of the early opposition leadership, were six who were eventually to turn to the King.[49] Especially noteworthy, perhaps, was the continuing role of Sir Francis Seymour, an opposition leader from the days of Phelips and Eliot.

Close to the top are the six men who were named to five committees (Crew, Digby, Hotham, E. Hungerford, Lytton and Whistler). There were thirteen, also, who were named to four of those studied (Bagshaw, Cage, D'Ewes, Gerrard, Glyn, Hyde, Maynard, Owfield, Palmes, Peard, Stapleton, White and Widdrington). Only in the latter list does some indication of the influence of towns appear.

From the lists of the committees selected in January 1641 to survive we have drawn the names of between sixty and seventy men to whom we can with assurance refer as members of the opposition 'organization' in the early weeks of the Parliament. The exact nature of their political relationships and their methods of operation must be left to surmise; but certainly the opportunities these men had had to know each other and to work together before November 1640 must be taken into account. Undoubtedly the frequent overlapping of appointments must have interfered with the work of the special committees we have studied. Deliberate absenteeism was probably less of a problem; the rounding up of laggards was hardly needed among the men whose names we have found. Although their attack on the royal administration may not have been managed in the most efficient way there can be no doubt that the reforming group kept the reins securely in their hands. There were enough opposition men of parliamentary experience and legal training in each committee to make sure that the business would be pressed forward.

---

[1] The publication of *The Rise of the Revolutionary Party in the English House of Commons, 1603–1629*, by Williams M. Mitchell, New York, 1957 [Oxford, 1958], after the first draft of this paper had been written, provides support for the method of studying leadership which is here used.

[2] Douglas D. Brunton and D. H. Pennington, *Members of the Long Parliament*, Cambridge, England, 1954; Mary Frear Keeler, *The Long Parliament, 1640–1641*, Philadelphia, 1954.

[3] Wallace Notestein, ed., *The Journal of Sir Simonds D'Ewes*, New Haven, 1923 (hereafter cited as *D'Ewes*); Willson H. Coates, ed., *The Journal of Sir Simonds D'Ewes*, New Haven, 1942.

[4] J. H. Hexter, *The Reign of King Pym*, Cambridge, Mass., 1941 [Oxford, 1941].

[5] S. R. Gardiner, *History of England from the Accession of James I to the Outbreak of the Civil War*, 10 volumes, London, 1883–1884, IX, 223.

[6] *Ibid.*, IX, 238.

[7] Mitchell, *op. cit.*, has shown effectively in his study of the Parliaments of 1604–29 the relationship between the growth of the committee system and the rise of a parliamentary opposition in the reigns of both James I and Charles I.

[8] *Ibid.*, 121–2, 164–5.

[9] Cf. Hexter, *op. cit.*, 84–7; Keeler, *op. cit.*, 29–30.

[10] Gardiner, *op. cit.*, IX, 238.

[11] *D'Ewes*, 173.

[12] *Commons Journal*, II, 66–7 (hereafter cited as *C.J.*); *D'Ewes*, 242–5.

[13] *C.J.*, II, 34.

[14] *Ibid.*, 74–5, 101.

[15] *Ibid.*, 91.

[16] *Ibid.*, 45.

[17] *Ibid.*, 52.

[18] *Ibid.*, 24, 42.

[19] *Ibid.*, 50.

[20] *Ibid.*, 56.

[21] *Ibid.*, 26, 27. The names of committee members are listed in this paper in alphabetical order, rather than in the order in which they appear in the *Journal*. There Pym's name is first. Since he became the principal spokesman for the committee he was apparently chairman, although it cannot be stated definitely that he was assigned to this place when the committee was set up. Cf. Mitchell, *op. cit.*, 87.

[22] *C.J.*, II, 25; *D'Ewes*, 243 and note.

[23] Coates, *op. cit.*, 51 and note; W. H. Coates, 'Some Observations on the Grand Remonstrance', *Journal of Modern History*, IV, 4–7.

[24] The twenty-four names are as follows: E. Bagshaw, T. Barrington, H. Belasyse, A. Capel, J. Clotworthy, J. Colepeper, J. Crew, G. (Lord) Digby, W. Erle, M. Fleetwood, H. Grimston (the younger), J. Hampden, R. Harley, P. Heyman, E. Kirton, G. Peard, W. Pierrepont, J. Pym, B. Rudyard, O. St John, J. Selden, F. Seymour, J. Strangways, T. Widdrington.
The statements regarding political affiliations here and later in this paper are based upon *D.N.B.* and Keeler, *op. cit.*

[25] *C.J.*, II, 65.

[26] *Ibid.*, 44.

[27] *Ibid.*, 50.

[28] *Ibid.*, 34.

[29] *Ibid.*, 46.

[30] *Ibid.*, 45.

[31] *Ibid.*, 53.

[32] *Ibid.*, 52.

[33] Among those who had emerged as leaders of the opposition in the Parliament of 1628, as indicated by appointment to a great many committees, were Barrington, Erle, Fleetwood, Heyman, Pym, Rudyard and Selden. Mitchell, *op. cit.*, 121, 164–5.

[34] *C.J.*, II, 65, 66.

[35] J. O. Halliwell, ed., *The Autobiography and Correspondence of Sir Simonds D'Ewes, Bart.*, 2 volumes, London, 1845, II, 247.

[36] *C.J.*, II, 44, 74–5, 101.

[37] *Ibid.*, 34, 50, 55.

[38] *Ibid.*, 45.

[39] D'Ewes records (p. 141) that Sir Edward Hungerford sat in the chair at the meeting on December 11th, and that Sir Francis Seymour spoke. Neither of these men was named in the list in the *Journal*. The discussion this day involved the conduct of a former sheriff of Wiltshire (Sir Edward Bayntun, M.P. for Chippenham). Hungerford was serving for Chippenham, and Seymour was a Member for Marlborough, another Wiltshire constituency.

[40] D'Ewes had urged the naming on the committee of sheriffs who had been called before Star Chamber for not collecting ship-money. *D'Ewes*, 108.

[41] See note 39 above.

[42] The twelve former sheriffs named in *C.J.* had, with the exception of D'Ewes, served in the office before the ship-money period. They were R. Ashton, E. Ayscough, N. Barnardiston, S. D'Ewes, E. Dunch, H. Grimston (the elder), T. Hutchinson, O. Luke, W. Lytton, G. Palmes, W. Purefoy and R. Sutton. Sir Francis Seymour, who attended at least once (see note 39 above), was sheriff in Wiltshire, 1625–6. All of these former sheriffs were of the reform group in 1640.

[43] *C.J.*, II, 38, 46, 47, 50, 109, 145.

[44] *Ibid.*, 68.

[45] *Ibid.*, 53.

[46] In addition to Eliot and Hobart the list of aggrieved M.P.s includes: H. Belasyse, Crew, W. Erle, Hampden, P. Heyman, D. Holles, Hotham, W. Long, Pym, Selden, Strode and Valentine.

[47] *C.J.*, II, 91.

[48] *Ibid.*, 34, 50, 55.

[49] Capel, Colepeper, Kirton, Palmer, Seymour and Strangways.

English Pamphlet Support for Charles I,
November 1648–January 1649

★

William L. Sachse

I N the early autumn of 1648 few could have realized that within a matter of months the life of King Charles would have run its course. It is true that as the King's predilection for playing one side against another had become better known, and the uneasy peace of 1646 and 1647 had given way to a short sharp war with the Scots, dire indictments of the royal conduct had been noised abroad. And yet, despite so ill an omen as the Army resolution at Windsor prayer-meeting, negotiations for some kind of peaceful settlement were to continue. The backing and filling that had gone on for months that stretched into years seemed likely to continue indefinitely as a Parliament dominated by moderate forces pursued the possibility of reaching an accord with the King.

But on November 20th, 1648 the pace was quickened, and a new and fateful urgency was introduced into British politics. For on that day a lengthy manifesto, known as 'The Remonstrance of the Army', was presented to the Speaker of the House of Commons by a deputation of officers and was ordered to be published forthwith.[1] This pronouncement, as Masson has written, 'was intended as a kind of Pamphlet to the English Nation setting forth the Army's views in a reasoned shape, and the programme of action on which they had resolved'.[2] It argued for the principle, *salus populi lex suprema*, justified the Army's conduct and position with regard to Parliament, emphasized the accountability of kings, identified Charles I with the wars and woes of recent years, and declared that Charles, because of his duplicity and unteachability, had forfeited popular trust and made his own restoration a political impossibility. Near the end came the specific demands of the Army, of which only the first need concern us. This was: 'That the capital and grand author of our troubles, the Person of the King, by whose commissions, commands, or procurement, and in whose behalf and for whose interest only, of will and power, all our wars and troubles have been, with all the miseries attending them, may be specially brought to justice for the treason, blood, and mischief he is therein guilty of.'

It is clear that the revolutionary character of the Remonstrance, which was primarily the work of Henry Ireton, was recognized at once. To William Prynne it was 'destructive to the Law of the Land and to the Fundamental Constitutions of the Kingdom', while Marchamont Nedham, in one of the first printed rejoinders, sought to prove 'that it tends to subvert the Laws, and fundamental Constitutions of this Kingdom, and demolish the very Foundation of Government in general'.[3] The King himself about this time could not shake off a deep pessimism. On November 29th he wrote Prince Charles: 'We know not, but this may be the last time We may speak to you or the world publicly. We are sensible into what hands We are fallen ...'[4]

That time was on the wing, that a decisive hour was at hand, became increasingly obvious. For in scarcely more than a fortnight the Army had assured itself of a compliant Commons through the offices of Colonel Pride, and in scarcely more than a month arrangements were on foot for the extraordinary tribunal which was to sit in judgment on the King. In the meantime representations, frequently of military origin, calling for the arraignment of Charles as the master delinquent, were being tendered from various parts of the kingdom. It was not only evil councillors now who must make amends, but royalty itself. It appeared that the exponents of Charles's monarchy must either speak out or to all practical purposes for ever hold their peace.

And speak out they did, despite obstacles impeding the course of free expression. The years of war and political manœuvring between 1642 and 1649 produced a remarkable outpouring from the presses of the capital, chiefly in the form of brief pamphlets and broadsides. To this the final weeks of the King's life proved no exception; indeed, judging from Thomason's entries, the months of November 1648 and January 1649 were not often surpassed in output, at least after the opening year of the war. It has been said that public discussion of the King's trial by way of the printed page was not tolerated by Parliament. From such censors as Gilbert Mabbott, and Colonel Henry Whaley and Theodore Jennings, who were appointed to serve with Mabbott in mid-January 1649 Royalists could expect no favours. Mabbott, reappointed to the licensing office in the autumn of 1648 at the recommendation of General Fairfax, was well known for his opposition to further negotiations with Charles and for his levelling tendencies. Whaley was Advocate-General of the Army, while Jennings was to become a sort of factotum of the Council of State. Yet the fact that on January 5th, 1649 an order came forth suppressing unlicensed books and pamphlets, as well as the commissioning of additional watchdogs, indicates that a close supervision was more easily projected than effected, and probably bears out Clyde's remark that 'the general carelessness of the licensers of news-books contrasts with the activity of the Government in legislating for complete control of the press'.[5] Moreover, in James Cranford, a Presbyterian divine who had served as a licenser since 1643, Charles's defenders had a friend at Court who was willing to place his imprimatur on such works as *The Humble Advice And Earnest Desires* of Zacheus Breedon and his clerical colleagues and John Gauden's *Religious & Loyal Protestation*. We may conclude that there were many leaks in the dike, and while some measure of success might be attained in controlling the serial news-book publications it was impossible to prevent the appearance of individual pamphlets whose titlepages frequently gave no clue as to author, printer or bookseller.

It was to this device that Charles's defenders turned as they sought a vehicle for propaganda. The catalogue of the Thomason tracts, as well as those of other collections, indicates that in the ten weeks between the promulgation of the Remonstrance and the decapitation of the King about a hundred pamphlets, directly concerned with the political crisis, made their appearance. The publications of January 1649 bear ample testimony to the prevalence of republican ideas. Yet of these hundred pamphlets about a third may be described as unequivocally opposed to the proceedings designed to bring the Stuart monarch to the block.

In authorship and content these writings present an interesting cross-section of the political and religious opinions held by moderates and conservatives of the day. In some cases, as we might expect, the mantle of anonymity makes it impossible for us to identify the author. At the opposite pole are works by well-known polemicists and publicity-seekers like Marchamont Nedham and William Prynne. The latter was to compose no less than half a dozen pieces in support of Charles during these weeks; imprisonment seemed only to stimulate the flow of his pen. Clergymen are, of course, represented, but judging from signed works the pamphleteers were for the most part laymen. The

Presbyterian clergy, for reasons that will appear below, were more in evidence than their episcopalian brethren. Only two of the latter—John Gauden and Henry Hammond—can be identified. No bishop appears to have entered the lists, though Henry King and John Warner were to bemoan Charles's fate shortly after his execution. In several cases the Presbyterian protestations profess to speak for the clergy of a locality; in one instance the names of fifty-seven London ministers are appended by way of attestation.[6] The King, by the publication of his rejoinders, was given a voice denied him before the Commissioners who tried him. But no noble authorship is discernible in the works of his defenders, and only Sir Francis Nethersole and Clement Walker can be definitely set down as members of the country gentry. Two women, Mary Pope and Elizabeth Pool, are encountered. The latter, a sort of Cromwellian Joan of Arc, was rather a narrator of visions than a pamphleteer; but 'Mistris Pope', who is described as a salter's widow, was by the early weeks of 1648 in the black books of the Commons for her *Treatise of Magistracy*, which they found to be 'very Popish, full of Salt, and Feminine-Malignancy'.[7] Charles's supporters, unlike their opposites, made comparatively little use of collective declarations and petitions; but, in addition to the pronouncements of the Presbyterian clergy, we find in the Thomason collection two such representations from the citizens of London. From the newly regulated universities we hear nothing. According to Madan not a single piece is known to have come from the Oxford Press between October 1648 and May 1649.

In many cases it is impossible to determine the exact date of publication. But the Thomason catalogue and, in some cases, internal evidence make it clear that they were pretty well scattered throughout the period. The publication of the Army's Remonstrance elicited a reply from Marchamont Nedham by the end of November, and another rejoinder, *A Cleare Answer To the Armies late Remonstrance Against Accomodation So far as to justifie their former Remonstrance for Accomodation*, probably came out about this time. Early in December William Prynne, muffled we are told to conceal the scars of Laud, spoke at length to the Commons in an attempt to induce them to accept the King's most recent offer as satisfactory. But this address was not published until late in the following month, when it appeared in a somewhat augmented form.[8] Towards the middle of December a number of anti-

Remonstrance works came from the press. One was *A True Relation of the Officers and Armies forcible seising of divers eminent Members of the Commons House*, to which was appended a letter purporting to show that the Remonstrance and attendant proceedings were serving to 'drive on the Jesuits and Papists Designs'. About the same time William Sedgwick, a Puritan divine, rebuked the evil spirit which held the Army captive,[9] and an anonymous tract, *Independency Stript & Whipt, Or, Iretons Petition, And The Royall Proiect Examined and Confuted*, saw the light. Still another, entitled *The Recoyle of ill-cast and ill-charged Ordinances*, indicted the framers of the Remonstrance for 'seditious impiety'.

Meanwhile, advocates of the revolutionary cause were making answer in their turn. Just before Christmas Thomas Collier, a Baptist, countered Sedgwick's *Justice upon the Armie Remonstrance* with a vindication of that document, and three weeks later Sedgwick (despite his changed position in *A second view of the Army Remonstrance*) received another reply in a lengthy treatise stressing the sovereignty of the people and the subjection of kings to law.[10] The altered tune of William Prynne, made particularly apparent in his *Briefe Memento To the Present Unparliamentary Iunto Touching their present Intentions and Proceedings to Depose and Execute, Charles Steward, their lawfull King*, which appeared early in January, evoked the satirical *Mr William Prynn his Defence of Stage-Plays* and, late in the same month, *Prynn against Prinn*. The telling qualities of John Goodwin's *Right and Might well met*, a vigorous justification of the Army's conduct, are well demonstrated by the pamphlets which followed in its train; rebuttals by Sir Francis Nethersole and John Geree were succeeded before the month was over by Samuel Richardson's *Answer To The London Ministers Letter*, in which Geree's Καταδυνάστης: *Might Overcoming Right* came under unfavourable review.

And so the fat was in the fire; the thrust and counter-thrust of pamphlet controversialists, so highly developed and keenly appreciated in seventeenth-century England, pointed to one facet or another of the many-sided problem. Was the King the chief shedder of blood, primarily guilty of the losses of life and treasure which England had sustained? Was he guilty at all? Even if culpable, could he be brought to account by a human agency? Under what authority, with what justification, did the Army act as it kept its sovereign in durance vile, sought to put the worst construction upon his actions, effectively terminated peaceful negotiations between him and his people, nullified the last vestiges of Parliament's representative character and erected an unprecedented tribunal, manned with its own creatures, determined primarily not on judicial investigation but on condemnation?

The essential innocence and good intentions of the King were naturally presupposed by his supporters. The anonymous author of *The Charge Against The King discharged: Or, The King cleared by the people of England, from the severall Accusations in the Charge, delivered in against him at Westminster-Hall* sought to rebut the aspersions of the opposition in connection with such common points of attack as the Spanish match, the death of James I, the Rochelle campaign, forced loans, coat-and-conduct money and monopolies. Charles stood acquitted on all indictments, being charged 'with what you can not take cognizance of ... falsely, maliciously, illegally, unreasonably'. The Remonstrance of the Army was 'writ in blood', and Charles would deny their supposition that he intended slavery for his people and autocracy for himself: so ran the argument in *A Cleare Answer To the Armies late Remonstrance*.

In general, however, the pamphleteers did not attempt to represent Charles as faultless—not before the royal martyrdom. Perhaps they felt that too sweeping an allegation of the royal innocence was poor propaganda: it would evoke rejoinders on the subject of royal duplicity and intransigence, it would raise questions better left at rest. Kings were not without their flaws, and Charles I was by no means perfect: Gauden the Episcopalian, Burges the Presbyterian, and Sedgwick the mystic could agree in this. To err is human, wrote Gauden, and Sedgwick found both sides guilty in this respect.[11] Cornelius Burges would go further. Acknowledging the 'woeful miscarriages of the King ... to be many and very great', he called upon his readers to pray 'that God would both give him effectual repentance, and sanctify that bitter cup of Divine Displeasure, that the Divine providence hath put into his hand; as also that God would restrain the violence of men, that they may not dare to draw upon themselves and the Kingdom the blood of their Sovereign'.[12]

Regardless of past error and misdemeanour, Englishmen were assured that the royal intentions were now good. Certainly they compared favourably with those of Parliament and the Army.

To Sedgwick the King was demonstrating a 'fatherly and large spirit'; he was a man to be trusted. Answering the Remonstrance, Nedham declared that Charles had already granted more than the world had supposed Parliament would demand: what were men to expect? On the other hand the Army-Parliament forces were following an uncompromising and merciless course. They were culpable in that they would not 'accommodate upon these Condescensions' of their sovereign, but would war upon him to the death.[13] The Army's 'present propositions' were unlike 'former pretences for Peace'; those had shown some regard for the King's rights, honour and safety, these were bloody and designed to disturb the State.[14] Now, wrote Gauden, 'in cool blood' the Army was bent upon destroying its lawful ruler after he had 'cast himself into His Subject's Arms, and was received with all assurances of Safety and Honour'.

That the proceedings against the King were illegal in the eyes of God and of law-abiding men (at least law-abiding Protestant Englishmen) was the general burden. As Burges wrote, the execution of King Charles 'in the present way of trial' is 'not agreeable to any Word of God, the principles of the Protestant Religion ... or the fundamental Constitution and government of this Kingdom ...' Some took the conservative politico-religious line that monarchs, even under the English dispensation, were accountable only to God. As an anonymous author wrote:

> We are so far from bringing his sacred Majesty into a Trial for any other, or the Accusations in the Charge given in upon Saturday last against him, that we stand fully assured (admitting all and every of them true) that by the clear and revealed Will of God in his Word, and the Laws of this Realm, he remains liable unto that supreme Judicature of Almighty God only, who hath passed an irreversible Act of Humane Indemnity unto him, and his lawful Successors ... [15]

There was no halting-point between subjection and rebellion. He that 'resisteth the power, resisteth the ordinance of God', so St Paul had taught, even as the persecuting Nero held sway. Deposition was unjustifiable as a usurpation of God's authority, for is it not he who 'removeth kings, and setteth up kings'? Sir Francis Nethersole reminded John Goodwin that he had once written that royal lives are to be regarded as 'consecrated corn meet to be reaped and gathered only by the hand of God himself'.[16]

More in conformity with English legal tradition was the argument that the king can do no wrong. And so, declared the Presbyterian ministers, he cannot by any written law 'forfeit his Crown and Life to his people'. If evils occur in governmental administration, the Council must answer; if in the course of justice, the judges. To the argument that it is palpably unjust to punish the servant yet let the master go free, it was rejoined that, while it is undeniable that he who gives a commission is more blameworthy than his instrument, yet 'humane Laws and penalties look at safety, as well as demerit'. To punish a king 'is like to set all on a flame'; therefore they are left to God 'to avoid inconvenience'. But 'if the King can have no Instruments, He can do no mischief'.[17]

Coupled with the concept that the king could do no wrong was the age-old interpretation of high treason. The trial of Strafford had given new scope to the doctrine set forth in the great statute of 1351. But William Prynne, at least, was willing to take his stand on the traditional reading. With characteristic boldness this veteran controversialist warned the survivors of Pride's Purge, whom he called an unparliamentary junto, that it was still high treason to 'compass or imagine the deposition, or death of the King ...' Carried away by his sense of personal grievance as an excluded member, he went on to assert that since the Rump Parliament was not a duly constituted legislature its Members acted only as private men, and therein lay themselves open to the penalties of treason.[18] This consideration of a private as opposed to a public capacity would seem to weaken the argument, but that Prynne counted on the legal weight of the old dispensation cannot be doubted. He underscores it again in his *Articles of Impeachment of High Treason, Exhibited By The Commons of England, In A Free Parliament*, where Cromwell, Ireton, Pride and a dozen others, accused of subverting the laws and liberties of England, are credited with 'a traitorous intent to depose, murder and destroy' the sovereign.

Apart from Prynne, however, the pamphleteers tended to steer clear of any direct reference to the proceedings against Charles as treasonous. At first glance this seems strange. The explanation probably lies in the vulnerability of a large proportion of the writers and their partisans. The ancient law of treason cut a wide swath. Certainly the Presbyterians were well aware that they were regarded by thoroughgoing monarchists as scarcely less culpable than the officers and politicians who were actually engineering the destruction of the throne. Had they not compassed or imagined Charles's death by preaching, launching and conducting a war against him? Their opponents—Milton, for example—never allowed them to forget this, and they were constantly on the defensive in the late 'forties. Signifying their 'utter dissent' from the fateful proceedings, the ministers of Banbury and Brackley protested that 'the dethroning or death of his Majesty, in prosecution of justice, never entered into our hearts'. Burges, a former royal chaplain who became a vice-president of the Westminster Assembly, insisted that the Presbyterian clerics did not engage with Parliament to hurt the King's person but to prevent his party 'from doing further hurt to the Kingdom; not to bring his Majesty to justice ..., but to put him into a better capacity to do justice ... not to dethrone, and destroy him, which (we much fear) is the ready way to the destruction of all his Kingdoms'. In still another protestation, 'Conscientious Presbyterians' explained that they had supported Parliament in order to remove wicked men from about the throne, not to 'pluck Him out of it'.[19] Nevertheless, many must have been uneasy as they considered how their words and actions would be regarded should unyielding exponents of the traditional monarchy gain the upper hand.

While, for tactical reasons, the King's defenders might side-step an orthodox argument, they would relentlessly attack the doctrine that the people possessed an overriding authority, an ultimate sovereignty, which could call kings to account and if necessary punish them, the argument that, in the last analysis, the apologists for revolution looked to as they wrote of *salus populi* and of a royal treason more heinous than the same crime at the hands of subjects. The 'persuasion that the community of the People is the Supreme power', and that the king is inferior to it and responsible to it, Hammond found to be the negation of Scripture, reason and history. In all of Holy Writ, only 1 Peter ii. 13, 14 ('Submit yourselves to every ordinance of man for the Lord's sake') might be regarded as favourable to such opinion. Where, he asks, is the historical evidence that 'this supreme power [was] vested in the whole Community originally?' Even if such evidence could be adduced, is not God's judgment to be preferred over human precedents? And is not the idea of a people recalling their trust in a ruler 'contrary to the end of all Government, quiet, and peace, and probably the parent of all confusion in the world, which is much worse than the hardest subjection?'[20]

With this position the other writers would in general concur. But the highly individualistic William Sedgwick, variously described as Presbyterian, Independent, Anabaptist, Seeker and Fifth Monarchy man, put his peculiar stamp on the issue. Taking a more positive approach than Hammond, he pointed out in his denunciation of the Army Remonstrance that the King 'had and hath a true and lawful right in the Kingdom and to the Kingdom, as good as any man hath to any thing he possesses ...' Further, it is the people's right to have a king. And so, 'he having a right to his Crown, and his People a right to him, it was as just for him and his party to stand for their right as for any other party to uphold theirs'. Here Sedgwick sees no supremacy in the people, but rather a kind of condominium with the king, rooted in mutual responsibility, respect and toleration. Not concerned with history and convinced that Charles is a man of goodwill, he provided in his *Justice upon the Armie Remonstrance* (December 11th) something of an antidote for the blindly partisan treatment of motives and events usually encountered in the works of the time. But Sedgwick, it appears, had not made up his mind. Though he was to eulogize the King in *The Spirituall Madman*, which appeared on December 20th, a few days later he brought out *A second view of the Army Remonstrance*. In this he effected a *volte-face*, confessing that he had interpreted the Army's intentions unjustly and identifying it now with the welfare of the people. No other Royalist writer appears to have undergone such a change of outlook while Charles yet lived; at least none demonstrated it so publicly. We cannot fathom the workings of his mind. Anthony À Wood calls him 'a conceited whimsical person and one very unsettled in his opinions';[21] others would be even less charitable. But his friends, no doubt, saw the directing hand of God in his altered course.

In any case the argument that the proceedings against Charles could be justified by the omnipotence of the people was adjudged invalid, for the simple reason that a majority of Englishmen did not support the Army-Parliament measures. They were twenty to one against the programme, wrote Gauden, while even Sedgwick declared that not one man in a hundred would agree with what the Army declared to be the public interest. 'The whole Peerage of England, distaste rigour against the person of the King,' declared John Geree, 'and I think three parts of four in the House of Commons are in their mind. The generality of the people of the Land detest it; the Ministry ... stand amazed at it, as most dishonourable to Religion ...'[22] One of the questions raised by a 'well-meaning man (that durst think truth in private)' was whether a ruler over three kingdoms was to be condemned and executed by a minority in one of them.[23] The affections of Scotland, at least officially, were not subject to doubt. About January 18th Members of the Scottish Parliament disclaimed any knowledge of or participation in the Army's proceedings against King or Commons on the part of 'either this Kingdom or any Person therein'.[24] Nor, Geree suggested, was 'all fair weather in Ireland'.

The claim that quality, not quantity, should be weighed was regarded as a device to secure factional control, a most dangerous and fallacious justification for political action. Only after Sedgwick had reversed his stand would he write that the Army was 'rightly and truly the people, not in a gross heap, or in a heavy, dull body, but in a selected choice way ...'[25] Nedham noted with distaste that the Army's Remonstrance was founded on this principle and on the concomitant notion that the Army alone is a competent judge of the people's safety. If it be argued that the 'godly People of the Land' who have petitioned for justice on delinquents, high and low, are to be reputed the community of the realm, it should be pointed out, wrote Hammond, that these petitioners (mostly from the military) are not a thousandth of the people of England, and that all the evidence of their godliness visible to him is 'their desiring liberty for themselves and others, and therefore Justice on those who stand in their way to that liberty'. Are there not, he asked, many more 'godly meek men' who would prefer to see Charles restored to his throne? If it is alleged that all power is originally in the people, a popular majority must be respected: 'other men's saying that they are not Godly, and that themselves are so can never exclude them from their Birthright'. If the Army desires to be accounted 'the Conservers, and not Conquerors' of its countrymen's liberties, it will poll the people to discover whether they prefer the subversion or continuance of the established Government, and assure them of its submission to their decision.

We have here the classic, and from the liberal point of view the unanswerable, refutation of the revolutionary programme, in this and after ages. Then and later, confirmed Revolutionaries would ignore or attempt to discredit such tactics—witness the behaviour of contemporaries as great as Cromwell and Milton. But in doing so they would lay themselves open to the charge of self-interest. The 'well-meaning' author of *Six Serious Quæries* called upon Englishmen not to suffer 'a rash inconsiderate number of Hot-spurs (of mean condition and broken desperate fortunes for the most part) out of private malice, fear, or designs to secure and enrich themselves by the ruins of others of better fortunes and quality ...' Elsewhere, the seekers after Charles's life were labelled seekers after his inheritance, the disposition of which had been prearranged.[26]

In representing the narrow, selfish and dictatorial character of the Army's programme the pamphleteers made the most of Pride's Purge. Here, wrote Geree, was an action 'neither defensible by the rules of solid Reason, nor Religion'. It was sheer usurpation for the Army to exclude and imprison the unacceptable members. In 1642 Charles I had but sought the arrest and impeachment of half a dozen legislators, and had aroused the fear and resentment of his subjects; how much more drastic was the action of the military. The King had merely attempted to launch judicial proceedings against a handful of traitors; the Army had effectively annihilated a free Commons because all the Members did not subscribe to the soldiers' philosophy. The Rump was no Parliament, declared Prynne, 'but rather a Conventicle or Junto'; what it did had no validity. It should adjourn until force was removed and all Members could sit and act. Then it could continue to seek a *modus vivendi* with Charles; certainly it would set its face against the High Court of Justice.[27]

With but one exception the Royalist pamphleteers stood shoulder to shoulder in indicting the extraordinary procedure of this court as barbarous, illegal and unprecedented. The most indefatigable burrowings into the books of Scripture, the laws of nature or the annals of men were alleged to reveal no shadow of a pattern for such a mockery. In all the Old Testament, wrote Prynne, 'there is not one precedent ... of any one King ever judicially impeached, arraigned, deposed, or put to death by the Congregation, Sanhedrin, or Parliaments of Judah or Israel'. As for the New Testament, how could one get around Romans xiii. 1, 2 and Titus iii. 1? No Protestant State had ever defiled its hands with the blood of its kings.[28] Even among the most barbarous nations, declared Nedham, 'the Persons of Sovereign Princes have ever been held sacred ...; and though in many Kingdoms they have been regulated by force of Arms, and sometimes (for the security of the grand Rebels) deposed, and afterward privately murdered; yet in no History can we find a Parallel for this, that ever the rage of Rebels extended so far, as to bring their Sovereign Lords to public trial and execution ...' Englishmen, in recent years, had been more than once reminded of the fate of Edward II and Richard II; several pamphlets describing their downfall had come from the press. But, Prynne insisted, their cases were quite different from that of Charles I. They had been forced by Roger Mortimer and Henry of Lancaster to resign their crowns in a formal manner, and subsequently deposed as unfit to reign, by a sentence in a full Parliament. There had been no judicial trial and both had been guaranteed good and honourable treatment. Later Mortimer had been impeached, condemned and executed for murdering Edward II in Berkeley Castle. But in any case the present Parliament had solemnly protested 'that they did never suffer these Presidents to enter into their thoughts'.[29]

The impression is strongly conveyed that it is not so much the doing of a king to death as his public arraignment on a capital charge that left the pamphleteers aghast. As 'E.S.' (probably Edward Stephens), a secluded Member, pointed out to Lord Fairfax, to kill a king by private conspiracy and for particular interests is an impiety deserving extreme punishment; 'but for Subjects to Solemnize their Sovereign's murder with a pretended legality, and usurp the power to be themselves his Judges must needs appear a very monstrous prodigy, and affrightful to every loyal contemplation: and the rather, because the act being by order, consent or connivency, made a national crime, will hardly be expiated without a national ruin'.[30] Only Elizabeth Pool saw any merit in the trial. This woman, who twice appeared before the Army Council to disclose her visions, believed that while God had permitted them to secure the King's person, he prohibited the forfeit of the royal life. But Charles should be brought to trial in order that he might be 'convicted in his conscience'.[31] What she appears to mean is that while vengeance is the Lord's and not the Army's, the royal offences should be formally demonstrated and the King made aware of them.

But if the King must suffer trial, surely a more august and representative tribunal, providing a more equitable procedure, than the High Court of Justice should be erected. How could an eighth of the membership of the Commons, acting under military constraint, fashion a suitable court? Charles should be judged 'only in full Parliament in the most solemn and public manner, before all the Members of both Houses', as was Strafford. Was not an Act of Parliament or at least an ordinance of both Houses required? Perhaps he should be tried by his peers—whoever they might be. Surely justice was not to be expected from the Commissioners, men 'who are professed Enemies to the King, and by their Remonstrances, Speeches and actions, profess they desire his blood and seek his life ...' And at least the King should have the benefit of liberty and time, and the advice of learned counsel 'to make his full defence' and counter the disadvantages of 'a dangerous unequal trial'.[32]

Thus did the pamphleteers attack the prosecution for ignoring and perverting both the law of God and of his Englishman. But there was yet another charge to be delivered, associated not with the fortunes of Israel or the shaping of the medieval constitution, but with Charles himself and the events of years just past. Had not the most explicit pledges been exacted that, regardless of political and military developments, the royal person was to be preserved? In over a hundred remonstrances and declarations, Prynne told the Rump, Parliament had professed to the world that it 'never intended the least hurt, injury, or violence to the King's person, Crown, Dignity, or posterity ...'[33] Singled out for special notice were parliamentary protestations of May 3rd, 1641 and October 22nd, 1642, the Commons's Declaration of April 17th, 1646 and the Solemn League and Covenant. By the first of these, which according to Rushworth 'was generally taken by the Members then present, and by others afterwards', the obligation to 'maintain, and defend his Majesty's Royal Person, Honour, and Estate' had been solemnly confirmed.[34] The second protestation, made the day before the battle of Edgehill, had stated that 'no evil intention to his Majesty's Person, no design to prejudice his just honour and Authority', had prompted the taking up of arms. More than three years later, when the Scots were seeking to drive on a speedy accommodation with the vanquished monarch, the Lower House professed its intention of maintaining the old Government of king, lords and Commons, and of requiring of Charles only such powers as would prevent the recurrence of civil conflict. This manifesto had been prepared to counteract the Scottish influence, which was by no means generally acceptable. But the Royalist writers made something of the argument that, since the King had not been captured in the field but had been surrendered by the Scots 'upon express promise ... that no violence should be offered to his Person', Englishmen were in duty bound to preserve his life.[35]

Most important of all guarantees of Charles's security, at least in the eyes of the Presbyterians, was the Solemn League and Covenant, to which the House of Commons subscribed on September 25th, 1643. Those that took the Covenant were by the third article obliged 'to preserve and defend the King's Majesty's person and authority, in the preservation and defence of the true religion and liberties of the kingdoms, that the world may bear witness with our consciences of our loyalty, and that we have no thoughts or intentions to diminish His Majesty's just power and greatness'. To the opposing controversialists, who dwelt on the unjustifiability of absolute and perpetual oaths in general and on the conditional nature of this one in particular, the Presbyterians would not give an inch. Herein, they insisted, lay an irrefrangible obligation, for was not covenant-breaking, like rebellion, as the sin of witchcraft? Will not the Covenant 'stare in your faces, your consciences, and engage God himself, and all three Kingdoms, as one man against you, if you should proceed to depose the King, destroy his person, or disinherit his posterity?' We must not risk God's wrath, warned the ministers of London; clergymen should exhort their charges to adhere to the Covenant and not be seduced by the Agreement of the People.[36]

Not only were the Army's transactions to be regarded as illegal and immoral, they were also impolitic. The destruction of Charles would bring about the continuation of alarms and wars, if not the utter destruction of the kingdom. Consider, the country ministers suggested, what English history taught; how, after the deposition of Edward II and Richard II, a 'Deluge of blood and calamities' engulfed our ancestors. The niceties of restraint were cast to the winds as the tribulations of fifteenth-century England were held up as the wages of unseating a king. Did not the chroniclers tell of two hundred thousand lives 'sacrificed by offended Justice' to avenge Richard II? The Army's programme would not only injure religion and weaken England by damaging the union with Scotland, but might well lead to a bloody conflict between Englishmen and a combination of Scots and Irishmen, bent on avenging Charles and setting his son upon the throne. Surely Prince Charles would not stand idly by without making a bid for his patrimony. Peace in Germany would afford plenty of mercenaries, and the disunity of those that had fought his father would play into his hands. Foreign princes would seize the opportunity to invade the island, wrote Breedon and his confrères. They may have known of King Louis' declaration 'against the most horrid Proceedings of a rebellious Party of Parliament-men and Soldiers in England, against their King and Country', published in Paris on January 2nd, and calling upon other princes to make similar proclamations. The unrestrained Prynne apparently felt that foreign aid would be unnecessary; ten thousand Englishmen to one, he wrote, would join with Scots and Irishmen to put Prince Charles upon his rightful throne.[37]

Whether or not the prolongation of armed conflict was to be expected, the destruction of the throne would certainly bring insecurity in life and estate to Englishmen. The trial, protested the Presbyterian ministers, was but a prelude to slavery and ruin. A deplorable infringement of the rights of Parliament and the liberties of London had already occurred; an army raised for 'the preservation of ... our Religion, Laws and Liberties' was engaged in activities tending to 'the manifest Subversion of them all'.[38] What body, what individual, could lay any claim to security if Majesty itself could be destroyed by violent hands? What shrub was likely to escape the axe if the tall cedar fell?

In seventeenth-century England, religious principles and precedents, whether or not they constituted the primary motivating force, were rarely ignored by propagandists. Particularly was this true at a time when a great army, characterized by a religious enthusiasm rarely encountered in military history, and acknowledging the direction of the Almighty in all its works, had gained control of the nation's fortunes and was bent on remodelling its

constitution. The Royalist writers did what they could to convince
their readers that the Draconian course of the Army and its
supporters could hardly be identified with Christian precept.
'Such', wrote Gauden, 'hath been the violence of praetorian
Soldiers, Janizaries and Mamelukes, such as have followed a
Caesar, or a Scylla, or a Marius, not knowing the mind of God in
Christ; But never of any Christian Soldiers, living in the power oi
Godliness.' His co-religionist, Hammond, scored those who
believed that only by further blood-letting, from which no
delinquent should be spared, could the offences of recent years be
fully expiated in the sight of God. He adduced 'peaceable-
mindedness, and charity, and the contrite heart ... [as] the special,
if not only sacrifices, which we find mentioned in the Gospel',
and suggested that a resolution to shed no more blood would be
'a more Christian probable means to pacify God' than a further
effusion. And, he added, if God does require such a sacrifice, what
right have the officers to be 'Gentile Priests'? Did not Christ
himself disclaim the office of a judge?

The doctrine of king-killing, it was pointed out, was of popish,
and particularly Jesuitical, origin. It had never been tolerated in
Protestant lands; the reformed religion was yet to be 'stained with
the least drop of blood of a King'.[39] Was England to set an in-
famous precedent? If so, how could Englishmen look Papists in the
face, whom they had so often reviled for 'their derogatory doctrine,
and damnable practices against Kings, or any in supreme
authority'? So queried John Geree. Sir Francis Nethersole, like
Geree a sharp critic of John Goodwin, called upon that divine
to explain his position as a defender of the Army at the risk of
being regarded as a professor of Jesuitical principles: 'the first
and only Minister of any Reformed Church, that ever was of this,
by yourself stiled Jesuitical, opinion' that kings might be deposed
and executed. Prynne, in his *Briefe Memento*, reminded Members
of Parliament of the oath of allegiance by which they signified
their detestation and abjuration of 'that damnable doctrine and
position, that Princes which be excommunicated or deprived by
the Pope, may be deposed or murdered by their Subjects, or any
other whatsoever'. But Prynne was not content, here and elsewhere, to indict as unprecedented and shameful the resort to
regicide by Protestants; he went on to blame the Catholics for the
crisis which now confronted the land. It was the Jesuits and popish

priests that had 'overteached and instigated' men who should have known better to prosecute such treasonable designs; Papists had induced the Army to purge the Parliament and to destroy the King. To such lengths could the polemical art be stretched in 1649!

The reader of these protestations and apologies, indictments and invectives, encounters little in the way of concrete proposals for the solution of the national imbroglio. There is, of course, a general plea for clemency, sometimes couched in terms of considerable fervour. Thus Gauden calls upon the Army to achieve as a crowning triumph 'the Conquest of yourselves: by overcoming what you conceive evil and blameable in another, with such unquestionable goodness in yourselves'. But while urging magnanimity he sets forth no practical programme. That further negotiations with Charles would result in a satisfactory outcome was doubtless generally believed, and is stressed in some of the pamphlets. Marchamont Nedham countered the Remonstrance with an appeal for accommodation. Mindful of the increasing suspicion with which Englishmen had come to view Charles's motives and actions, the author of *A Cleare Answer* declared that while 'the dangers of accommodation are but probable, and scarce that', those of rejection and execution must be regarded as 'inevitable'. He suggested that the King's careful regard for his position should be looked upon as a hopeful sign, pointing out that treaties are most likely to be broken by rulers who care not what they grant. Others saw in the truncated Parliament an instrument of oppression which should be blunted at once, and called for disbandment or adjournment until the full membership could sit. The Presbyterians of Banbury and Brackley petitioned Lord Fairfax for a programme which included the restoration of the secluded Members and the suspension of all proceedings against the King's Crown and life, 'until advice [be] had (in point of Conscience) with the Reverend Assembly of Divines, and the Church of Scotland, touching the several Oaths, that lie both upon us and them, and in point of prudence, with the Kingdom of Scotland, who are jointly concerned with us in his Majesty'. The recognition of the Army's all-important position in English politics is seen in the representations made directly to Fairfax and the Army Council; and there is more than a hint that the Commander-in-Chief, unlike the more intransigent Ireton and Cromwell, might be expected to heed a reasonable argument and intervene personally to save the King's life. He must, wrote 'E.S.', rouse himself against 'these blasphemers'; he should read Quintus Curtius Rufus on Bessus and Darius, and not be tempted to infidelity and ambition. Hammond closed his *Addresse* with the plea that, if the Army Council remained obdurate, Fairfax should interpose his hand and rescue Charles.

There is no reason to doubt that these pamphlets were intended primarily to convert the advocates of regicide and a violent break with the nation's constitutional past to the spirit of moderation and compromise. We can say this, fully recognizing the concern of the Presbyterians in squaring their conduct during the First Civil War with their expressed abhorrence of violent measures as the King's life neared its close. That the pamphleteers failed in their main purpose is undeniable. Most of them must have realized how precarious was the King's cause. Written after formal proceedings against Charles had been launched these pamphlets must be regarded as eleventh-hour appeals for clemency and justice, and not as elaborate defences of the Stuart monarchy as an institution. The approach to the problem is along well-worn political and religious channels, with almost no regard for economic considerations. None stands out, to be reread by later generations, as does Milton's *Tenure of Kings and Magistrates* or Goodwin's *Obstructours of Justice*. Though the English monarchy was to prevail in due season, its supporters in its greatest hour of need are for the most part forgotten; their opposites, pursuing a more novel theme, have attracted far greater attention. This is not surprising. The literature of revolution is more exciting than that of restoration, and in the long run the monarchs of Europe would be more challenged than justified. Yet these writers, ineffectual as they were in salvaging the royal cause, preoccupied as some were in placing their own actions in a better light, should not be ignored. In their various pamphlets they give a voice to the largely inarticulate majority of the time.

[1] *A Remonstrance Of His Excellency Thomas Lord Fairfax, Lord General Of The Parliaments Forces. And Of The Generall Councell Of Officers Held at St Albans the 16. of November, 1648.* Abridged versions were also circulated. For this and other pamphlets I am obliged to the Folger Shakespeare Library and to Union Theological Seminary.
[2] David Masson, *The Life of John Milton*, New York, 1946, III, 616.
[3] *Mercurius Pragmaticus*, November 21st–28th, 1648; Marchamont Nedham, *A Plea for The King And Kingdom; By way of Answer to the late Remonstrance of the Army.*

[4] James Heath, *A Chronicle of the Late Intestine War*, London, 1676, 191.

[5] William M. Clyde, *The Struggle for the Freedom of the Press from Caxton to Cromwell*, London, 1934, 180.

[6] *A Serious and Faithfull Representation Of the Judgements of Ministers Of The Gospel Within the Province of London.*

[7] *Mercurius Elencticus*, January 5th–12th, 1648.

[8] *The substance of a Speech Made in the House of Commons by Wil. Prynn of Lincolns-Inn, Esquire.*

[9] *Justice upon the Armie Remonstrance.*

[10] *The Armies Vindication.*

[11] John Gauden, *The Religious & Loyal Protestation, Of John Gauden Dr. in Divinity; Against the present Declared Purposes and Proceedings of the Army and others; About the trying and destroying our Sovereign Lord the King*; William Sedgwick, *Justice upon the Armies Remonstrance.*

[12] *A Vindication Of The Ministers of the Gospel in, and about London, from the unjust Aspersions cast upon their former Actings for the Parliament, as if they had promoted the bringing of the King to Capitall punishment.*

[13] *The Charge Against The King discharged.*

[14] *A Cleare Answer To the Armies late Remonstrance Against Accomodation.*

[15] *The Charge Against The King discharged.*

[16] 'Ο Αὐτο-Κατάκριτος. *The Self-Condemned. Or, A Letter To Mr Jo : Goodwin.*

[17] Zacheus Breedon et al., *The Humble Advice And Earnest Desires Of certain* well-affected Ministers, Lecturers of Banbury ... and of Brackly ..., *To his Excellency Thomas Lord Fairfax ...; and to the Generall Councell of Warre* ; and *The Charge Against The King discharged* ; and *A Cleare Answer.*

[18] *A Briefe Memento To the Present Unparliamentary Iunto.*

[19] *An Apologeticall Declaration Of the Conscientious Presbyterians of the Province of London.*

[20] Henry Hammond, *To the Right Honourable The Lord Fairfax, And His Councell Of Warre: The Humble Addresse Of Henry Hammond.*

[21] *Athenae Oxonienses*, London, 1813–20, III, 894.

[22] Καταδυνάστης : *Might Overcoming Right. Or A Cleer Answer to M. John Goodwin's Might and Right well met.*

[23] *Six serious Quæries, concerning the Kings tryall by the High Court of Justice.*

[24] *A Necessary and Seasonable Testimony Against Toleration And the present proceedings of Sectaries and their Abettors in England in reference to Religion and Government.*

[25] *A second view of the Army Remonstrance.*

[26] *Heare, heare, heare, heare, A Word Or Message From Heaven.*

[27] *Briefe Memento.*

[28] *Ibid.*

[29] *Ibid.*

[30] *A Letter of Advice, From a secluded Member of the House of Commons, To his Excellency, Thomas Lord Fairfax.*

[31] *A Vision : Wherein is manifested the disease and cure Of The Kingdome.*

[32] *Six serious Quæries*, and *A Letter of Advice, From a secluded Member.*

[33] *Briefe Memento.*

[34] John Rushworth, *Historical Collections : The Third Part*, London, 1692, I, 241, 242.

[35] *Briefe Memento*; Breedon et al.; see also Gauden.

[36] Mary Pope, *Behold, Here Is A Word Or, An Answer To The Late Remonstrance of the Army*; and *Briefe Memento* ; and *Serious and Faithfull Representation*; Burges.

[37] Breedon et al.; E. S., *Letter of Advice*; Geree; *Briefe Memento.*

[38] *Apologeticall Declaration*, and *Serious and Faithfull Representation.*

[39] Burges.

' Of People either too Few or too Many '

The Conflict of Opinion on Population and its Relation to Emigration

★

Mildred Campbell

THE American scholar summering in London soon learns that leisurely walks in whatever choice environs lie about him offer rewards second only to those of the archives among which he has come to work. Happily on occasion the one supplements the other. Returning recently from such an expedition I crossed the Strand at St Clement Danes, and turning right into the circular street that forms the Aldwych Crescent, paused alongside the impressive façade of Australia House for a better look at one of its large display windows. There gazing out, amazingly lifelike in a modern three-dimensional way, was a happy-faced family group, introduced as the Pollards of Brasted, Kent. But the backdrop of the scene was a broad expanse of golden prairie wheat. A snug ranch-house occupied a part of the foreground, and sheep of no Kentish breed nibbled the grass close by. One gathered at a glance that the Pollards had emigrated to Australia. The accompanying script, moreover, was clearly designed to convince the passer-by that if all were not well with him he might do far worse than to follow their example.

On that particular evening this scene was bound to have attracted my attention, as I had all of that day and the previous one in the Public Record Office, less than a quarter of a mile away, poured over the accounts of another emigration story: 'how to people with people' His Majesty's plantations in the New World—Virginia and the Barbados. Details of the inducements to settlers differed greatly from those outlined in the above exhibit. But the arresting thing was the similarity of their basic appeal to that which had taken the Pollards to Australia: a subsidized passage across the sea, either free or cheap land in amounts that the little man of an island race could never hope to own, and better opportunities for himself and his children than they could reasonably look forward to at home.

One was struck anew with the recurrence and the importance of the emigration motif in the past three centuries and a half of England's history. Articles in the current press throughout the summer reporting emigration to Australia and Canada brought once again into focus the question that has plagued Englishmen at intervals from the first century of colonial settlement to our own day—namely, whether the departure of so many people to distant lands is to be looked upon as a national asset or liability. This and subsequent queries were debated in Hansard and the daily press: What of the rate of population growth? What kind of people were going? Should skilled workers be permitted to leave the country?[1] New elements, of course, have entered the picture, as changed conditions at home and abroad raise new issues. But much, including the diversity of opinion on the subject, strikes a familiar note. This essay proposes another look at the problem as it appeared to Englishmen in the seventeenth century, when for the first time in their history emigration and population became matters of national concern.

It has now been fifty years since George Louis Beer wrote his classic work on *The Origins of the British Colonial System*, followed shortly by other volumes that carry the story forward.[2] His studies broke new ground and turned up much material hitherto unused. All students in the colonial field continue to be in his debt. But history keeps its vitality partly because other findings lead to the questioning of accepted interpretations. Beer's concern with the way in which seventeenth-century theories regarding population affected the contemporary view on colonies and emigration made him perhaps more than anyone else responsible for the treatment of that question which soon made its way into the standard treatises, and eventually into the textbooks. There, as is customary, it fell into more rigid lines than its author had designed. Modifications of certain particulars came in the 'thirties; but to a marked degree a pattern was established that has held its own throughout the years in practically every standard work dealing with the subject.

This traditional interpretation needs no lengthy recounting. Most of us were brought up on it, in full or slightly modified form. It presents England under Elizabeth and the early Stuarts as a growing and prosperous country. In the midst of this prosperity, however, idleness, crime and unemployment were rife, and hundreds suffered poverty on a scale hitherto unknown. Parallel with these conditions arose the belief that the country was over-populated and that its numbers were increasing at an alarming rate. If this were not actually the cause of the above ills, it at least greatly hampered their cure. Hence the first half of the century welcomed the colonial projects as a means whereby the harassed nation could rid itself of its 'surplusage of people'.

From the standpoint of the State it was this belief in over-population, Beer thought, which furnished the chief stimulus for the early emigration. From the point of view of the 'emigrating individual' it was political and religious motives which in the first half of the century determined his course. The appeal of adventure and the lure of riches were recognized as present with some, but 'not to any extent whatsoever' did they leave 'because of economic pressure at home'.[3] The coming of the Civil Wars brought emigration to a close, the traditional view holds, and after that event the prevailing attitude on population changed. It was then thought that England's people were decreasing in numbers and hence not keeping pace with the nation's capacity to produce. From about the middle of the seventeenth century onwards, therefore, emigration was regarded as a 'pernicious phenomenon' and a 'positive evil' which gradually 'dried up', except for a few obnoxious groups whom the country was glad to get rid of. Instead of the sturdy Puritan settlers of the earlier days, undesirables and 'foreign Protestants' made up the bulk of those who were sent to replenish colonial populations.[4]

Beer himself did not quite strip the story to so bare a framework. But his emphasis was such that any qualifications were pretty well lost sight of in the ensuing years. Historians in the 'thirties disposed to push back to a still earlier date the roots of mercantilist thought which they found in the same sources Beer had used, placed less emphasis on over-population as the chief stimulus of the State to early colonial enterprise, giving somewhat more weight to economic motivation. But the basic assumption that contemporaries were overwhelmingly convinced that England was over-populated and were consequently desirous of ridding the country of its 'surplusage' has remained for the most part unchallenged. Indeed Klaus Knorr, the most recent writer to deal at some length with colonial theories, says in reply to one critic that cast doubt on Beer's over-population theory, that after a complete review of the evidence he is forced to conclude that 'he [Beer] and the textbook version are substantially right'.[5]

No one working in the field will be disposed to throw overboard in its entirety the traditional picture. Indeed, its first premise—

namely, that the Elizabethan and early Stuart period was one of growing prosperity in which, nevertheless, many Englishmen faced poverty and unemployment hitherto unknown—has been strengthened and in part at least explained by later research. For if the 'Tawney century' has not solved all of the problems in that seeming paradox it has at least thrown light on many of their complexities. We know more about why prices had doubled and were still rising; more of the vagaries of rents and land tenures whereby it could happen that the fortunes of one tenant rose while those of his neighbours fell, why one landlord flourished while another near by suffered 'decay'. We have more information about the mobility of labour, and about slumps in trade and in particular industries. And we are beginning to learn something more of the earlier humanitarian efforts to attack the problem of poverty and child delinquency along lines other than those set down in the Poor Laws and the Statute of Apprentices. All of this knowledge, however, tends merely to underline the fact of economic and social distress in the midst of growth and prosperity. The parts of the picture that appear to call for further study are those dealing with the nature of contemporary opinion regarding population and emigration; the degree to which English emigration 'dried up' from the Civil Wars onward; the probable way in which both theory and practical need affected the shaping of official emigration policy in the second half of the century; and something more of the kind of people who emigrated during the years.[6] Current demographic studies which are adding to our knowledge of the actual population growth of the seventeenth century are of absorbing interest.[7] But since it was what people *thought* was taking place that affected emigration attitudes and policy, it is only the opinion concerning population that will here concern us.

It is quite clear from an examination of Beer's sources and those of other scholars who have followed in his footsteps why they thought the Elizabethans and their immediate successors were all obsessed with the idea of too many people. The literature which they were reading was full of it. Indeed, had the evidence been more sparse, or less convincing in tone, they might have searched further afield with somewhat different results. But on the face of it, both in quantity and substance it is impressive.

It dates from the earliest plans of settlement. Hakluyt made use of it in his famous *Discourse on Western Planting*. In 1583 Christopher Carleill, Walsingham's kinsman, planning to take a hundred men to the 'coast of America', gave it as one of his reasons for undertaking the enterprise. It was the 'rankness and multitude of increase in our people', and the 'evident danger that the number and infiniteness of them' would be to the commonwealth that furnished one of the chief themes for the sermons of Symonds, Crashaw and Crakanthorpe, and it was emphasized in letters, broadsides and pamphlets of members of the great companies that forwarded the colonization work, both those who went and those who stayed at home. These writings are set forth with all of the force and imagery of which the age was master: 'Our multitudes like too much blood in the body do infect our country with plague and poverty ... our land hath brought forth, but it hath not milk sufficient in the breast thereof to nourish all those children which it hath brought forth.'[8] 'The people do swarm on the land as young bees in a hive in June', one declared, and the 'young bees' were urged 'to swarm and hive themselves elsewhere'.[9] Others sought authority from the Scriptures: 'If thou beest much people, get thee up to the woods and cut trees for thyself in the land of the Perizites and of the Giants, if Mount Ephraim be too narrow for thee.'[10] These are mere samples. It is a body of literature well known to every student of colonial origins.

Beer and others found it convincing. And an author reviewing the evidence almost forty years later, though he admits that it often shows 'very crude notions of the prevailing distress', yet concludes that a careful reading of these sources will dispel any doubts that their authors were sincerely convinced of their country's overcrowded condition.[11] But is it their sincerity that is really the point at issue? Is it not rather whether we take as typical of the 'general opinion' on population only the testimony of those who, sincere or otherwise, were to so great a degree concerned as promoters, investors or participants—sometimes in all three capacities—with the colonial ventures? These men were not merely reflecting contemporary opinion, they were helping to create it.

Indeed, opinion favourable to emigration had to be created if those precarious toeholds that had been gained at such cost on the distant shores of Virginia, New England and the West Indies were to be maintained and strengthened. There was no lack of interest and curiosity about the New World, and many in an age that had money to invest were ready to gamble on shares offered by one of the joint stock companies, or buy chances in a Virginia lottery. But when the question was put as to 'who would venture their persons, and who their purses', those in the first category were never enough. The time would come when the recruiting agents would have powerful allies in friends and kinspeople already settled 'beyond seas', and ready to help provide for the newcomer. The time would even come when a harassed judge would complain that young people committed misdemeanours on purpose in order to receive a court sentence for transportation to America. But that time was not yet. 'People which is our greatest need' is a phrase that echoes like a refrain throughout much of the literature of the first century of settlement.

This being the case it would have been surprising had there been no attempt to link the need for settlers to the current increase in poverty and unemployment. That there was such a segment of opinion at hand to be used and enlarged upon, there can be no doubt. It is also true, however, that among certain contemporaries the exact opposite opinion prevailed. In fact, one needs go little beyond well-known writings of the period which lie outside the colonial literature to discover that population was a subject on which there was a genuine conflict of opinion.

Englishmen appear to have been interested in the subject especially from early Tudor times on. The recurrent problem of enclosures, the constant reports concerning 'decayed' towns, and as the century progressed the growing consciousness of international rivalries and competition abroad, continued to bring home its importance to many of the statesmen and thinking men of the kingdom. Thomas More, looking to the ancients for guidance on social as well as moral questions, believed that there was a proper or *right* number of people for every commonwealth and that such regulation as would achieve this number was both the concern and obligation of the State. This idea of the proper balance keeps cropping up. 'For if the country be never so rich, fertile and plentiful of all things ... yet if there be of people either too few or too many ... there can be no image or shadow of any commonwealth.'[12] Something of this kind, of course, was implicit in most of the arguments which favoured emigration as a means of cutting down numbers.

But by no means did everyone believe that the current problem was one of too many people. As Renaissance statesmen and thinkers both on the Continent and in England became more imbued with the idea of a strong national state, and more aware of the political and economic threats which such states placed upon each other, the greater was their tendency to identify national strength with a large population. And the subsequent question with each was whether his own state was secure in that respect. Machiavelli had also turned to the ancients on this question; principally to the Romans who made a large population the first prerequisite of a strong state.[13] And Machiavelli was being read all over Western Europe. Bodin spoke out strongly on the subject: 'One should never be afraid of having too many subjects or too many citizens, for the strength of the Commonwealth is in men.'[14] He was also a great believer in colonies; but the argument of the promoters we have quoted would have appeared upside down to him. For he did not approve of colonies because they would rid the country of excess population, but of a large population because it would enable a nation to colonize and still have plenty of people left at home for military and other uses. Other French writers made a large and industrious population the necessary prop for national wealth and strength, and their counterparts are to be found among the German, Dutch and Spanish.[15] The same was true in England. 'As the wise husbandman maketh and maintaineth his nursery of young trees to plant', it was said in 1549, 'so should politic governors provide for the increase and maintenance of people, so that at no time they may lack to serve his highness and the commonwealth.'[16] Men sought authority in the Scriptures as well as the classics. And from Latimer on to the end of the seventeenth century one finds writers quoting from the Book of Proverbs that 'in the multitude of people is the King's glory, but in want of people is the destruction of the Prince'.

Whether or not Thomas Starkey's famous *Dialogue* can be taken as a literal presentation of the views of the two Tudor scholars and men of affairs whom he made his spokesmen, matters less than the fact that it points up in a realistic way some of the problems which England faced at the close of Henry VIII's reign. It is significant that the first weakness pointed out by Reginald Pole in his diagnosis of the ills of the Commonwealth, was 'the lack of people and the scarceness of men'. To his assertion that these were the first prerequisite of a strong state, Thomas Lupset was made to reply: 'Sir, Meseemeth this ruin of cities and towns ... argueth nothing the scarceness of people but rather the negligent idleness of the same.' It may be that the device of having Lupset take the other side in the debate is in order to give Pole the opportunity to drive home his view, apparently Starkey's own, that 'in times past many more have been nourished therein and the country hath been more populous than it is now'.[17] But in the light of other evidence one is inclined to believe that the points of view presented by the two men actually mirror the differences of opinion that one might have found in any group that chanced to fall into a discussion of the question. Points similar to Pole's arguments were made in a slander case in 1549 by a witness who declared that England was a country 'such as would both keep thrice as many people as it doth and also bring forth and keep plenty of all things for their nutriment',[18] a sentiment usually associated with the later Stuart period.

A much more penetrating economic analysis than that of Starkey, *The Commonweal of this Realm of England*, almost certainly the work of John Hales, came a few years later. Here, too, the author lamented the decay in England's population, holding it in a measure responsible for her backwardness in trade and industry among her neighbours. It may be significant that when the tract was first published in 1581, thirty years after it was written, the remarks on population were allowed to stand, though other parts, considered by the editor to be no longer true because of changed conditions, were altered.[19] Hales was particularly eager to keep skilled workers from emigrating. Things 'should be wrought within this Realm' to sell abroad—another forerunner of an argument that was later to become a commonplace.

That there was diversity of opinion on the subject of population was itself a matter of comment among contemporaries. William Harrison said that there were some who affirmed 'that we have already too great store of people in England'. He was himself critical of those who blamed the increase in poverty on over-population, and warned that if there should be an invasion they would discover that 'a wall of men is far better than stacks of corn and bags of money'. 'It is an easy matter to prove', he said, 'that England was never less furnished with people than at this present.'[20] It would not have been as easy to prove as he thought, but

'Political Arithmetic', by which Englishmen would try their hand at statistical analysis and proof, was still a good half-century away.

It is well known that Francis Bacon favoured plantations; but this was not because he was worried about over-population. Quite the contrary! He declared before the House of Commons in 1607 that England had once been far better peopled than she then was. And in the outline of his projected treatise on 'The Greatness of Britain', a work either never finished or else lost to us, Bacon gave as the second point among those things most 'solid and principal', that 'true greatness consisteth essentially in population and breed of men'.[21] A few years later Thomas Mun expressed similar belief in the strength of a large population though his book remained unpublished until 1664.[22] In 1636 Robert Powell published his pamphlet on 'Depopulation', declaring it to be 'a treatise necessary in these times'.

It is clear, therefore, that there was not unanimity but diversity of opinion both on the actual state of population and on what it ideally should be. Indeed, some men, probably in the process of working out their opinions on the matter, were not always consistent in their own views. Hakluyt's name often heads the list of those who were said to have thought England over-populated. And he did indeed speak of how England had 'grown more populous than ever before', and talked in favour of sending 'our superfluous people' to America. Yet a careful reading of Hakluyt shows that he considered this situation not the result of over-population as such, but of an unenlightened and ineffective public programme for keeping people at work. 'If this come about', he said, 'that work may be had for the multitude, where the Realm hath now one thousand for the defence, the same may have five thousand: for when people know how to live, and how to maintain and feed their wives and children, they will not abstain from marriage as now they do ... I dare truly affirm that if the number in this Realm were as great as all Spain and France have, the people being industrious, there should be victuals for all.' England could, he thought, if proper use were made of resources, set a hundred thousand people 'on work'.[23] The evil was not in over-population *per se*, but in the proper handling of labour. In somewhat the same fashion John White, friend of impoverished Dorset fishermen, said in a passage often quoted from his famous *Planter's*

Plea, 'that we have more people than we do or can profitably employ, will I conceive, appear to any man of understanding'. Yet it must be noted that he also said: 'But the idleness or unprofitable labours of our people arise not from our numbers, but from our ill government.'[24] It was, he thought, an effective use of laws already made that was most needed, not 'transportation'. Men in this period were groping in the field of both theory and practice towards a fuller grasp of economic principles. The precepts which had moulded the thinking of many of them were in theological and philosophical rather than economic terms. But circumstances were forcing their thoughts in that direction. Many, often in a rather vague way, related population with subsistence, and even subsistence, a few were thinking, need not be left to blind chance or divine direction.[25] Others foreshadowing Malthus, looked to war, pestilence and fire to be somehow the natural regulators.[26]

But these men who have been quoted were writers and men of affairs. What of the point of view of the ordinary Englishman? Did the man who was neither concerned with colonial ventures nor troubled his head too much about the national good think that the country was over-populated? That is, of course, more difficult to say. His ideas on the increase or decrease of population, if he had any, would almost certainly be determined by what he observed in his own city, town or countryside. Harrison had bolstered up his views on the loss of population with the remark: 'I know what I say by mine own experience.' But experience would tell a different story in different parts of the realm.

Probably most Londoners—and London was the centre of operations for many of the colonial activities—would feel certain that England was growing more populous—too populous, perhaps, for its own good. Twelve large granaries and storehouses for coal were put up in 1610 as a precautionary measure against famine, 'such is the late unspeakable increase of people within and about the city, as well strangers as natives'.[27] Edmund Howes who continued Stow's narrative spoke of the tremendous building programme in 1614, 'for these late years so much increased in people'. Highways and highway repairs, owing partly to the same reason, had, it was said, gone on at a more rapid rate in the past twelve years than in the preceding fifty.[28] Thomas Dekkar, playwright and self-appointed expert on all aspects of London life, unwittingly anticipated Malthus when he wrote of the effects of the Plague of 1625: 'We flatter ourselves that the Pestilence serves but as a Broom to sweep Kingdoms of people, when they grow rank and too full.'[29]

Contemporaries spoke of the large numbers of foreigners coming to London in these years; but also much of London's increase, it was always pointed out, was at the expense of other parts of England.[30] For prosperity and good times in general prevalent under Elizabeth and the early Stuarts were neither continuous in point of time nor uniform throughout the country. Hence there was great mobility, particularly among large groups of workers, more than was heretofore suspected.[31] The casual observer might well mistake mobility of population for either increase or decline. Coventry in mid-Tudor times was said to have been reduced within a few years from a population of three thousand to fifteen hundred.[32] Leicestershire men declared in 1612 that their villages had been reduced by half in the past years.[33] Local Yorkshire records tell the story of constant complaint of decay of both wealth and numbers of inhabitants, a situation thought not to have changed until the Civil Wars were over. Lincoln was said to have suffered decreases as a result of the decline in the wool industry from late medieval times, and in 1607 a Parliamentary Commission was set up to inquire into the rural depopulation of that shire.[34] Yet in Northamptonshire, not far away, there were thought to be too many and to spare.[35] Either because of changes in trade routes or trade controls a number of port towns including Newcastle, Hull, Boston and Lynn to the north-east, and Southampton, Weymouth, Bristol and Chester to the south and west were listed among the 'decayed' towns at the close of Elizabeth's reign, though Bristol was certainly on the threshold of great growth.

Londoners suffering from the Plague fled to the countryside. But neither did country towns and villages escape that scourge; and because there were fewer people there to be wiped out the losses may have seemed even greater. If conditions were favourable population decreases would be temporary; but a neighbourhood might never within the lifetime of those who were left, regain its former populousness. There were no pollsters to take samplings of opinions from people scattered here and there throughout the realm. But it is clear that local conditions differed greatly, and available evidence indicates that there, too, diversity rather than any degree of unanimity marked the prevailing thought on population trends.

Much less was said about emigration as such than in the second half of the century. Its full implications were not yet generally known or appreciated. In the main, people were sympathetic with the colonial ventures and eager to have them succeed; hence were ready to lend a sympathetic ear to the notion that there were many people who might well be spared, yet individuals were not wanting who sensed the trend of certain things to come.

We have already seen John Hales worrying about the emigration of young craftsmen to the Continent long before there was any colony in the New World to bid for their services. Others also were concerned because more things were not being made in England to be sold elsewhere. Indeed most of the arguments that were to become the stock-in-trade in later years had already been voiced in the earlier period. The Proclamation of 1637, designed to prevent the embarkation of those who had not taken the oath of allegiance and conformity, has often been said to have sprung from fear lest the Puritans set up a factious centre outside England that would in time damage the mother country. That was one of the reasons for it. Another was that some were already feeling concerned about the loss of the people themselves and their skills.

Francis Bacon who deplored the get-rich-quick methods of some of the promoters early warned against the short-sightedness of taking 'the scum of people and condemned men' as the first settlers. But the planters were for the most part to find out that mistake by bitter experience. They found, as Bacon also advised, that it was farmers and handicraft men who made the best settlers. The poor and the condemned continued to be sent as they could be absorbed; for that was in accord with public policy. But the farmer and the craftsmen came soon to be the most valued settlers, and because of conditions at home it was often they who listened most readily to what the New World had to offer.[36] The strength of the religious motive among the prospective settlers of New England is not to be belittled. Indeed, religious nonconformity is an enduring and activating force throughout the whole emigration story. But to fail to take account of the relation of economic conditions to the Puritan exodus is totally unrealistic and contrary to the records which are left to us.[37]

The relationship was not lost on contemporaries. The departure of Puritans, as such, would strike many as good riddance of bad rubbish, but they did not like to see skilled workmen go. Secretary Coke was concerned about the loss of ships' carpenters that Winthrop had taken to New England. Letters to Laud expressed concern over the 'intent of divers clothiers of great trading' to go to New England, and pointed out the danger of many parishes being impoverished. A sad lament was written on the 'poor ruinated town of Hingham', when almost that entire Norfolk village transported itself to a new Hingham in Massachusetts. Emanuel Downing described one emigrant, Will Stephens, as 'so able a shipwright as there is hardly another to be found in this kingdom'. It would be strange if there had not been those who began to wonder how many Will Stephenses the country could afford to lose. Special mention was made in 1641 of the 'multiplicity of vexations' that beset tradesmen and artificers which 'did impoverish many thousands and so afflict and trouble others that great numbers, to avoid their miseries, departed out of the kingdom, some into New England, and other parts of America, others into Holland, where they have transported their manufactures of Cloth, which is not only a loss by diminishing the present stock of the kingdom, but a great mischief by impairing and endangering that peculiar Trade of Clothing'.[38]

Hence it is clear that the sentiment that was to grow to much greater lengths in the second half of the century was already in the making. In fact, another argument that was also to make its way near the close of the century—namely, the idea that emigration might in the end prove a boon to population growth at home —had at least been brought to the attention of Englishmen in the early period. It came by way of the Italian Giovanni Botero, whose *Treatise Concerning the Causes and Magnificence of Cities*, published first in 1598, included a full and thoughtful treatment of colonies. An English translation of his work was published in London in 1606. Here it can scarcely have failed to catch the eye of some of those men who were that very year launching the Virginia enterprise. In his attempt to answer the question 'What shall we say of Colonies?', Botero turned also to the ancients as did so many of his contemporaries. 'Were they a good help to the greatness of Rome, or no?' He found an unequivocal reply in the affirmative. Questioning further whether emigration would in the end tend more to depopulate or to increase the population at home, he recognized the weight of conflicting arguments but his own theory pointed to an eventual increase: 'For if any man think, by taking the people out, and sending them to colonies elsewhere that the city thereby came rather to diminish than increase; happily for all that, the contrary may happen.'[39] It was an argument that would find able supporters before the century closed.

And what of the traditional view of the second half of the century? It may be had in practically any standard treatise. As one writer expressed it, the over-population theory which led to the pro-emigration sentiment in the early part of the century 'gave place about the middle of the seventeenth century to the belief that the country was under-populated'.[40] Another describes the twenty years from 1640 to 1660 as a time 'during which the communities of the New World lost touch with the old'. The Restoration, he says, 'renewed some of these contacts, but not the greatest of all, the continued emigration in due proportion of the home population'. After the Restoration 'new immigration was scanty' because 'English thought was by this time unfavourable to the emigration of useful English citizens, which it held to be a draining of the mother country's strength. The Proprietors, therefore, sent out few mature Englishmen, but looked rather to the older colonies, to Scotland and to the Huguenots of France for the peopling of the new domain.'[41] An excellent work on the Puritan migration says that 'With the beginning of the Civil Wars it [emigration] rapidly dried up owing to the impossibility of finding transport ... The great exodus was over.' Not again, the author says, until the nineteenth century would there be so many people leaving England.[42]

Again, as in the earlier period, one readily admits a certain amount of validity to the traditional view. But parts of it need further clarification, and some of it considerable modification. Here, too, there was greater diversity of opinion on both population and emigration than has sometimes been thought, as well as considerable change of emphasis in the course of the half-century. It is, moreover, important to find out what the official emigration policy actually was, and something of the conflicting demands that faced the men who formulated it. Finally we need to know the extent and nature of the English emigration that actually did take place after the Civil Wars.

Any consideration of the opinion on population under the later Stuarts must first of all take note of the emergence of a new type of person—the population expert. He was perhaps less important to his age than his successors in later years would be to theirs; but he was, after all, of his age. Whoever had expressed himself on matters of population in the earlier period had done so in terms of policy, or on random and usually limited observation. In the Restoration years and later, England boasted several individuals who were seriously trying to establish some sort of measuring rod whereby population trends could be determined.

It is a far cry from John Graunt's rather clumsy work with the inadequate mortality rolls of London parishes to the refined methods of the modern demographer. Even so, it was important enough at the time to gain him entry on the King's recommendation to the newly organized Royal Society, which his friend and colleague William Petty helped to found. Here men with new ideas met at intervals to read papers to each other on all manner of subjects that interested them, properly indifferent to the verdict of posterity which would call some of them crackpots, and others men of scientific vision ahead of their time. Population came to be a matter of interest to them. Graunt appears to have worked up the first figures; but Petty elaborated them, published them and later did more work of his own.[43] And before the century was over, Matthew Hale, Charles Davenant and Gregory King had all published population studies. These men have had ample treatment elsewhere. But it is pertinent here to note that although they arrived at somewhat different numerical results and from different approaches they all came to the conclusion that, despite periodic losses, Britain's population was increasing rather than decreasing. They did not, moreover, consider emigration something to be afraid of.[44]

But if the experts agreed on the general trend, by no means did everyone agree with the experts. There were those who, not taking the long look of the student of population but observing certain current phenomena, were definitely concerned about the loss in manpower. A country engaged in civil warfare unfortunately has to count the losses on both sides. Local records and the markers in country churches give ample testimony that there was scarcely a hamlet in all England that had not lost men on one side or the other, often both, during the struggle between King and

Parliament. In addition, wars with both the Dutch and French came at intervals throughout the century. In terms of modern warfare the losses in these wars were notably small. But people in rural communities—and despite its growing towns and cities England was still rural—would be conscious of every gap.

Ravages of the plague were particularly bad during the Civil Wars and at intervals afterwards. The ghastly scenes that Pepys and Evelyn have portrayed of the London of '65-6, where seven thousand were said to have died in one week, should not blind one to the losses suffered in provincial towns and country places at that same time and in succeeding years.[45] In London, also, on the heels of the Plague had come the Great Fire; so that in the place where men in the first half of the century had been most aware of population growth there were now the most spectacular exhibitions of population losses. It is small wonder that people expressed concern. Certain proposals offered to Parliament in 1670 stated that 'There is nothing so much wanting in England as people ... the two last Great Plagues, the Civil Wars at home, and the several wars with Holland, Spain and France have destroyed several hundred thousands of men, which lived among us.'[46] Sir William Coventry in 1670, gave as his first reason for the diminishing of rents that 'We have fewer people than heretofore.'[47]

It is, of course, expressions of this kind that have led to the assumption that it was the prevailing belief after the Civil Wars that the country's population was decreasing. Certainly there were those who thought so. Yet a careful study of available evidence shows a less widespread belief that population was actually declining than a growing realization of the value of a large population. Sometimes the evidence is subject to different interpretations. Does the M.P. who said in 1673 that 'We labour under a poverty of people'[48] mean that population was decreasing, or simply that England had not as many people as she needed and could use? Certainly on every hand one encounters the growing belief that England's future strength lay in developing a more productive society. Some thought in terms of increasing agricultural production. Perhaps even more emphasized the need for industrial and mercantile growth; for the picture of England as the maker of things for the whole world, advocated a hundred years earlier by John Hales, was growing apace.

The term 'mercantilism' has become somewhat suspect in late years, and with good reason if a fixed system of policy and action is implied. But despite differences, and a good deal of vagueness of detail among seventeenth-century writers, no one can question the fact of a body of opinion, both lay and official, which held that England's road to national power and wealth lay in her development as a strong maritime and industrial nation, seeking ever to enlarge her trade with the rest of the world in the hope thereby of providing a balance in her own favour. There was nothing new in this idea to the seventeenth-century business man. English merchants, with at least the blessing of the Crown and often its connivance, had envisaged national wealth in terms of trade for a long time. It is true, however, that greater overall planning and a stronger emphasis on industrial output, together with an increased consciousness of international rivalries and the strategic manœuvring they called for, characterize the English, especially from the Restoration onwards. They were envious of the Dutch, and afraid of the French. And dozens of tracts less celebrated than that of Mun, were published to attest the interest of business men and the general public in commercial and industrial betterment. Growth of output either for home or foreign consumption called for a large population, more farmers and craftsmen, and more trained seamen to man the ships, British built, that would carry her products to distant markets. 'People and plenty are commonly the begetters of one another', it was said.[49] Some placed their hopes in density of population rather than mere numbers, pointing with increased envy to little Holland with its large and productive population.

Yet in the very nature of this programme lay conflicting demands which if not sensed in the beginning were in time to become obvious both to the public, and more quickly to those directing national policy. For in addition to increased agricultural and industrial output at home the development of colonies as a concomitant factor in the growth of a strong maritime state, was an idea that steadily rose in favour. Both economic and strategic considerations seemed to call for this development. Colonies would furnish military and naval bases for keeping French, Spanish and Dutch rivals at bay; and would help train seamen for both the Navy and merchant ships. They would provide English manufacturers with materials which they would otherwise have to buy from foreigners, and would furnish additional markets for home-manufactured goods. These are the chief elements in the decision to sustain and develop colonies. They were at least implied in the first Navigation Acts, and emerged more clearly in the hands of Restoration statesmen and the various trade and colonial organizations that had charge of the implementation Colonial policy. Clarendon later wrote that soon after the Restoration he had used all of his endeavours to bring His Majesty to have great esteem for his plantations, and to encourage the improvement of them.[50] He succeeded well. The late Stuart monarchs, particularly Charles and James, maintained a personal and active interest in colonial matters.

The programme thus set forward envisaged both the maintenance of colonies already under way and the planting of new ones. But it had earlier become apparent that nothing was so necessary in the beginning years of a colony as a constant supply of people. Even the older colonies, as their records constantly reveal, were only periodically beyond that need. Thus far the demand had been met almost entirely by English emigrants. But continued emigration would clearly come into competition with the labour demands of a more aggressive programme for increased output at home; unless, indeed, the colonies could do with the undesirables, vagrants, convicts or people like the Quakers who were thought to be making a nuisance of themselves at home. That they could and should do with such was a comfortable notion that made great headway. It left out of account several considerations, including the fact that promoters had through the years learned to be more discriminating about the material required for colonial building; that servant recruiters had grown more expert in their business of persuading people to go; and that with friends and kinsmen on the other side as a drawing-card, and conditions not wholly ideal at home, more people might now wish to go of their own accord than was earlier the case.

It is true that during the actual years of civil warfare English shipping to the Colonies was greatly curtailed; but to speak of the twenty years from 1640 to 1660 as a period 'during which the communities of the New World lost track with the old' is scarcely borne out by the evidence. It is clear from the writings of Winthrop and others that even during the war years New England was constantly in touch, following the course of events and agonizing over 'the miseries' of old England. In that colony, indeed, the stream of passengers ran for a while somewhat in reverse, as Puritan leaders hastened home to take part in the wars or to be ready to share in the gains; and some who had planned to come over decided 'to stay in England in expectation of a new world' they hoped to see emerge. But despite shipping difficulties there was a great deal of going back and forth, as thanks were offered for the safety of ships that have 'carried those of the Lords family between the two Englands'.[51] New England did cease to be the goal for emigrants that it had been in the 'thirties, but this came about for other reasons than the 'drying up' of emigration to the New World. The course of emigration shifted, but it did not stop.

Colonies with Royalist sympathies, such as Virginia, likewise kept close touch with what was going on, and as soon as the fighting was over and unsettled conditions brought the usual crop of post-war difficulties in England emigrant recruiters found new fields for their activities. Immigrants came into Virginia by hundreds and thousands. Political prisoners banished to the colonies under the Commonwealth and Stuart régimes have had their due—and more attention than their figures warrant. It is the stream of common folk, farmers, artisans and labourers who left for the New World in the unsettled years of the commonwealth and later under the Restoration that have for the most part gone unnoticed. Their going did not go unnoticed by their contemporaries. In fact, by the latter part of the 'sixties, emigration had become a subject of public agitation. A number of factors contributed to the anti-emigration flare-up. The acts of the early 'sixties against nonconformists had made transportation a punishment for some. It was also becoming known that others were voluntarily turning in the direction of America. The generous terms offered people who would settle the new province of Carolina may have been a subject of conversation. It is quite possible that the news had got around concerning the exodus of scores of cloth-workers from the towns and villages of Somerset, Gloucestershire and Wiltshire, and also that hundreds of young farmers were going. Mention has already been made of the gloom that followed upon the losses from the London fire and from the plague in London and provincial centres. Hence it was in these years—the decade following the late 'sixties—that the dangers facing the country from emigration began to be pointed up in some of the most forceful pamphlet literature of the entire half-century, and for a time emigration was made the scapegoat for all ills, past, present and to come.[52] Feeling ran so high that Lord Ashley took note of it in his Memorial to the King in 1669. His opening paragraph set forth an excellent summary of that part of the national programme that emigration might harm:

> First, I take it for granted that the strength and glory of your Majesty and the wealth of your kingdoms depend not so much on anything as in the multitude of your subjects, by whose mouths and backs the fruits of and commodities of your land may have a liberal consumption ... and by whose hands both your Majesty's Crown may be defended on all occasions, and also the manufactures of both your natural and foreign commodities improved by which trade and your Majesty's revenues must necessarily be increased.[53]

If it be admitted, said Ashley, that emigration were responsible for the things with which it was being blamed 'then recovery must be by using all rational and just ways to invite foreigners in, and stop the drain that carries natives away'. Hence at this time and in the following year (1670), Ashley argued for a greater toleration for all dissenters except Roman Catholics and Fifth Monarchy men, one of the reasons for his plea being that such action would be a means of 'increasing population'; that is, it might act as a stay to emigration. In the meantime other efforts were made to meet the demand of the colonies for more people. Some years earlier a greater use of intercolonial migration had been suggested. In the Barbados a particular economy had developed that called for the large planter and many slaves, leaving little or no room for the small farmer. Hence it was thought that the latter group might be used elsewhere. The Barbados, it was said in 1667, should serve 'as a nursery for planting Jamaica, Surinam and other places'.[54] And, indeed, as such it was used until the desire for more whites to offset the predominantly coloured population caused the Barbadians to become alarmed at their own depletion.

Other possibilities, which had also been for some time the subject of Whitehall talk, came now more and more to the fore. They included the encouragement of more Irish and Scottish emigrants in order that the English might be kept at home; the sending of

'Foreign Protestants', earlier thought of as a means of augmenting English labour at home; and the continued transportation of vagrants, beggars and other 'noxious' people. It is, I believe, the reiteration of these tenets, in both the official and unofficial literature of the day and the body of anti-emigration pamphlets published in the late 'sixties and in the 'seventies, that is responsible for the stereotype so often presented for the entire second half of the century—namely, a belief in current depopulation and the triumph of anti-emigration sentiment that resulted in a 'drying-up' of English emigration after the Civil Wars.

That the above tenets became a kind of ideal and one often repeated is quite clear, and some headway was made towards their realization. Irish, Scots and Foreign Protestants did come to figure more largely in the minds of planters who sought settlers, but none of these groups came in large numbers until in the eighteenth century. Intermigration among colonies, as stated above, was also periodically effective; but few colonies for long had people to spare.[55] The poor and condemned continued to be sent to the limit of what the colonies could or would absorb. But despite these extra sources of supply English emigrants, many of the very type which the country wished least to lose, continued to go throughout the century and on into the next.

A full analysis of the kind of people who were going and the reasons for the continued flow of English emigration must await further study, but the official policy under which it was allowed to go forward and some indication of its extent are directly pertinent. The fact that during the height of the anti-emigration sentiment the shaping of colonial policy was in the hands of men who were themselves head over heels in colonial activities has long been known; but its possible bearing on the emigration policy that was actually made has not, I think, had the attention it deserves.

We have seen how the Earl of Clarendon in the first year of the Restoration was zealous in colonial enterprise, and sought to enlist his sovereign's interest. Even more, after the reins fell from Clarendon's hands, did Charles Stuart surround himself with a group of men to whom colonial ventures were a veritable hobby. Adventurous spirits in the age of Drake and Raleigh had found outlets for their interest in the New World in voyages of discovery. Under the later Stuarts, for such men as Lord Ashley, Arlington, the Berkeleys, Sir John Colleton and others, the New World offered ventures of a different kind. The hope of building up or retrieving personal fortunes was still, as it had always been, a main spur to such ventures. But there were those who were also ready to risk fortunes already in hand: 'I am now making myself a plantation', Ashley wrote to Thomas Lynch in Jamaica, 'and intend to throw away some money in making some experiments there.' His plans were to try to grow cocoa trees and other new products, and he was asking Lynch for seeds, roots and directions for planting.[56] This was typical of the spirit that prompted the Carolina venture. The eight proprietors, receiving their charter in 1662, reserved twenty thousand acres apiece for themselves, to be settled and developed, and they worked to persuade well-to-do friends to follow their example.

Already most of these men had had experience with colonial affairs. Charles II had scarcely arrived in England before a set of *Instructions* issued in his name, probably the work of Clarendon, was sent to the newly appointed Council for Foreign Plantations. One section gave special attention to emigrants. Colonies which needed a steady supply of servants were not to be left unprovided for 'in so essential an assistance'. Englishmen at home were to have better protection from servant recruiters who had learned to make a business of their trade and sometimes duped people into going against their will; and 'vagrants and others here noxious' were to be transported. The *Instructions* clearly stated, however, that 'such as are willing to be transported thither and to seek better fortunes than they can meet with at home may be encouraged thereunto'.[57] The Council followed up their instructions with a fact-finding survey based on questionnaires that were sent to colonial governors. The queries asked for detailed and exact information (more detailed and exact than many colonial administrators could readily produce) concerning their numbers, the increase and decrease in population in the past seven years, the estimated number of white servants needed to keep up the supply and the like.[58]

Again in 1662 the new Committee of the Council of Plantations added certain demands to the survey, but stated unequivocally that: 'It being universally agreed that People are the foundation and Improvement of all Plantations, and the people are increased principally by sending servants thither. It is necessary that a settled course be taken for furnishing them with servants.'[59]

The emphasis on servants was entirely justified. The system by which young men and women could go to the colonies with their passage paid, serve under indenture four or five years, receive at the end of their term land or other benefits and be free thenceforth to mould their own fortunes, was steadily proving its worth. Much can be said both for and against indentured service as a practice, but there is no gainsaying the fact that it was through this means and the 'headright' system, under which a man paying his own passage could enter at once into land and receive additional acres for servants and members of his family, that the mainland colonies from New York southward and the West Indies were peopled.[60] Because the servant's term was relatively short it called for constant replenishment. Short of an actual prohibition against it there was not likely to be a drying up of English emigration as long as these two practices continued.

But for various reasons the new colony of Carolina did not thrive, and by the late 'sixties it became clear that either it would have to be abandoned or new measures taken for its success. The proprietors decided on the latter course, determining to assume greater personal supervision of it. In actuality this meant that for the next few years Lord Ashley, soon to be Earl of Shaftesbury, and his trusted secretary John Locke, kept personally in touch with every detail of its growth. Ashley in 1669, two years after Clarendon's fall, was arriving at the height of his political power. He was on intimate terms with the King, and a member of all three groups then dealing with trade and colonial policy.[61] This combination of circumstances, each separately well known, has, I believe, an importance in the shaping of emigration policy at a time when public feeling against emigration was running high that has not been fully recognized.

Lord Ashley, it has already been noted, took account of the anti-emigration agitation in his Memorial in 1669 by saying that 'if it be admitted' that the decrease in population was responsible for the ills it was blamed with, a policy must be inaugurated for bringing foreigners in and stopping the departure of the native English. But at no time in his career was this 'Adventurer' more convinced of the eventual benefit of colonies to the nation than he was at this period. And during the next two years he was to learn from the point of view of a personal promoter just how much the success of a colonial venture depended on having both the numbers and the kind of people it needed.[62]

The first ships for the revived Carolina project landed in 1670. In the ensuing months letters to Ashley from Joseph West, Thomas Owen, Stephen Bull and others in charge in the colony were replete with details concerning its needs. No request appeared as often as the appeal for people: 'People which is our greatest want.' At one time it was said that five hundred more would render them secure, and a thousand more make them 'a perfect settlement'. Sometimes the plea was in specific terms: 'I hope your Honour is thinking of sending a supply of servants from England ... we find that one of our servants we brought out of England is worth two of the Barbadians.' Again the request is 'that the servants hereafter sent may be husbandmen or tradesmen'. And again: 'Do not send us the poor yet awhile, they but eat us out.'[63]

To these pleas Ashley reacted as any other promoter would whose heart and his money were bound up in an undertaking (Carolina 'which is my Darling'): he tried to get them what they asked for. To both Owen and Stephen Bull he wrote that 'the Projectors intend not to slacken our hands till we have brought such an addition of people to you as you have mentioned will be sufficient ...'[64] And the records are dotted with references to individual Englishmen and their families, of small worth and great, whom Ashley persuaded to go. One is to be granted twelve thousand acres because it is thought that he will 'plant in a short time with people that he will carry over from hence'. Another promises that he will bring over 'forty able persons', and so it went. That there was awareness of the unpopularity of appealing publicly for people is evident from a letter that Peter Colleton wrote to Locke asking for a map of Carolina to send to John Ogilby, author of the famous Travel and Road Guide. Ogilby wanted it for a projected book on America. Indicating that he had promised the map, Colleton wrote to Locke: 'And if you would do us the favour to draw a discourse to be added to this map in the nature of a description such as might invite people *without seeming to come from us* it would very much conduce to the speed of settlement.'[65]

These details of the Carolina story are not in themselves important. It was some years before that colony pulled its own weight, and the total numbers going during those early years were never great. But they are important because they suggest the possible influence that these requests, dinned constantly in his ears—requests which he worked personally to meet—had on Shaftesbury's thinking. For it was during those same two years (1670-2) that he was the leading spirit in the Council for Plantations, which formulated the basic principles of colonial policy that were to stand throughout the remainder of the century and beyond.[66] A part of the Council's task was to define emigration policy. With anti-emigration sentiment at its height restrictive measures even to the point of prohibiting any English except the poor and 'noxious' from going would almost certainly have met with the public favour. But despite the gesture in that direction that was made in the King's Memorial no such drastic step was taken. To be sure, Colonies 'thinly and weakly inhabited' were advised if possible to secure people from 'other of our plantations which are overstored'; but this alternative was added: 'or from any part of these our dominions'. The 'poor and noxious' were still to be sent; and the usual stand was taken against 'spiriting', resulting this time in a statute which made it a capital offence to force people to go against their will. A good deal has been made of that part of the Council's policy. What has been widely overlooked is the fact that the *Instructions* outlining the above programme also specifically stated that all such persons 'that are willing and that shall desire to go to seek a better condition there than what they have at present at home' were not only to be permitted to go but should 'by all means be encouraged'.[67]

Were excuses needed to satisfy anti-emigration sentiment, the opening of Pennsylvania in 1682 could be justified in terms of ridding England of a 'noxious' part of its population, the Quakers. But no strings were put on Penn's crusade for settlers; and never was promotion work more carefully planned nor more successful. The Dutch, Swedes and Finns in small numbers were there already when the English began to 'throng in'. The first to go with Penn were largely Friends; but soon all kinds were going including hundreds of farmers and skilled workers; for news of good treatment, and of fine land and plenty of it, spread rapidly. Penn, speaking of the 'divers nations' represented in his colony, said concerning the number of English, that they were 'equal to all the rest'.[68]

Even in New England, where the economy did not rest on the large servant overturn, the population was increased by immigrants from England.[69] We do not have the accurate statistics we should like for any of the colonies in the seventeenth century, still less do we know the relative growth from natural increase and from immigration. But a number of studies based on different approaches provide us with some conception of the general increase, and particulars have been reckoned from a variety of sources. It is estimated that the population of the mainland colonies increased from approximately seventy-six thousand in 1640 to two hundred and ten thousand in 1689, and two hundred and fifty thousand by the end of the century.[70] And by every estimate made the English far outnumbered all others until the end of the century, nor did they cease going then. There were, of course, ups and downs as colonial economy adjusted itself to the Navigation Acts, and other factors affecting emigration came into play. There were years when the Barbados had people to spare, and other years when she had not enough for her own needs; and periods such as that from 1649 to 1662 when Virginia's population jumped from an estimated fifteen thousand to forty thousand,[71] to the late years of the century when her increase was small, and Pennsylvania and other areas were the chief attraction.

Professor Wertenbaker, working from the Virginia land patents, reckons the average immigration to Virginia until the close of the century at fifteen hundred to two thousand per year. 'Even during the Civil War and Commonwealth periods, this average seems to have been maintained with surprising consistency.'[72] It was these periods, it will be recalled, during which it was said that 'the communities of the New World lost touch with the old'. Mr Wertenbaker says further that an examination of the head-right lists shows here and there an Irish or a Scottish name, and on very rare occasions one of French or Italian origin;[73] but he estimates the entire non-English strain at about five per cent. The Maryland land office records show a total of more than twenty thousand arrivals to that colony between 1633 and 1680, of whom the greater part were English.[74] Corresponding figures come from the English side. Upwards of ten thousand indentured servants, only a handful of whom were Scots or Irish, left the port of Bristol alone from 1654 to 1685.[75] The numbers going from London would not have been less, probably more.[76] If the first six years can be taken as a key the servants leaving Bristol were predominantly farmers and craftsmen, and we know that hundreds of their kind were paying their own fares.[77] Emigration from England was far from drying up after the Civil Wars.

From the early 'eighties on, moreover, the pamphlet literature concerned with colonies and emigration shows a somewhat different emphasis. There were still occasional diatribes about people leaving the country, as there would continue to be throughout the next century. But it appears now to have become something of an accepted fact that if there were colonies, regardless of other sources of supply, there would also inevitably be emigration from England. The debate now turned oftener on the degree to which the losses in emigration were offset by other gains. For whatever doubts had existed in earlier years there was no gair saying the fact that in the later years of the century the colonies were paying off, and more and more handsomely.

One enthusiastic writer, calling his pamphlet *Plantation Work—the Work of this Generation*, claimed that the Almighty in every age has some special work that can 'properly be called generation work'. In this age it was the plantations; and he warned Christians to be cautious in opposing them, lest they 'be thought too narrow-breasted by after ages'. It was a sign that the Lord's 'set time to favour Sion' had come because 'so many good men and women have inclined to go thitherward'.[78] When Josiah Child had argued in the 'sixties that 'We have not the fewer but the more people in England by reasons of our English plantations', almost nobody had agreed with him. But when his pamphlet was published again near the end of the century there were other men talking along the same lines: Francis Brewster, John Houghton, the irate Barbados planter who wrote a long and graphic dissertation to prove that the plantations had not diminished England's population;[79] and an unknown writer whose approval of keeping the colonies replenished rested on his belief that the time had come when 'the plantations do not more if so much depend upon the interest of England as the interest of England doth depend on them'.[80] Four years before the close of the century Gregory King published the most detailed population study that had yet been made, showing, as modern students of demography agree, that despite emigration England's population was increasing.[81] The debate on that question would later be renewed with vigour among the eighteenth-century population experts. Meanwhile, English men and women, singly, in twos and threes, sometimes in large neighbourhood groups, made their way to London or Bristol, or one of the lesser ports, to secure passage on a westbound ship, going 'to seek a better condition there than what they have at present at home'.

[1] Practically all of the debates on the Empire Settlement Bills (1922, 1937, 1952, 1957) illustrate the point. See especially *House of Commons Debates*, VOL. DLXIII, 428–31, 522. For samples in the periodical press, see A. Maude, 'Flight from Britain', and the Reply to it by R. West, in *The Spectator*, February 1st, and March 29th, 1957; Arthur Bryant, 'Should Young Men and Women Be Encouraged or Allowed to Emigrate?' *Illustrated London News*, February 23rd, 1957; and L. Birch, 'Long, Long Queue to Leave Britain', *The Reporter*, March 7th, 1957.

[2] *The Origins of the British Colonial System, 1578–1660*, was first published in 1908, MacMillan, New York. The citations that follow are from the reprinting of Peter Smith, New York, 1933. The story was continued in *The Old Colonial System*, VOLS. I and II, first published in 1913, reprinted, Peter Smith, New York, 1958. The first of Beer's books dealt with the later period: *British Colonial Policy, 1754–1785*, New York, 1907 (reprinted 1958).

[3] *Origins*, 46, 52.

[4] See notes 40, 41 and 42.

[5] Klaus E. Knorr, *British Colonial Theories, 1570–1850*, University of Toronto Press, 1944, 42, 45. The view that he argues against is that of E. A. J. Johnson, a scholar whose work I have found helpful. See especially Johnson's *American Economic Thought in the Seventeenth Century*, London, 1932, and *Predecessors of Adam Smith*, New York, 1937 [London, 1937].

[6] The last point, though a part of the traditional thesis in need of revision, goes beyond the scope of this paper; hence it will be but briefly touched on here. A fuller study is in preparation. See also note 77.

[7] The tremendous interest in current population studies is probably responsible for turning the attention of some of the demographers to its historical aspects. See J. C. Russell's remarks on seventeenth-century population in his Introduction to *British Medieval Population*, University of Mexico Press, 1948; W. Taylor, 'Some Aspects of Population History' in *Selected Readings on Population Theory and Policy*, edited by J. Spengler and O. Duncan, Glencoe, Illinois, 1956. A new French survey is, André Toulimon, *Histoire de la Population*, Paris, 1956. The volume that will cover the seventeenth century in A. G. Ploetz, *Raum und Bevölkerung in der Weltgeschichte* is not yet out. Older but still useful surveys are, René Gonnard, *Histoire des doctrines de la population*, Paris, 1923; Pierre Reynaud, *La Théorie de la population en Italie du XVIe au XVIIIe siècle*, Paris, 1904; and the best of the older English surveys is C. E. Strangeland, *Pre-Malthusian Doctrines of Population*, Columbia Studies in History, Economics and Law, XXI, No. 3, New York, 1904. See note 77 for reference to a recent article on the sources used by Gregory King and a revaluation of King's work. For the prominent place population has come to hold in the thinking of English economic history see H. J. Habbakkuk, 'The Economic History of Modern Britain', *The Journal of Economic History*, XVIII, December 1958, 486–501.

[8] Robert Gray, *A Good Speed to Virginia*, London, 1609, B4.

[9] W. Simonds, *Virginea Britannia*, London, 1609, 21–2.

[10] 'God's Israel', it was said, 'is much like that plot which we have now in hand for Virginia.' The above reference is to Joshua xvii. 15.

[11] Knorr, *British Colonial Theories*, 45.

[12] Thomas Starkey, *A Dialogue between Reginald Pole and Thomas Lupset*, ed. K. Burton, London, 1948, 56.

[13] *The Prince*, Chapter IV; *The Discourses*, BOOK II, section 3. Though in his *History of Florence* Machiavelli seems to believe that in a small territory the population may grow beyond the capacity of the country to support it. See *History of Florence*, BOOK I, Chapter I. See also G. Botero, *The Reason of State*, P. J. and D. P. Waley, Yale Press, 1956 [London, 1956], BOOK VII, No. 12.

[14] *Six Books of the Commonwealth*, Tooley translation, Oxford, 1955, BOOK V, Chapter II.

[15] Antoyne de Montchretion, *Traicte de l'Oeconomie Politique*, Funck Brentano, ed., Jacob Bornitius, *Partilionum Politicarum*, BOOK IV; An introduction to other Continental writers may be had in C. E. Stangeland, *Pre-Malthusian Doctrines*.

[16] Lansdowne MSS., 238, f. 292.

[17] Thomas Starkey, 75–7. See Starkey's later discussion on the need of a larger population and methods of increasing it, pp. 137–41.

[18] Minutes of Privy Council, Lansdowne MSS., 238, f. 292.

[19] *A Discourse of the Common Weal of this Realm of England*, ed. E. Lamond, Cambridge, England, 1929. See editor's Introduction regarding authorship and alterations.

[20] *The Description of England*, Furnivall edition, London, 1877, BOOK II, Chapters X, XIX, 215–16, 306–8.

[21] *Works*, Spedding, Ellis and Heath, London, 1879. VOL. VII, 48.

[22] *England's Treasure by Forreign Trade*, in J. R. McCulloch's *Tracts on Commerce*, Cambridge, England, 1952, 184, 190. McCulloch thought the tract was written between 1635 and 1640. W. P. Ashley (Economic Classics edition) dates it as 'probably about 1630'.

[23] *The Original Writings and Correspondence of the Two Richard Hakluyts*, Hakluyt Society, Series II, VOL. LXXVI, 176, VOL. LXXVII, 234–9, 337.

[24] *Force's Tracts*, No. 3, 9–11.

[25] See Bacon, 'Of Sedition and Troubles', *The Essays*. English Classics, London, 1900.

[26] See Gerard Malynes, *The Ancient Law*, London, 1685, 164. This was an old theory and one often repeated. See Machiavelli, *Discourses*, II, 2, 5; Charles Cock, *A Survey of the Household of God on Earth*, London, 1651, 49.

[27] John Stow, *Annales*, continued and augmented by Edmund Howes, London, 1631, 996.

[28] *Ibid.*, 1014, 1021.

[29] *The Plague Pamphlets of Thomas Dekker*, ed. F. P. Wilson, Oxford, 1925, 143.

[30] See plan presented to Parliament in 1641 which advocated giving special privileges to other towns in order to draw off some of the population from London. Henry Robinson, *England's Safety in Trades Encrease*, London, 1641, 5.

[31] E. E. Rich, 'The Population of Elizabethan England', *Economic History Review*, 1950, Series II, VOL. II, No. 3, 247–66.

[32] William Dugdale, *Antiquities of Warwickshire*, London, 1656, 96.

[33] W. G. Hoskins, ed. *Studies in Leicestershire Agrarian History*, Leicester, 1949, 68–71.

[34] J. W. F. Hill, *Tudor and Stuart Lincoln*, Cambridge, England, 1956, 22.

[35] H. M. C. Reports, *MSS of Lord Montagu of Beaulieu*, 109.

[36] These are the groups who as time goes on get more and more attention in the promotion literature, and are oftenest requested by the planters.

[37] The most usable local records dealing with social and economic conditions are those of Essex, housed at the Record Office in Chelmsford. They consist of Quarter Sessions Records, deeds and many miscellaneous documents. Excellent records of both town and country are also at Norwich, and there is good material on Suffolk at Bury St Edmunds and the Ipswich Free Library.

[38] *A Remonstrance on the State of the Kingdom*, 1641. Seligman Collection, New York Public Library, E. 979. I am indebted to R. Colie for this reference.

[39] *A Treatise Concerning the Causes of the Magnificencie and Greatness of Cities*, London, 1606, 33–6.

[40] J. F. Rees, 'Mercantilism and the Colonies', *The Cambridge History of the British Empire*, 564.

[41] J. A. Williamson, 'The Colonies after the Restoration', *ibid.*, 235, 249.

[42] A. P. Newton, 'The Great Migration', *ibid.*, 249.

[43] See Walter Wilcox's estimate of Graunt and his discussion of Petty's relations

with Graunt in the Introduction to the *Natural and Political Observations*, Hollander Economic Tracts, Johns Hopkins Press, 1939. Cf. Introduction of C. H. Hull to *The Economic Writings of Sir William Petty*, Cambridge, England, 1899.

[44] Mathew Hale, *The Primitive Origination of Mankind*, 1677. The best of Davenant's ideas on population and emigration are in 'Of the Use of Political Arithmetic' and 'On the Plantation Trade', in *Discourses on the Public Revenues and on the Trade of England*, London, 1698, Parts I and II (3).

[45] Outbreaks of smallpox were particularly bad in Oxford in 1661, 1675 and 1683. See Ruth Fasnacht, *History of the City of Oxford*, Oxford, 1954; also Conrad Gill, *History of Birmingham*, Oxford, 1952, *passim*.

[46] *The Grand Concern of England Explained*, London, 1673, 13.

[47] Sloan MSS, 3828, f. 205.

[48] *Grey's Debates*, 1667, I, 41, 56; 1673, II, 155.

[49] Samuel Fortrey, *England's Interest and Improvement*, Cambridge, England, 1663, 4.

[50] Clarendon, *Autobiography*, Oxford, 1827, III, 407.

[51] John Winthrop, *The History of New England from 1630 to 1649*, edited by James Savage, Boston, 1853, II, 91, 103-4, *passim*. See interesting account of this movement in William Sachse, *The Colonial American in Britain*, Madison, 1956, H. 89-90, 117, 137-45.

[52] It is not just in Samuel Fortrey, William Coventry and the other oft-quoted pamphleteers that one finds this sentiment during these years. It crops up in the debates in Parliament (*Grey's Debates*, I, 41, 56), gets into the wording of the Statutes (*Statutes of the Realm*, 1671, v, 748) and is carried across the sea (Letter of Jonathan Atkins, CO.1/29/2 ff. 91-2). A somewhat less well-known pamphlet is the anonymous *The World's Mistake in Oliver Cromwell*, London, 1668. See also speech of 'Mr Gorges', Eg. MSS. 2395, f. 490.

[53] Reprinted in Christie's *Life of the First Earl of Shaftesbury*, London, 1871, VOL. II, Part VI, Appendix I.

[54] *Cal. S.P.C.* 130, 309, 1657. See inducements offered by Carolina sponsors to settlers in Barbados, P.R.O. Shaftesbury Papers, 30/24/48, No. 441. See also letter of Sir John Yeomans, on Act passed by Barbados Assembly in 1670 to prevent depopulation, *ibid.*, No. 47; and concern of Governor of New York that so many were thinking of leaving there for Carolina, *ibid.*, No. 77.

[55] Samuel Fortrey had argued for the immigration of Foreign Protestants as early as 1663. See *Grey's Debates*, I, 41, 56; II, 155. For an act affecting Irish and Scottish servants see 15 Car. II, C 7, No. 5.

[56] P.R.O. Shaftesbury Papers, 30/24/48, No. 55.

[57] Journal of Council for Plantations, 1660-1664, P.R.O. CO.1/59/1 (123).

[58] *Cal. S.P.C. 1661-1668*, Nos. 24, 32.

[59] P.R.O. CO.1/18/90-6.

[60] Of course it is not true that New England has no indentured servants as has sometimes been thought, but the New England economy did not demand them as did that of other colonies; and there was neither the shipping for which they were sought as cargo nor the inducements of large amounts of land to draw them. Both of the Winthrops spoke of the difficulty of getting servants. For this, and examples of servants in New England, see *The Winthrop Papers*, Mass. Hist. Soc., VOLS. I-IV (consult index); and Letter of John Winthrop, jr., in 1660, in *Mass. Hist. Soc. Publications*, Series V, VOL. VIII, 67.

[61] See C. M. Andrew's discussion of the organization and administration of plantation matters at this time. *British Committee, and Councils of Trade and Plantations*, Johns Hopkins Studies, 1908. An interesting recent treatment of policy is in A. Thornton, *The West Indian Policy Under the Restoration*, Oxford, 1956.

[62] Ashley gained a new grant of land in the Bahamas in 1670. He already had interests in Barbados, Guiana and Carolina.

[63] All of these letters are in the P.R.O. Shaftesbury MSS, 30/24, Bundle 48. It is significant that in the Fundamental Constitutions prepared for the colony, progression upwards from one rank in the proposed feudal scale to another was to depend partly on the numbers of people an individual could bring over.

[64] *Ibid.*, No. 55, 37.

[65] Ogilby's book on *America* was published in 1671. The part on Carolina contains

the paragraph Colleton wanted, the only one of the colonies for which Ogilby gave any sales talk.

[66] C. M. Andrews, *British Committees, Commissions and Councils of Trade*, Baltimore, Maryland, 1908, 108.

[67] Instructions to the Council for Foreign Plantations, 1670 (signed by Arlington) Bodley, A 255, f. 147, No. 10; North MSS (Rhodes House, Oxford) S1.

[68] 'A Further Account of the Province of Pennsylvania, 1685' in *Original Narratives of Early Virginia*, A. C. Myers, ed., New York, 1912, 260. Penn came in the autumn of 1682. It is estimated that by the following July there were three thousand then. 'People now went from all parts of England to Pennsylvania; as from London, Liverpool and Bristol especially.'

[69] See Letter of Edward Randolph, *Cal. S.P.C. 1885–1888*, No. 824. See also Stella Sutherland, *Population Distribution in Colonial America*, Columbia University Press, 1937 [Oxford, 1936], 31–2.

[70] G. N. Clark, *The Later Stuarts, 1660–1714*, Oxford, 1934, 344. See particularly the work of the Committee of the A.C.L.A. on a study of national stocks in the colonial population in the *Report of the American Historical Association* 1931. This committee concluded that at the end of the colonial period the population was 60–70 per cent English. Since the bulk of the Scots, Irish and Europeans came in the eighteenth century the percentage would have been much larger at the close of the seventeenth. Stella Sutherland, *Population Distribution in Colonial America*; and E. Greene and V. Harrington, *American Population before the Federal Census of 1790*, Columbia University Press, 1932 [Oxford, 1932], A. T. Barck and H. Lefter, *Colonial America*, New York, 1958 [London, 1958], 133, 171.

[71] 'New Description of Virginia', Peter Force, *Tracts and Other Papers*, VOL. II; Eg. MSS, 2395 f. 356b.

[72] T. J. Wertenbaker, *Planters of Colonial Virginia*, Princeton University Press, 1958, 35.

[73] *Ibid.*, 36.

[74] Index to Early Settlers in *MSS of Maryland Land Office*, Annapolis, VOL. I.

[75] See 'Servants to the Foreign Plantations' in Corporation MSS at Bristol.

[76] We know that at least one thousand servants left London in the year 1683–4. See servant indentures in the Middlesex Guildhall and in the Folger Library.

[77] This subject has been partially dealt with in my chapter in *Seventeenth-Century America*, edited by James M. Smith, University of North Carolina Press, 1959, and will be more fully treated in a book that is in preparation.

[78] 'W.L.', *Plantation Work—The Work of this Generation*, London, 1682.

[79] *Groans of the Plantations*, London, 1689.

[80] Rawl. MSS, A 478, ff. 48–52.

[81] *Natural and Political Observations and Conclusions on the State and Condition of England*, London, 1696. See D. V. Glass on Gregory King in the *Eugenics Review*, January 1946. See also note 7, and in *Population Studies*, III, 1950.

The Admiralty in Conflict and Commission, 1679–1684

*

William Appleton Aiken

THE achievements of the British Navy during the last forty years of the seventeenth century hardly helped that service to sustain the great reputation which it had acquired under Robert Blake in the time of the Protectorate. Isolated victories during the second and third Dutch Wars, the endeavours to strengthen the fleet made by James, Duke of York and Samuel Pepys, and the limited success of Admiral Russell at La Hogue failed to conceal the fact that from the restoration of Charles II until the accession of Queen Anne the Royal Navy left much to be desired. What could account for this decline? No single explanation will alone suffice. But among many causes for naval inefficiency during this period the transformation of the Admiralty Commission into a political football after 1679, to be kicked about at the King's whim, must be accounted a paramount factor.

Early in that year Charles tried to strengthen his position by a conciliatory policy of compromise between the court and country parties. To effect this he made skilful use of a scheme proposed by Sir William Temple for a reorganization of the Council. Accordingly he reduced that body to thirty members, representing moderate elements from court, country and the new opposition, and then proceeded to institute a similar policy in other departments of the administration. Before this time the Duke of York had served as Lord High Admiral of England, but upon his refusal to take the oath of office in accordance with the terms of the Test Act he had been forced to resign. Charles then placed that office in commission and appointed, among others, the Lord Chancellor, the Lord Treasurer, the Lord Privy Seal, the Lord Chamberlain and the two Secretaries of State to serve under the leadership of his cousin Prince Rupert, with Samuel Pepys as Secretary. When Danby fell and Charles found himself faced with a new and hostile Parliament, he reconstituted this commission along lines corresponding to contemplated changes in the Council.

On Easter Sunday, April 20th, 1679 he dissolved the old Council and next day swore in as many of the proposed new Council as were present. At the same time he declared his intention to make Sir Henry Capel, k.b., Daniel Finch, eldest son of the Lord Chancellor, Heneage Finch, Sir Thomas Lee, Sir Humphrey Winch, Sir Thomas Meres, Edward Vaughan and Edward Hales his commissioners for executing the office of Lord High Admiral. Sir Henry was accordingly sworn in as Privy Councillor by virtue of his appointment as First Commissioner.[1]

These honours reflected a studied objective on the part of Charles and Danby to split the opposition with a promise of restrictions upon a Catholic king. Thus Sir Henry took his seat at the council table along with his illustrious elder brother the Earl of Essex. As for Finch, he might in a sense be said to have succeeded his father at the Admiralty, but he also represented moderate Court and Tory elements whom Charles hoped would co-operate with him in his new policy of conciliation. Sir Thomas Lee had opposed the Court in the past but not consistently and may even at one time have been its pensioner. He had supported measures favoured by the Finches, had been a friend of young Daniel and a close political associate of Sir Thomas Meres and Edward Vaughan. These last two men had long shown moderation as leaders of the country party against the Court, which had hoped to have Meres as Speaker in the new Parliament of 1679. An orator of 'tireless fluency' and a consistent churchman, Meres was something of a political chameleon who belonged in reality to no party.[2] Sir Humphrey Winch and Edward Hales rounded out a commission which revealed, quite as clearly as did the new Council itself, those elements upon whom the King would rely for support during the impending crisis over the fate of the Dukes of York and Monmouth. As secretary to these commissioners Charles appointed Thomas Hayter, a Quaker, to succeed Samuel Pepys.

He furthermore endowed them with powers equal to those enjoyed previously by Prince Rupert and his colleagues, which retained considerable authority in the King's own hands. These limitations proved unacceptable to his new incumbents, however, so that after several stormy interviews they managed to obtain a commission 'to run in the fullest terms of any Lord High Admiral'. They drafted these terms themselves and finally won royal approval for them in a document which bears the date May 14th, 1679.[3]

A contemporary wit remarked that if it were true that an oyster did 'gape and shut according to the tide, when it is out of water, it would at least be a better oracle of the sea than this new commission'. The flippancy was warranted. With the single exception of Hayter, few of these men had the slightest knowledge of the matters now entrusted to their care. Faced with a host of complex problems their inefficiency exceeded all expectation.[4]

Many years later Finch recalled how they were first treated with contempt, and in mockery called the 'Land Admirals'. He confessed frankly that he had 'no knowledge of sea affairs', although, he added, 'I was (as all Englishmen are or should be) very fond of the fleet'. He then proceeded to speculate as to why the King should have constituted such a commission at all. Overlooking the obvious explanation that Charles sought merely to gain the support of moderate men of both parties, he reached the naive conclusion that it must have been because His Majesty imagined that, being impartial, they would economize in such a fashion as men trained to the sea could never do, and especially since Parliament had now pared down their budget to three hundred thousand pounds a year. Out of this sum the King apparently expected them to defray the expenses of a war with Algiers, 'which required a squadron of ships at the mouth of the Straits and many more convoys for merchantmen than otherwise were needful'. Perhaps, indeed, Charles, with his 'great skill and delight in shipping and knowledge of his sea officers', hoped to direct those matters himself and leave his commissioners to deal with strictly financial matters alone, which, Daniel felt, 'by application' they might soon master.[5]

But in point of fact these commissioners soon found that 'application' was not in itself a sufficient means to resolve their difficulties. From the start they embraced two mutually exclusive policies. They had absolutely no money; yet they expected to refit all ships then in service that had fallen into disrepair, and in addition to build thirty new ones, a measure for which Daniel himself had favoured an appropriation in 1677.[6]

The most pressing problem which these new commissioners should have faced concerned the fate of Tangier. This outpost of empire and strategic key to control of the Mediterranean had fallen to England as a part of the dowry of Queen Catherine of Braganza. The English had ringed it with forts and constructed a tremendous mole to protect its harbour. In addition to the garrison a naval squadron had been stationed there for some years under the command of a vice-admiral, currently Sir John Narborough. But maintenance of this stronghold involved serious problems. The French desired to oust the British. A faction at Court, led by Lord Sunderland, advised its sale or abandonment; while the country party, in bitter conflict with the Court at this time over the Exclusion Bill, vociferously advocated that it be retained. On April 7th, 1679 the opposition introduced a Bill into the House of Commons, which would have annexed Tangier to the English Crown. But when they linked its passage to the King's consent to exclusion they overplayed their hand. Prorogation killed it.

If the opposition had carried the measure it would have entailed heavy additional expenditures, but even in existing circumstances Tangier proved a costly financial burden. The presence of hostile Moorish forces required the importation of all foodstuffs. Maintenance of fortifications and the refitting of ships on station cost more money than was available. Military and naval defences alike languished in a state of disrepair. Yet, from the point of view of far-sighted statesmanship, Tangier clearly remained an asset. A sudden flood of pamphlets bore eloquent testimony to this fact and should have attracted the attention of all men at Whitehall seriously concerned with English foreign policy.[7]

The new commissioners, however, appeared indifferent to the problem. Aware of the financial dilemma, they limited their horizons to the domestic scene. On December 29th they addressed to the Navy Board a 'Letter of Retrenchment'. In the name of economy they would dismiss the three most experienced members of the Board. Certain offices within the Admiralty were also to be combined. The number of clerks in various departments were to be reduced and certain allowances to others entirely abolished. At the same time, although there was not enough money in the treasury to finance naval administration, they would embark upon a construction programme that was to cost, at a conservative estimate, three quarters of a million pounds.[8]

The results were deplorable. Men sat daily in the dockyards at Chatham, drawing down pay but without enough material to keep them busy. The Navy needed new stores and fresh supplies if these workmen were to be employed. These were ordered, apparently on the theory that the Navy Board could defray expenses out of non-existent funds. Work at this rate reached a standstill. Authorities could not turn up enough money to pay wages. Many a man faced an ugly prospect of starvation.

In 1680 arrears for payment of men in active service amounted to over eleven thousand pounds, which by November had increased to more than fourteen thousand. The situation improved gradually throughout 1681 and 1682, but another crisis blew up in the winter of 1683 and another in August of that same year. Meanwhile, seamen were paid by a system of credit notes which were often not honoured in time to save the wretched recipients from their creditors or from unprincipled speculators.[9]

Despite their ignorance and inefficiency the commissioners were not entirely to blame for these conditions, for country gentlemen in Parliament had no conception of the cost of maintenance of so great a navy. Their appropriations were as consistently inadequate as supply was apt to be misappropriated. After 1681, moreover, Charles never summoned another Parliament. Hence, the commissioners soon had to depend for income solely upon royal revenue.

These difficulties were increased by the advantage which sea captains, clerks and officials took of inefficiency in high places. Corruption was everywhere rampant, and in no place more than in the fleet itself. Both clerks and sea captains kept false muster-books. In 1683 Daniel Finch's old schoolmate George Legge, now Baron Dartmouth, reported that nine hundred men at Tangier drew pay, according to the musters, for two thousand seven hundred. But the worst and most common abuse of all was the 'good voyage'.

In order to protect the merchants as well as Government shipping from the threat of piracy upon the high seas, men-of-war could carry bullion as cargo. For this service a captain received due payment, usually in the form of a small percentage of the value of his burden. Ships of the line, however, could only transport gold and silver in the course of regular duty which might require them to sail towards the desired port of destination. So much for a theory constantly abused in practice by corrupt officers, who shipped all sorts of cargoes at a heavy price and fabricated orders not only for single bottoms but even for entire squadrons. Thus a timid trader would gain illegal protection for his merchandise at a price almost as ruinous as that exacted by those freebooters against whom he craved defence. All efforts to stop these procedures would certainly fail unless the Admiralty could raise sufficient funds to pay adequate wages to naval commanders then in Government employ.[10]

One of the worst offenders in this respect was Admiral Arthur Herbert, who succeeded Sir John Narborough as Commander-in-Chief of the English squadron stationed near Tangier for the defence of the straits. Herbert had gone to sea in 1663 at the age of sixteen and had commanded his own ship in both Dutch wars. He had served in the Mediterranean under Allin, Spragge and Narborough, and was fully aware of the vital significance of Tangier. Pepys and his patron Lord Dartmouth, on the other hand, despised him for the vicious corruption of his private life. Abusive and arrogant, he sometimes extorted as much as twenty-five per cent of the value of various cargoes carried on his men-of-war, which money belonged by right to the King. Herbert justified his conduct on the grounds that His Majesty owed him three times as much in arrears as he was now able to gain by plundering him.[11]

Charles unfortunately encouraged this attitude by telling officers that they were fools not to do as others did. Such indifference towards the encouragement of a conscientious respect for regulations on the part of the Crown obviously discouraged young officers from any proper or thorough performance of duty. Hence the practice of 'good voyages' continued.[12]

But this was not the only problem with which the commission had to contend. On many of these excursions captains would lie for four weeks at a time off the coast of Spain or Portugal 'drunk and merry'. Admiral Herbert, in such a state of revelry, once stripped his surgeon stark naked, tied him up in his cabin by the toe and brought women in to laugh at the wretch in his humiliating plight. Brutal debauchery of this sort was rife from one end of the Barbary Coast to the other. At Tangier many officers had houses ashore, living in open licence with their whores and their men like a bevy of oriental pashas. Royal stores and money were employed over long periods of time to build domiciles for these creatures. Each house cost the Government anywhere from a thousand to twelve hundred pounds. Everyone spoke of the splendour of Herbert's establishment, where his women were 'visited and attended, one after another, as the King's are'. Some said his captains waited upon him at his rising and going to bed. They combed his periwig, brushed him and helped him on with his coat. Most servile among them was young Francis Wheeler, whom Herbert made captain of a ship although he had never served as a lieutenant, a step required in the promotion of any officer. Some said that Wheeler, as one of Herbert's most 'vicious confidants', forced the Admiral's hand, since he knew so much about him that his superior dared not offend him. For the same reason Pepys reports that the Admiral also promoted his own barber-valet Hastings to command a ship of his own.[13]

Luxury and vice combined to destroy all sense of discipline in the minds of commanding officers. Herbert was as lazy in the execution of orders as Daniel Finch and his fellow-commissioners were diligent in drafting them. He refused to hold councils of war or to keep a journal, supposedly the required duty of every captain. He further upset disciplinary standards by allowing his lieutenant to set the watch and fly the Admiral's flag aboard his ship when the Admiral was ashore, an honour allowed only to the eldest captain of the squadron in the absence of the commander.[14]

Favouritism of this sort established an unfortunate pattern. But even Finch had his favourites in the fleet whose interests he defended. After a single voyage his cousin Dering pretended to be a lieutenant, yet could not so much as cast the time of the tide at London Bridge when the day of the month and the moon's age were given him. He was therefore told to make another voyage, which he did, and returned to find himself a captain. As such he refused to obey the orders of his superior, a squadron commander. This officer went at once to protest the matter to the Navy Board and to the King. On the way he met Finch, who, to save his cousin, told the old seaman that the youth should ask his pardon before the ship's company if he would only agree to say nothing more of the matter. Dering had hitherto supplied Daniel with information about evil conditions in the squadron under Herbert's command. Thus favour, nourished upon ties of blood, drew further strength from considerations of an essentially practical nature. Daniel was now a man of some influence at Court. The commanding officer had no choice. He had to let the charges against Dering drop.[15]

Other gentlemen besides Dering found advancement in the service for equally reprehensible reasons. Henry Killigrew had been a lover of the Duchess of Cleveland, who presumably persuaded the Duke of Grafton, her natural son by the King, to grant Killigrew the right to fly a pennant from the masthead of his ship, although this was actually an honour reserved only for senior captains. Yet this favoured paramour of a royal mistress seemed less obnoxious than some of his associates. When Pepys went aboard Killigrew's ship, the *Montagu*, he 'dined most delicately' and remarked that not only was his ship 'the finest and neatest kept' but also 'his manner of living the neatest and most like a gentleman that I ever saw of any man, and his civility to me extraordinary'.[16]

Many officers, however, showed superior merit in the service at that time. Captain John Benbow, the son of a tanner from near Shrewsbury, had run away to sea as a boy, served as a petty officer off the north coast of Africa and now had command of a merchantman. Captain Cloudiseley Shovel, as gallant a tar as England ever bred, began his career as a cabin boy. He first leapt into the limelight 'upon an accident relating to a fox called "Teague", which the Duke of York had aboard his ship'. On another occasion he swam for a quarter of a mile under fire of the enemy to carry the orders of his commander to a subordinate officer on another ship. As early as 1679 Shovel in the Mediterranean had gained a reputation as a 'very discreet and brave officer'. He and Benbow had both risen from the ranks and were known as 'tarpaulin' commanders. Birth, however, did not necessarily indicate a distinction between gentlemen and tarpaulins. 'Gentlemen' included all those men who were neither bred to the sea nor interested or industrious enough to learn the art of good seamanship. Captain Hastings, Herbert's *valet de chambre*, ranked quite as much as a 'gentleman' in this sense as did Wheeler or Killigrew. A crisis almost invariably revealed the shortcomings of a gentleman, when a commander who did not know every rope, block and tackle by name, and who had no care and knowledge of his mast or rigging, inevitably failed to get full service from his ship at a time when it was most needed. Herbert's enemies described him as very ignorant in these matters. Wishing his men to hoist a certain sail they told how he would shout, 'Haul up that whichum, there!' with a 'kind of jest', adds Pepys, 'to disguise his not knowing the name of it.' Yet Herbert, for all his faults, did not lack ability as a commander, although his reputation was probably as much exaggerated by his friends as it suffered damage from the biased testimony of those who disliked him.[17]

Few gentlemen had either the taste, temperament, time or experience to make first-rate sailors, in spite of what their friends might claim. Most of them went to sea to make their fortunes. Only a few felt obliged to master their trade as a means to that end. In the Mediterranean, Captain Edward Russell alone fulfilled this ideal. Some thought that he knew more about navigation than any officer afloat. A dumpling of a man, with cherry cheeks and an excellent sense of humour, he quarrelled with Herbert, complained that the ship which he commanded 'sailed indifferently like a haystack' and reported it unfit for service. He wished to be recalled. When the Admiralty refused to oblige him he swore that once returned to England he would never go to sea again, and made peace with his old enemy. This was characteristic, for 'Cherry' Russell was everyone's friend at one time or another and no man's friend for long. During 1682 he struggled to foster good relations with Finch. The friendship lasted exactly ten years, although from the start they made an ill-sorted pair, for Russell led a most unsavoury private life and never lost an opportunity to flaunt this fact with great vulgarity both in conversation and correspondence. Such were the men who served at sea with whom a bewildered commission tried to deal.[18]

We know that Finch, at least, took cognizance of all these facts. He complained of jealous rivalries between captains and condemned their persistent efforts to win preferment for their favourites, for whom they would order pay without reference to the instructions which alone would entitle them to it, and whose extravagant accounts they would order passed and paid without the proper vouchers to justify them. He bemoaned their youth and the fact that none of the merchants knew them, since they never would suffer the hardship of long voyages in merchantmen. This meant, of course, that in times of peace they remained unemployed. Long periods of inactivity ashore stimulated ceaseless pressure for pensions and half-pay. This added a heavy financial burden to the limited appropriations set aside for the Navy without any equivalent compensation or return.

Even when young gentlemen *did* receive training at sea in

accordance with the principles advanced by the King's Institution of Volunteers, Finch observed that more often than not it proved inadequate. Tarpaulins under whom these had served feared lest they might lose the favour and assistance of persons of interest or quality who sponsored the striplings. They coddled them and refused to employ such harsh or severe discipline as sound training might demand. The new commissioner felt that 'gentlemen might make greater improvements than others of a mean birth, if they would use equal application and industry'. But he sadly allowed that 'the age was too loose to expect, either from them or their officers, such an education as would entitle them justly to a preference'. The fact that these volunteers might get to be lieutenants before a tarpaulin was half out of his apprenticeship disturbed him, since this frequently meant that a warrant officer or even a ship's master could never rise higher in the service, even when he could better command a ship than his young captain. Obviously this destroyed morale. Hence, as Finch himself states: 'I ... always endeavoured to support and prefer those brave tarpaulins, who had ventured their lives in defence of their country, though I could not always succeed.'[19] Had he, by chance, when he wrote these words, overlooked or forgotten the case of his nephew Dering?

No doubt he needed a friendly agent in the Mediterranean during these years, as he likewise needed encouragement at Whitehall. Dering provided the one; but the other proved more difficult to find. Conflicting and incompatible temperaments lay at the root of his problem in both places. Serious difficulties appear first to have arisen within the commission itself as a consequence of certain shifts in royal policy caused by a variety of interrelated factors. The question of the succession, the passage of the first Exclusion Bill, the failure of schemes for limitation of the sovereign powers of a Catholic ruler, the intrigues of Shaftesbury and Monmouth and the King's pressing need for money combined to force Charles to prorogue and then dissolve his third Parliament on July 12th, 1679. He summoned a new one for October 7th, but prorogued it when it met and never summoned it again until October 21st, 1680. The period of the long prorogation produced many changes in the complexion of that coalition upon which the King had hoped to ride out triumphantly the storms of the past year. He dismissed Shaftesbury. Halifax and Essex retired.

Charles then appointed two young courtiers, Sidney Godolphin and Lawrence Hyde, younger son of the late Lord Chancellor Clarendon, as commissioners of the treasury. Meanwhile feverish negotiations continued behind the scenes with Shaftesbury and other leaders of the opposition. These failed, as the King may have expected.

All these events had repercussions at the Admiralty. During February 1680 Sir Henry Capel gave up his seat at the Council and shortly thereafter resigned his post as First Commissioner. He and his brother Essex had long followed the same course in politics. Like Daniel Finch, Sir Henry had defended Arlington in 1674, and in the Parliament of 1679 had supported Seymour's scheme for limitations. But apparently, during the period of the long prorogation and after the failure of the King's half-hearted negotiations with Shaftesbury, he decided to follow his brother's example. Thereafter he became a vociferous and violent supporter of exclusion. Finch now succeeded him as Privy Councillor on February 4th, and as First Commissioner two weeks later. Meanwhile Sir Thomas Lee and Edward Vaughan had resigned. This left several vacancies on the Board.[20]

To fill them the King appointed William, Viscount Brouncker, and Sir Thomas Littleton. So did the issue of exclusion alter the composition of the commission. The new First Commissioner took a dim view of these changes. He described Brouncker as 'corrupt' and regarded both of them as 'creatures of the Duke [of York], poor and needy'. Personal prejudice must have coloured his judgment in this case, since Brouncker could boast of his skill in languages, mathematics and medicine as well as of longstanding friendship with Pepys, Boyle and Evelyn. President of Gresham College and member of the Royal Society, he might well have esteemed the Duke, if only through long association with naval affairs. This gave him an advantage at the Admiralty which Finch could scarcely claim. When superior knowledge collided with superior rank, friction was bound to ensue. As for Littleton, he had served as Treasurer and Victualler of the Navy and so had also had experience which Daniel sorely lacked. In Parliament he sometimes favoured and at other times opposed the stand taken by the Finches on various issues. His intrigues with Arlington and the King which finally precipitated the dissolution of Parliament in 1681 may well have created the impression that his interests were closely bound up with those of the Duke of York, while his friendship with Bishop Burnet would hardly endear him to Finch, whose arrogance and self-assurance soon combined to create hostility between these new associates and their chief.[21]

Thomas Hayter's promotion, on February 24th, 1680, to become assistant to the Comptroller of the Navy increased these tensions. John Brisbane, his successor, had once been Secretary of the Embassy and Agent for Maritime Affairs at the Court of Versailles. Pepys confessed that he now received his new post only 'for want of other ways of gratification'. He did at least have some slight knowledge of the sea, for he had been on the north coast of Africa with an English squadron in 1669–70. Furthermore, Pepys liked him and found him a pleasant man, learned and scholarly, with an easy pagan attitude towards life. Finch, however, described him as 'a Scotchman of no fortune, ... false, perfidious and wicked'. The judgment sounds biased, but from Brisbane's own letters it would appear that he worked by every underhand means to undermine Daniel's reputation and authority.[22]

From this time forth the First Commissioner took small pleasure in meeting the new obligations thrust upon him. Most annoying was the manner in which he found offices given to those who least deserved them. Although he did manage to get Hayter a pension of four hundred pounds per annum, in most cases he could neither hinder nor concur in the decisions of his fellows. On one occasion they resolved to appoint a 'worthless beggar' as storekeeper at Cadiz for the use of the squadron under Admiral Herbert. Daniel refused to sign the warrant. His colleagues complained to the King. Summoned to attend His Majesty, Finch explained that 'the character of the man was such that he was not fit for that trust', and he added that 'they who thought otherwise were enough to execute their own resolution and that if this man performed his duty, they would have the credit of having recommended him'. He concluded with the observation that since there was no need for a First Commissioner to act against his own opinion in compliance with the majority, so, too, there was no reason why he should take a share in the blame if the fellow failed to do his duty. Apparently what he hoped to avoid in this fashion was establishing any sort of principle which might oblige him in the future to sign his name to any orders which the other commissioners might favour contrary to his own better judgment.

With patient indifference Charles replied: 'Go and agree it among yourselves.'

As they left the royal presence Littleton asked Finch whether he would now sign the warrant. 'No,' came the answer, 'for I do not understand that the King commanded me to do so, and without such a command I never shall.'[23]

Meanwhile reports from Daniel's friends at Tangier brought rumours of corruption and abuse. As yet no names were mentioned. But the system worked both ways, for as early as 1680 Brisbane was writing long letters to Herbert about an unspecified 'master of knavish tricks'. Then, during the winter of 1681, the Admiral came under direct attack when he quarrelled with the Governor of Tangier. Herbert's temperament did not help. He was overbearing and irascible, while Captain Russell called him 'impertinently jealous'. He was also irreverent and profane. It was said that he habitually called his chaplain 'ballocks' before company until he finally drove him from the fleet with the mounting obscenity of his ridicule. In March and again in April came further complaints of imperious conduct and neglect of duty. In desperation Brisbane wrote and begged Herbert to 'receive without scorn one mighty comprehensive piece of advice, which is, that you would so live towards God as you may be at peace with Him, and then you will find a calm within, that will either make you friends by softening your wild temper or make your enemies ashamed'.[24]

Several months before these words were written Finch had an opportunity to escape from the discomforts of his post at the Admiralty. With the rise of Lawrence Hyde early in 1680, Robert Spencer, Earl of Sunderland, became Secretary of State. An exquisite and unprincipled opportunist, Sunderland was in speech and conduct 'as venomous as deadly nightshade'. He loved intrigue and office above life itself and would stoop to almost any trick, no matter how devious, to retain it, but in the violent debates over exclusion during the autumn of 1680 he played a poor hand by supporting that Bill in the Lords. On the thirty-first of January, 1681 Charles dismissed him.

One day at about this time, when the King happened to take a seat next to the Lord Chancellor upon the woolsack in the House of Lords, he told Heneage Finch that he intended to make Daniel Secretary of State to succeed Sunderland. Taken completely by surprise the Chancellor thanked His Majesty, but said he thought his son too young and inexperienced for 'a station of so great weight'. To this Charles replied: 'Why should you only, of all my Ministers, be against your own son?' Daniel himself continues the tale:

> My father came home and told it me, but not without showing great concern, apprehending that this would take me from him to attend the constant service which that office required; and my wife was so possessed with that thought and so extremely grieved at it that she told me that if I did take this place she would never leave my father, whom she loved as much as if he had been her own. And indeed it was very irksome to me to leave my father in so disconsolate a state as he was from the time my mother died, and under great infirmity of body too, being a cripple with the gout.[25]

In these circumstances the young man declined the royal offer and remained at the Admiralty to pursue the same quarrelsome course, while the King appointed Daniel's uncle Edward, Viscount Conway, as Secretary. The circle of the Finches had now reached its peak of power and influence with Daniel at the Admiralty: his father, Lord Chancellor; his brother, Solicitor; one uncle, Sir John Finch, serving as British Ambassador in Constantinople; and another uncle serving as Secretary. During this same year, moreover, Charles rewarded his faithful Chancellor with the earldom of Nottingham. Automatically the Chancellor's son now assumed the courtesy title of Lord Finch. This promotion may well have tended to inflate his sense of self-righteous certainty. Two weeks later, at any rate, an open breach occurred between him and Brisbane over the Secretary's right to open all letters directed to the Admiralty on His Majesty's Service.

Then, in August 1681, a more serious dispute broke out over a scheme of Herbert's to establish convoys for merchantmen in the Mediterranean. It appears that the Admiral insisted in a letter to the Secretary of State, Sir Leoline Jenkins, that it would be to His Majesty's interest to order all convoys to Spain and the Mediterranean placed henceforth under Herbert's command.

This, he argued, would save expense and at the same time would provide greater safety for the merchants. Charles concurred and told Jenkins to inform the commissioners accordingly. The Board agreed without hesitation, except for Lord Finch, who raised such objections as his colleagues could not answer. The King then ordered them to attend a committee of the Council, who, upon hearing the matter, were to report back to Charles and await his further pleasure. Daniel opened the case before the committee. None of his associates opposed him, yet they would only support him with a feeble 'yes' when he carefully explained how Herbert's scheme would provide a greater expense for the Crown and less safety for the merchants. On the other hand, he continued, the scheme would doubtless delight Herbert, who would line his pockets with fees paid by the merchants as collateral for their security. These arguments apparently satisfied the committee, who told him to set them down in writing. This he did and laid the document before the Council. Herbert's scheme was vetoed.[26]

Hard feeling thus engendered was not improved by the Admiral's habit, during the ensuing autumn, of opening and reading bills of lading and misappropriating stores. Yet by January 1682 Herbert had been brought to the point of admitting defeat. Brisbane alone prevented him from doing so by refusing to deliver a letter of submission to his adversary. So the struggle continued.[27]

The balance of faction on the commission changed at this time with the death of Sir Thomas Littleton. Rear-Admiral Sir John Chicheley and Sir Henry Savile together replaced him on January 20th, 1682. Sir John had had extensive experience at sea, and as a Tory his appointment would seem in all respects justifiable.

Savile received his post upon the insistence of his elder brother Lord Halifax. He was a witty, licentious rake and hard drinker who had received his education abroad. Confident and presumptuous, he liked the sea and the Duke of York but carried little weight as a politician. He had served on the *Royal Charles* in the battle of the North Foreland in 1666 and again under the duke six years later, and counted Brisbane, with whom he had once lived in Paris, as among his friends. There was not the slightest reason to suppose that he would share the interests, tastes or standards of Lord Finch of whom it was said he had 'a very mean opinion'.[28]

If Savile's temperament hardly suited Daniel's tastes, certain qualities which lent flavour to the entire Court of England's merry monarch likewise would disturb him. Such raffish levity as animated men like Savile found no counterpart upon the Finch estates. Had Daniel ruled over England instead of Charles, there would have been no royal bastard such as Harry, Duke of Grafton, to run a foot-race round St James's Park in the dead of winter for a purse of a hundred guineas. That attractive young peer outstripped his adversary 'by at least a quarter of a mile', even after he had allowed his opponent the handicap of an equivalent distance at the start. A scapegrace band of fine ladies and gentlemen applauded the victor, for everyone admired this natural son of the King by Barbara Villiers. Grafton himself was bluff, hearty and 'exceeding handsome'. He had been 'rudely bred' from early youth before the mast and had learned to know the ways of men from harsh experience rather than from books. Courage, blunt honesty and bad manners he brought with him when he came from the sea to Whitehall, where he soon developed an esteem for the probity of Lord Finch.

Daniel now accused Brisbane of attempting to undermine his reputation with Grafton, whom he regarded as 'a very gallant man, and extremely beloved by the seamen, with whom he was very familiar and often joined with them in their rough sports, and, had he lived, would have deserved to have been Lord Admiral'.[29] Apparently Brisbane had proposed to the King that Grafton be allowed to sit unofficially with the commission in order to better acquaint himself with such transactions as related to the Navy ashore as well as at sea, where he had already served for some years. This was to be done, not by putting him into the commission but by a mere verbal order from His Majesty. Lord Finch instantly opposed this as 'an overruling our commission under the Great Seal and an unnecessary reflection upon those employed in it'. He then went personally to the Duke of Grafton, 'to whom Brisbane had valued himself for this proposal', and explained his objections to the manner in which it had been suggested that His Grace be ordered to sit with them. Telling the story in his own words, Finch assured Grafton that he would 'be extremely glad of his company with us for his own sake, and indeed

upon my own account too, that he might see the proceeding of some of my brethren and judge how ill they served the king, ...'
and therefore:

> if he would allow me, that which he, or the King for him, had a mind to should be done, viz., by our summoning him constantly to the Admiralty, as we do the Navy Board, or any officers of the fleet occasionally. He took this very kindly. So I went to the King and proposed this to him, who approved of it. And the Duke of Grafton was very sensible of Brisbane's flattering knavery to him in putting him into a wrong way and was ever after my friend.[30]

During the summer of 1682 more friction developed between Daniel and Brisbane over the terms of a treaty arranged by Herbert with the Algerines. Each party now complained to the King behind the other's back. Charles, who must have been greatly harassed to find himself the father of a large and discordant family of officials, sided with Brisbane and Herbert, although Pepys, who should have been a competent judge in these matters, agreed with Lord Finch, especially in regard to his dispute with the other commissioners over an article in the treaty concerned with passes. In this case Daniel appears to have been justified in his claim that the clause had been inserted by Herbert 'expressly for the benefit of Brisbane'. This may be so, but the vindictive manner in which he attacked his enemies showed how gradually personal animosities had mastered his sense of discretion.[31]

Some time after the death of the Lord Chancellor, when Daniel had become second Earl of Nottingham, the commissioners took some undisclosed action, presumably concerning Sir Edward Villiers's proprietorship of Tynemouth light. Brisbane complained to the Lord Keeper North, who was no friend of the Finches and who apparently censured Nottingham, as Brisbane may have hoped he would. North brought the matter up in Council, where the King declared he found no fault in the action taken. The Lord Keeper then proposed that an Order in Council be issued to confirm their action. Nottingham continues:

> I said I could not thank my Lord Keeper for his proposal, for, if we had done amiss, no subsequent order could be a warrant or justification to us. And a warrant to do what

already was done must, in its nature, be improper and absurd. But if we had not done amiss, 'as your majesty has been pleased to declare', there was no need of an order. Nay, it would imply or have some appearance that we had committed a fault, 'of which your majesty has absolved us, and therefore, I hope no such order will be made'. And when he went out of the council chamber, he told the Duke of Grafton that what was objected to us was impossible to be true.[32]

All these petty feuds and intrigues could not fail to hamstring the efficiency of the commission, dominated as it was by Nottingham, swarthy of countenance, funereal in manner, positive, inflexible and jealous of authority. Small wonder that by January 1683 the star of the Finches sank rapidly. In that month his uncle Conway surrendered the Secretary's seals to Sunderland. His other uncle, Sir John Finch, his father and his wife were all dead, while his own position in office grew ever more precarious as a result of Brisbane's efforts to curry favour with Sunderland, whose power was now all but supreme.[33]

To make matters worse Admiral Herbert had returned to London when once it had been decided to evacuate Tangier, a policy promoted for domestic reasons by Sunderland. On August 22nd, therefore, the commission was renewed a third time in order to add Herbert as a supernumerary with salary. Presumably this must have doubled the tensions amidst which Nottingham was supposed to operate. With the death of Lord Brouncker on April 17th, 1684, Herbert became an ordinary commissioner and Lord Vaughan, a son-in-law of the Marquis of Halifax, was added as a supernumerary in the Admiral's place. Then, one month later, the commission was revoked by letters patent. It had survived for just over five years.

During this time changes at the Admiralty had tended to reflect the shifting sands of domestic politics. Born amidst royal attempts to attain an equilibrium through coalition of factions, exclusion had upset and altered the new commission. The rise and fall and rise of Sunderland had again affected it. Death played a part. Nottingham had survived in office through all these successive crises. Starting as plain Mr Finch he had ended up as Lord Nottingham. Without proper knowledge of sea affairs, bickering with his colleagues, complaining to the King, it seems surprising that Charles should have allowed him, or the commission itself, to function as long as it did. At times, indeed, it almost appeared as if His Majesty maintained them as a jest. Small wonder that inefficiency prevailed everywhere and that the Navy sank into a miserable state of disrepair. Yet Finch never quite seemed to lose credit with his royal master, who was even willing to offer him the secretaryship of State. With the passage of two hundred and seventy-five years, however, the spectacle of the Admiralty Commission between 1679 and 1684 looks less than edifying, if not almost disastrous.

Naval operations during the reign of William III would surely appear to confirm this statement. At the outbreak of war in 1689 the French caught both the British and the Dutch fleets woefully unprepared. Nottingham had by this time returned to office as Secretary of State for the southern department. Herbert, who had quarrelled with James II and then rallied to the cause of the Prince of Orange, ultimately took charge of the convoy which brought William over to England. As a reward for the transfer of his allegiance he became Commander of the Home Fleet, First Lord of the Admiralty and Earl of Torrington. Yet Herbert's performance thereafter at Bantry Bay brought little credit to the maritime reputation of his country, while his behaviour in 1690, during the indecisive engagement off Beachy Head, forced his court-martial and finally his retirement. It might seem, indeed, as if England no longer had the ships necessary to ensure the defence of her own coasts; while high-ranking officers lay under suspicion of cowardice and incompetence. When Admiral Russell succeeded Torrington some hoped to see the situation improve. Yet Russell's celebrated victory during the summer of 1692 off Cap la Hogue could hardly be said to have achieved its proper objective, which would require the destruction of the French Atlantic squadron rather than its mere confinement to defensive action.

Meanwhile death claimed new victims, when Nottingham's friend Grafton, after fighting with ferocious gallantry at Beachy, died of wounds that same summer beneath the walls of Cork. The subsequent fate of Sir Francis Wheeler, recently promoted to the rank of rear admiral, tarnished the English record more acutely. Caught in a hurricane off Malaga, his entire squadron dispersed. Some of his ships, mistaking Gibraltar bay for the straits, were dashed to pieces on the shore, while Wheeler's own flag-ship foundered in the height of the storm, with the loss of all hands save two Turks. The destruction or capture of the Anglo-Dutch merchantmen in this same year served further to underscore the bad state of affairs at sea.

Grafton and Wheeler were now dead; Torrington had retired; Russell saw only sporadic action after 1694. Of the 'old guard' in the days of the commission of 1679–84, Rooke, Shovel and Benbow, among promising captains, remained. New names, to be sure, had appeared. Days of glory lay ahead. Nevertheless a naval historian in the twentieth century may well ask whether the paralysing incapacity of the Admiralty Commission at the end of the reign of Charles II cannot in part at least account for the very tentative successes of the Royal Navy under William III, in contrast to the great victories of Rooke and Shovel at Vigo, Gibraltar and Toulon in the halcyon days of Queen Anne.

[1] Historical Manuscripts Commission, *Report on the Manuscripts of the late Allan George Finch, Esq.*, London, 1922, II, 53, Daniel Finch to his uncle, Sir John Finch, June 2nd, 1679; Navy Records Society, *Catalogue of the Naval Manuscripts in the Pepysian Library at Magdalene College*, ed. J. R. Tannier, London, 1903, I, Introduction, 57–8.

[2] Keith Feiling, *A History of the Tory Party, 1640–1714*, Oxford, 1924, 147.

[3] N.R.S., *Cat. Pepys. Libr.*, I, 57.

[4] N.R.S., *The Tangier Papers of Samuel Pepys*, ed. Edwin Chappell, London, 1935, 152.

[5] H.M.C., uncalendared Finch manuscripts from Burley-on-the-Hill, fragment of an autobiography in the holograph of Daniel Finch, Second Earl of Nottingham, undated and untitled but endorsed 'for my children', f. 4. (Subsequently referred to as *Autobiography*.)

[6] Draft of a speech in the hand of Daniel Finch, undated (*ibid.*) but reported in Anchitel Grey, *Debates in the House of Commons, 1667–1694*, London, 1763, IV, 124–5.

[7] Julian S. Corbett, *England in the Mediterranean*, London, 1917, 2nd ed., II, 388–96; David Ogg, *England in the Reign of Charles II*, Oxford, 1934, II, 657–9.

[8] P.R.O., Admiralty 1 : 3550, ff. 783, 793–8; N.R.S., *Cat. Pepys. Libr.*, I, Introduction, 62–3.

[9] P.R.O., Admiralty 1 : 3550, ff. 779–803, 819–21, 855; 3551, ff. 419–20, 475, 851; 3552, ff. 5, 45, 295, 431, 447, 843; 3553, ff. 281, 353; cf. also N.R.S., *Cat. Pepys. Libr.*, I, Introduction, pp. 60–5; Ogg, *op. cit.*, I, 261.

[10] P.R.O., Admiralty 1 : 3550, f. 747; 3551, ff. 447–8, 1009–19; 3552, ff. 185–9; N.R.S., *Tangier*, Introduction, xxxiii–ix, also 96, 144.

[11] N.R.S., *Tangier*, 106; Corbett, *op. cit.*, II, 396.

[12] N.R.S., *Tangier*, 182.

[13] *Ibid.*, II, 101, 117–18, 138, 204.

[14] *Ibid.*, 89, 90, 92, 122, 223, 225.

[15] H.M.C., *Finch*, II, 109, T. Walcomb to [D.F.], April 30th, 1681; 185, Dering to Nottingham, July 1st, 1683; N.R.S., *Tangier*, 132–3; for a sequel to this episode cf. 163, 168.

[16] N.R.S., *Tangier*, 46, 211.

[17] N.R.S., *Samuel Pepys's Naval Minutes*, ed. J. R. Tanner, London, 1926, 390; H.M.C., *Finch*, II, 120, H. Sheres to Mr Finch, September 23rd, 1681; N.R.S., *Tangier*, 106, 123, 225.

[18] N.R.S., *Tangier*, 226, 321–2; N.R.S., *Minutes*, 113; H.M.C., *Finch*, II, 94, Russell to Finch, December 31st, 1681; 104, Same to Same, March 17th, 1682; 117, Same to Same, August 10th, 1682; Bodleian Library, Rawlinson MSS., A 228, f. 306, Brisbane to Herbert, October 2nd, 1682; British Museum, Egerton MSS., ff. 77, 78, Russell to Herbert, December 10th, 1688.

[19] *Autobiography*, ff. 4, 5.

[20] The date is controversial. J. R. Tanner (N.R.S., *Cat. of Pepys. Libr.*, 58) gives 1681, so does Arthur Bryant (Arthur Bryant, *Pepys: The Years of Peril*, Cambridge, England, 1935, 352). But Bryant gives 1680 in his life of Charles II (Arthur Bryant, *Charles II*, London, New York, Toronto, 1949), as does Louise Fargo Brown (Louise Fargo Brown, *The First Earl of Shaftesbury*, New York, London, 1933) and Robert Beatson (Robert Beatson, *A Political Index to the Histories of Great Britain and Ireland*, London, 1803, I, 377). Writing to the Duke of Ormonde, February 3rd, 1680, Francis Gwyn remarks that he must have heard of Capel's withdrawal from the Privy Council and goes on to say 'it is supposed that Lord Brouncker will succeed Sir Henry Capel in the First Commissioner's place in the Admiralty ...' (H.M.C., *Calendar of the Manuscripts of the Marquess of Ormonde*, New Series, V, 270), while an anonymous letter to Ormonde, dated January 20th, 1680, mentions the possibility of Capel's restoration to the Admiralty (*ibid.*, 562). Finally, Cokayne in his *Peerage* also gives the date, 1680, under 'Capel'. Hence I have preferred the earlier to the later date.

[21] *Autobiography*, f. 6.

[22] N.R.S., *Minutes*, 257; *Autobiography*, f. 6.

[23] *Autobiography*, f. 6.

[24] British Museum, Additional Manuscripts, 19827, f. 55, Finch to H. Sheres, September 18th, 1680; f. 59, Lawrence Hyde to Mr Sheres, November 11th, 1680; Bodl., Rawlinson, A 228, H 231–232, Brisbane to Herbert, May 21st, 1680; f. 244, Same to Same, October 2nd, 1682; Same to Same, April 12th, 1681; H.M.C., *Finch*, II, 103, Col. Sackville to D. Finch, January 29th, 1681; N.R.S., *Tangier*, 168.

[25] *Autobiography*, f. 8; H.M.C., *Finch*, II, 109; Brisbane to Finch, April 28th, 1681; 110, Finch to Brisbane, May 10th, 1681.

[26] *Autobiography*, f. 6.

[27] Uncalendared Finch MSS. from Burley-on-the-Hill, Samuel Barber to S. Mitchell, October 27th, 1681; Bodl., Rawlinson, A 228, f. 268, Brisbane to Herbert, January 30th, 1682.

[28] H.M.C., 11th Report, Appendix, Part V, *Manuscripts of the Earl of Dartmouth*, 93, Sir Christopher Musgrave to Lord Dartmouth, September 24th, 1683.

[29] *Autobiography*, f. 7.

[30] *Ibid.*

[31] H.M.C., *Finch*, II, 170–5, Memorandum by Daniel, Lord Finch, May 1682; N.R.S., *Minutes*, 180; N.R.S., *Tangier*, 323.

[32] *Autobiography*, f. 7.

[33] Bodl., Rawlinson, A 228, ff. 348–9, Brisbane to Herbert, April 9th, 1683.

The Bishops in Politics, 1688–1714

★

F. G. James

'*The control of the Church was the heart of the English Revolution.*'

C. J. FRIEDRICH

THE conflicts of Stuart England cannot be explained by a single formula whether it be the old liberal epic of democracy v. absolutism or the Marxian dialectic of class struggle. Yet if one wishes to give priority to a single thread in the Stuart drama, that of religion might offer the best explanation of events. Cromwell came to see it in that light, so possibly did Charles I and certainly James II. The overt conflicts of the century—the Bishops' wars, the great civil war of 1642, the second civil war of '48, Cromwell's Irish and Scottish wars, Monmouth's rebellion and the final revolution of 1688—all could be called religious struggles. The relative importance of religious issues seems to have increased, also, as the century progressed. Taxation ceased to be a major cause for contention after 1660, while the abuse of the royal prerogative which gave the most concern after 1660, the dispensing and suspending power, became an issue specifically because Charles II and James II employed it to circumvent the religious policy of Parliament. Likewise after 1688 the most consistent differences between Whigs and Tories were religious in nature. Viewed from such an angle the central constitutional struggle of the era itself, that between Crown and Parliament, appears as a battle for control of the Church.

Although Anglican apologists regarded royal supremacy as divinely ordained, legally the Crown's power over the Church rested upon parliamentary statute. Even before the Reformation the Crown was wont to employ popular and parliamentary pressure against the papacy. When Henry VIII broke with Rome he had to seek parliamentary support. Under Edward VI and Mary Parliament was again called upon to sanction religious change, and the Elizabethan settlement bore the stamp of Parliament. Elizabeth I sought with reasonable success to exclude Parliament from ecclesiastical matters, yet she had considerable trouble with the Puritans. It was clear before her death that Parliament was becoming increasingly concerned with religious policy and would strive to control it in the reigns of her successors.

In England implicitly, as in Germany explicitly, the Reformation established the principle *cuius regio, eius religio—sed cuius regio?* *utrum regis aut parliamenti?* In most Continental States, Roman Catholic as well as Protestant, the new principle accelerated the trend towards absolutism. In England it raised the question of who possessed sovereignty: the ruler, Parliament, or even perhaps the people? To James I and Charles I the earthly control of God's Church obviously lay with his anointed king. Not so to the Puritans, to them neither king, nor bishop, nor priest had any more right to act in God's name than did the Pope. Consciously or unconsciously they rejected the basic premise underlying royal supremacy. By 1688 all parties had come to accept the fact that Parliament should determine religious policy. Although nowhere explicitly stated (and still formally denied by most Anglicans) this principle was the cornerstone of the revolution settlement of 1689. All that remained to be defined after that date was exactly what religious policies Parliament should impose upon the nation.

Before the Civil Wars the English clergy had been divided between Anglicans and Puritans. After the collapse of the Protectorate and the restoration of Charles II the Puritans were compelled to withdraw from the Established Church. From the time of the Clarendon Code to the flight of James II the Church of England was, if not a seamless robe, at least relatively united not only on religious questions but likewise on politics. It is not to be understood that the Restoration Church agreed on all matters of doctrine, liturgy or even in their attitude towards the King. Some of its members believed in comprehension or limited toleration, a few remained unreconstructed Laudians; more followed the moderate conservatism of Archbishop Sheldon; yet a common fear of sedition and schism, combined with a common desire to re-establish the strength of the Anglican communion, led them to co-operate.[1] They also shared a deep respect for, and loyalty to, the Crown as an institution. This does not mean that they were completely subservient to the royal will. When Charles II tried to ditch Clarendon the bishops stood by the minister. Again on the issue of the Declaration of Indulgence they took a firm position in opposition to Charles's policy.[2] But, since Charles II had the good sense to abandon his unpopular programme, they never faced the necessity of challenging royal supremacy. Throughout his reign the bishops voted with near unanimity on all fundamental issues: on the Clarendon Code, the Test Acts, the Exclusion

Bill.[3] Not only was the episcopal bench united, there is every evidence to show that the great majority of the lower clergy supported the episcopate in its acceptance of royal supremacy and in its resistance to any hint of republicanism. At the time of James II's accession and of Monmouth's rebellion the Church still remained staunchly loyal to the Crown. It took the clear threat of a Roman Catholic restoration to estrange the Anglican clergy.

On November 18th, 1685 James II opened the second session of his first and only Parliament. In his speech the King asked for a revision of the Test and Corporation Acts, making evident his intention to retain Roman Catholics in civil and military offices. As was customary the House of Lords voted thanks for the royal address; then, to the chagrin of the Court party, the earl of Devonshire proposed that a day be appointed for debating the King's message. In a forthright speech Bishop Compton of London supported the earl's proposal. He likened the laws of England to the dikes of Holland and Roman Catholicism to the encroaching ocean, concluding with the statement: 'I am empowered to speak the mind of my brethren, and in their opinion, and in my own, the whole civil and religious constitution of the realm is in danger.'[4] As he finished the Lords Spiritual rose to acclaim him. This solemn scene marked a momentous turning-point in both the history of the Church of England and of the English monarchy. The holy alliance of the Stuart restoration, that of 'Church and King', was cleft in twain. By the time of the trial of the seven bishops in the summer of 1688 the Church was almost as solidly aligned against James as it had previously been for him—and for once in its career it was also aligned with the Dissenters.

The unity of the Church in opposing James II arose as a response to an imminent danger. In short, it was negative. As soon as the danger had passed churchmen discovered they could not agree on a positive policy. Some clergymen became non-jurors; others disgruntled Tories, emotionally still half Jacobite; the rest, with varying degrees of resignation or enthusiasm, embraced the revolution settlement. Since virtually all Anglicans had accepted the doctrines of royal supremacy, passive obedience and the sanctity of hereditary monarchy, they could endorse the revolution only after an inward struggle which compelled them to formulate some kind of justification for their conduct. Common difficulties should, perhaps, have encouraged mutual toleration; unhappily the result was quite the contrary. Each faction seemed to suspect the motives and sincerity of all others. Until long after the Hanoverian succession churchmen were plagued by the heritage of 1688. As a consequence, during the closing years of the Stuart era the Church was more deeply divided by political partisanship than was the nation as a whole.

The divisive effects of the revolution upon the episcopal bench became apparent as soon as the Convention Parliament assembled in January 1689. The Commons promptly sent to the Lords a resolution that since James II had attempted to subvert the constitution and had abandoned the kingdom the throne had thereby become 'vacant'. The resolution precipitated a hot debate in the Upper House. Conservatives defeated a declaration that the throne was vacant by a vote of 55 to 41, but William's followers were able to stop a move to establish a regency by the slim majority of fifty-one to forty-nine, and thus clear the way for William to become king.[5] The bishops present supported the regency proposal thirteen to two, only Compton of London and Trelawny of Bristol opposing it.[6] The attitude of the episcopate was understandable. In view of the Church's traditional stand on hereditary monarchy churchmen wished to avoid naming William as the legitimate sovereign. Disillusioned as they were with James they were loath to recognize anyone else as a *de jure* ruler. The regency scheme offered a way out of their dilemma; its defeat proved a heavy blow. Now they must stand and be counted. Having won the initial victory, William's supporters set about to strengthen their position by requiring oaths of allegiance to the new King, oaths to which a sizeable minority of churchmen felt unable to subscribe. William, anxious to avoid alienating the Church, recognized the need for patience, but finally early in 1691 he deprived all non-jurors of their benefices. As a result of this purge six of the most conservative bishops, including Archbishop Sancroft of Canterbury, lost their sees. Actually the number should be raised to nine, as Cartwright of Chester had fled with James and two other non-juring bishops died before the formal deprivation.[7] Since between 1688–91 seven other sees fell vacant due to the death of the incumbent, William came to nominate sixteen of the twenty-six bishops during the first three years of his reign.[8] One of the paradoxes of the Revolution of 1688 is that while it established Parliament's control over religious legislation it afforded the Crown an unusual opportunity to exploit its remaining power of ecclesiastical patronage.

As a foreigner and only a conforming rather than a genuine Anglican, William had less interest in church appointments than his queen, who was a devout communicant of the Church of England. While Mary lived (until 1694) she exerted considerable influence upon church patronage; after her death William created a commission of churchmen to advise him on appointments. Nevertheless William always concerned himself with the choice of bishops.[9] It is obvious that he favoured Latitudinarians, both because he approved of their greater tolerance towards Dissenters and because he thought them more trustworthy politically. During his reign, in addition to the sixteen new bishops already mentioned, he had the chance to name five other new men making a total of twenty-one.[10] Of his twenty-one appointees only two or three can be classified as moderate High Churchmen and none of them as real 'Highflyers'. Really only one, Archbishop Sharp of York, turned out to be a consistent Tory. Four of the five bishops he rewarded by translation to a more lucrative see were also Whig Latitudinarians, and the fifth, William Lloyd, was the only surviving member of the pre-1688 era who showed sympathy with the Whig-Latitudinarian position.[11] William's record regarding episcopal appointments contrasts with his policy towards lay peers. As is well known he sought to stand above party, and among the twenty-four new laymen he raised to the peerage he included a number of Tories.[12] Evidently the one group he trusted least of all was the High Church clergy. Whatever his reasons, his policy on episcopal patronage must be considered the most important single cause for the transformation of the House of Lords from a predominantly Tory body in 1688 to one with a small but fairly definite Whig majority by 1702. The replacement of a dozen High Tory bishops by an equal number of Whig Latitudinarians represented a significant shift in a House where active membership seldom reached much over a hundred.

The impact of the Revolution of 1688 and William's subsequent episcopal nominations did not, however, result in a complete Whig bench; instead it changed the bishops from a nearly united bloc into a group of men divided between different factions of both political parties. There exists no full record of voting in the Lords, only fragmentary material. Members of the House of Lords enjoyed the right to register official protests against any Bill, resolution or decision, stating their reasons for opposition. These protests offer concrete information on the position of the signatories; there are also some unofficial accounts of voting divisions on certain issues; finally there exists a number of references to the stand of specific individuals on various questions. Taken together this evidence provides a reasonably clear picture of the position of perhaps three-fourths of the bishops; for the rest we must be more cautious. Of course, until the deprivation and replacement of the non-jurors episcopal attendance in the Lords was at a low point. When King William made his speech in favour of toleration in March 1689 only five bishops were in Parliament.[13] Furthermore their stand on toleration was not governed solely by party feeling. In the last years of James II's reign even High Churchmen like Archbishop Sancroft had co-operated with Dissenters against the threat of Roman Catholicism. As a result the bishops had virtually promised to work for the comprehension of conservative Dissenters within the Church of England, and for toleration for the remainder.[14] The flight of James II, however, had removed the chief motive for supporting comprehension; not only for many Anglicans but also for many of the Dissenters, who now hoped that under a Calvinist king they might gain full equality with the Established Church.[15] With only Latitudinarian bishops like Burnet continuing to work seriously for comprehension the scheme died in committee. On the other hand, whatever their inclinations, the bishops felt bound to accept the Toleration Act, and none of them appear to have voted 'against it. After all, the Toleration Act as passed did not abrogate either the Corporation Act of 1662 or the Test Acts of 1673 and 1678: the Anglican monopoly of political office remained intact.

A more useful issue for gauging the temper of the episcopal bench early in William's reign is one which came before the Lords in April 1690—a Bill to legalize the Acts of the Convention Parliament. Although there were still a number of episcopal vacancies twelve bishops were present at the time.[16] Most Tory peers opposed the Bill as a measure which would invest the recent revolution with an uncalled-for sanctity. Apparently, though accepting William and Mary, they preferred to live in sin with the new régime rather than have it established upon unimpeachable legal grounds. It is not clear which of the bishops besides Burnet supported the Bill, but half of the bishops present signed a protest against the proposed Act 'as being neither good English nor good sense'.[17] Of these six only one, Stillingfleet, had been raised to the bench by William.

Probably the most significant question during William's reign for which a full record of the bishops' vote exists is that of Fenwick's attainder. Fenwick was a Jacobite conspirator who had been arrested on suspicion of treason. The Whigs, fearing he might never be convicted, set out to attaint him. When the Bill of Attainder came before the Lords on December 23rd, 1696, twenty-one bishops were present (out of a total house of a hundred and seven).[18] Archbishop Tenison and Bishop Burnet both spoke strongly in favour of Fenwick's condemnation. They and ten more bishops voted for Fenwick's death.[19] Of these dozen bishops in favour of the attainder all were William's appointees save Bishop Lloyd. Nine bishops voted against the attainder, and eight of them signed a protest denouncing it: 'Because Bills of Attainder against persons in prison, and who are therefore liable to be tried by law, are of dangerous consequence to the lives of the subject, and, as we conceive, may tend to the subversion of the laws of the kingdom.'[20] The eight episcopal subscribers to this protest included six pre-1688 bishops and two of William's nominees, Ironsides and Kidder. Archbishop Sharp apparently voted against the attainder without subscribing to the protest. The Fenwick Bill was decidedly a party issue; in fact, one of the reasons why the Whigs preferred to attaint Fenwick rather than have a full trial was that Fenwick had implicated Whigs in his conspiracy. Tenison, when appealed to show mercy towards the accused, replied that a vote against the attainder would be construed as evidence that he believed in Fenwick's innocence: since he was convinced of Fenwick's guilt he had no choice but to support the Bill.[21] Apparently, however, Ironsides and Kidder saw the issue as one involving a basic constitutional principle, the protection of the rights of the individual against arbitrary punishment.

A somewhat similar case to Fenwick's was that of Sir Charles Duncombe. In 1698 a Whig-dominated Commons had imprisoned Duncombe in the Tower and passed a Bill of Pains and Penalties against him, by which he would be deprived of two-thirds of his property. Duncombe, a Tory goldsmith, had undoubtedly used his influence as receiver of excise to increase his fortune, but his legal guilt was debatable. The Lords dismissed the Commons's Bill by a single vote, the bishops present dividing eight to six against Duncombe along strictly party lines.[22] In similar fashion in 1701, when the Tories in Commons attacked the Whig Ministers for their part in the partition treaties, the episcopal bench seems to have responded in a purely partisan manner.[23] On the other hand, on some types of issues episcopal voting did not always follow logical partisan divisions. One would expect High Church bishops to be conservative on moral and theological questions, the Latitudinarians to be liberal. Yet in the Norfolk divorce in 1700 three of William's bishops, Gardiner, Patrick and Stratford, joined with Compton, Sprat and Trelawny in protesting the divorce, partly on the grounds that the case had not been begun in the ecclesiastical courts.[24]

In summary it seems safe to say that, although a dozen or more bishops led by Compton and Trelawny accepted William, only one of these pre-1688 bishops who lived beyond 1691 (Lloyd) came to embrace the revolutionary settlement with enthusiasm. Though at first thought of as a Whig, Compton voted consistently with the Tories after 1690, as did also Trelawny.[25] In fact Compton signed more Tory protests than any other bishop, and Trelawny ran him a close second. The six other pre-1688 bishops who served throughout William's reign (Beaw, Crewe, Mews, Sprat, Smith and Watson) may all be classified as passive rather than active supporters of the new régime.[26] These men, though they endorsed the revolution as the only practical way of preserving the Established Church, devoted their energies to protecting the church interest. Among the post-1688 bishops only Sharp threw in his lot with this group. At the opposite extreme were the bishops like Burnet, Patrick and Tenison who worked hard to build a Whig bloc in the Church. Most of William's appointees followed the lead of these Latitudinarians, but with some reservations.[27] On several important issues the bishops of all parties stood together: in opposing the Place Bill in 1692, in favouring the Triennial Act in 1693 and in supporting William in the conflict over the forfeited Irish estates.[28] Nevertheless William's reign witnessed the transformation of the episcopal bench from a united body of essentially Tory bishops into a divided but predominantly Whig group. The same forces which caused this metamorphosis among the Lords Spiritual altered the character of the Anglican clergy as a whole, though to a lesser degree. Among the rest of the clergy the High Church party remained in the majority. Thus appeared that marked partisan difference between the bishops and lower clergy which explains the convocation dispute that began in 1697 and lasted for nearly two decades. Historians have been wont to regret this cleavage within the Church. Turberville writes: 'With whichever side our sympathies may be, with High Church or Low, we must agree that it was an evil day for the Anglican Church when the nominal representatives of the Church in Parliament ceased to represent the Church as a whole.'[29] Perhaps, yet the Revolution of 1688 could hardly have proved permanent had it not created a strong Whig element among the clergy of the Established Church, and the Church Whigs could scarcely have been strong without the leadership of a majority of the bishops.

Before proceeding to a consideration of Anne's reign it is necessary to clarify what is meant in this essay by political parties. Recent scholarship has led to a re-evaluation of the English party system in the eighteenth century. Namier's brilliant analysis of politics at the opening of George III's reign has demonstrated that the terms Whig and Tory, as employed in the mid-eighteenth century, can hardly be said to denote political parties in the modern sense. In his recent book *English Political Parties in the Early Eighteenth Century*, Robert Walcott has argued convincingly that the Namier thesis can be applied even to Anne's period, once thought to be the very springtime of the two-party system. Rather than a conflict between Whig and Tory, he sees instead a political constellation composed of a dozen or so blocs or 'interests', revolving around the conflict between Court and country. To employ the traditional party labels, it would seem, is now almost to be guilty of an anachronism. Yet if older historians interpreted eighteenth-century politics too much in Victorian terms they did not invent those offending words Whig and Tory. The abundant political literature of William's and Anne's reigns bristles with them. Whatever the logic of the situation, contemporary public opinion approached almost all political questions from a two-party point of view. Burnet well expresses it when he writes: 'the high party, whom for distinction's sake I will hereafter call tories, and the other whigs—terms that I have much spoken against, and have even hated: but, to avoid making always a longer description, I must use them, they being now become as common as if they had been words of our language'.[30]

In identifying the Tories with the High Church Party, Burnet is guilty of Whig bias; not all Tories could be classified as High-flyers. Still, all Tories did pose as champions of the Established Church; indeed, this was possibly their chief source of strength. Conservative laymen as well as clergy felt an intense loyalty to the Church of England because it represented the institutional embodiment of traditional order. After James II and the Revolution of 1688 the Crown had lost much of its lustre. Tories could scarcely be expected to share the Whig enthusiasm for the Bill of Rights or for the régime it established, while only the naive could be thoroughgoing Jacobites. But every lover of Old England could rally to the defence of the Anglican monopoly. If 'Church and King' might no longer be a suitable battle-cry against fanatics, freethinkers and republicans, 'Church in Danger' would serve almost as well. Furthermore, in William's reign the High Tories had good reason to believe the Church endangered; Princess Anne herself agreed with them.[31] Did the King not sympathize with Dissenters; was he not subverting the episcopal bench by his choice of bishops? With an ideological expediency that would have shocked old Laud, the Highflyers devised a theory of ecclesiastical constitutionalism to meet the needs of the situation. Convocation, they decided, possessed powers parallel to those of Parliament. Not only would this concept blunt the power of the King, it would also reduce the power of the episcopate; the Lower House of Convocation could counterbalance the bishops as Commons did the Lords.[32] The sight of staunch Anglicans seeking to undermine royal supremacy and episcopal authority cannot help but remind Americans of the Federalists expounding States' rights at the Hartford Convention. Such tactics, however, were only temporary; the Highflyers still hoped for the return of happier times. Princess Anne, they thought, was one of them.[33] Soon the exile would be over, the temple rebuilt.

Except for her sister's short reign as joint sovereign, Anne represented the first English ruler since Charles I who could be called a sincere Anglican. There could be no question of her orthodoxy or her piety; in that the High Church Party was correct. Yet Anne possessed another characteristic which tempered her religious faith. Alone among the Stuart sovereigns she shared the outlook and prejudices of her fellow-countrymen. Her wily uncle had come to understand the average Englishman but he was never one himself. Though Anne lacked Elizabeth I's intelligence, she achieved through mediocrity what Elizabeth accomplished by insight; she succeeded in acting as the majority willed. If her love of the Church made her naturally favour Tories and distrust Whigs, she refused to become the tool of any extreme faction. She would not jeopardize the unity of the nation by alienating the Latitudinarians or Dissenters. Her episcopal appointments illustrate her cautious conservatism.

As a loyal churchwoman Anne took a deep interest in ecclesiastical preferment. For guidance she turned to several moderate High Churchmen among whom Archbishop Sharp appears to have been the most influential.[34] Anne also sought the advice of her lay ministers, and these, as we know, changed in party complexion.[35] As a result the political affiliation of her episcopal appointees reflect, partly at least, those of the party in power, although her distaste of Latitudinarians kept her from ever naming any of that group. Above all she attempted to choose men worthy of the episcopal office, refusing to be governed solely by their political position.[36] Her first three years she elevated three Tories to the bench, one of whom later became a 'Church Whig'.[37] During the period of growing Whig ascendancy, 1705–9, she named eight bishops—two of them definitely Tories, six moderate Whigs.[38] During the last four years of her reign, with the Tories in full political power, she nominated six men—all of them Tories and two of them real Highflyers.[39] It is also noteworthy that of the six bishops translated in her reign five were Tories.[40] Her appointments, then, clearly favoured the Tories, though to a lesser degree than William's had favoured the Whigs. The sum result of her preferments was to redress the balance which William had upset. When she died the episcopal bench was nearly equally divided between the two parties.

In Anne's day party conflict centred around two issues: the security of the Church and foreign policy. Underlying both, even when not explicitly stated, lay the basic question of the Protestant Succession. To put it another way, the Tories saw (or pretended to see) the chief threat to national security in the increasing political influence of Dissenters and freethinkers and in the reckless and costly war policy of the Whigs. The Whigs, on the contrary, stressed the need for national unity (of both Anglicans and Dissenters) against the popish power of France and the evil machinations of the Jacobites. The Tories feared a second Cromwell; the Whigs another James II. Viewed with historical hindsight across the prosaic decades of Georgian England the vitriolic pamphlets of Anne's day appear foolish or insincere, or both. But to a generation which read Clarendon, knew Huguenot refugees and remembered the trial of the seven bishops, talk of sedition, privy conspiracy, schism and rebellion in no way seemed ridiculous. The two English parties owed their existence to the armed conflicts of the past century. As long as there remained any possibility of another civil war partisan animosities were infused with an emotional intensity it is difficult for us to appreciate.

As has already been stated, the High Church wing of the Tories greeted Anne's accession with enthusiasm. Now they expected to deprive the Latitudinarians of their power and to restore the Church Party to its rightful influence in the State. Although they did not dare to work openly for the complete repeal of the Toleration Act, they lost no time in attacking the Dissenters by drawing up a Bill to tighten up the Test and Corporation Acts. According to the provisions of these Acts anyone who subscribed to certain oaths and who took communion in the Established Church could hold municipal and State offices. Since some Dissenters sincerely approved of occasional communion with the Church of England (as an expression of Christian brotherhood) and others practised it for political reasons, the Anglican monopoly of public office was obviously threatened, especially at the local level. Politicians in 1700 well appreciated the importance of controlling local patronage and elections as the basis for parliamentary power. The occasional conformity controversy became the focal point of a bitter partisan struggle during the opening year of Anne's reign. Nothing tells more about the political position of the different bishops than their stand on this issue. Fortunately we have nearly complete evidence on how they voted.

With Anne queen and a clear majority in the Commons, the Tories confidently introduced a strong Bill against occasional conformity in November 1702. By its provision any officer-holders who took communion in the Church of England (as all must to fulfil the requirements of the Test and Corporation Acts) and who subsequently attended a dissenting service would be fined and removed from office. Second offenders were to be subject to even heavier fines. The Commons passed the Bill with a big majority and sent it up to the Lords. Here the struggle began. Although Anne had created four new Tory peers and had appointed one new Tory bishop (Nicolson), the Whigs still slightly outnumbered the Tories in the Upper House. Anne herself fully endorsed the proposed Bill as did Godolphin, Marlborough and Nottingham—though the first two had misgivings as to the appropriateness of such a measure at a moment when they wished to unite the country behind the French war. Obviously the contest would be close. If all of William's appointees among the bishops voted with the Whigs the Bill would have little chance; but would they? Although Sharp was the only consistent Tory among William's appointees a number of William's other bishops had shown conservative tendencies. A move to protect the Anglican monopoly of political power made a strong appeal to all churchmen except convinced Latitudinarians. On the other hand the passage of the proposed Bill would undoubtedly divide the nation. On December 3rd, 1702 Lord Somers advocated an amendment to restrict the new Bill to persons covered by the Test Act alone; in other words, to exempt those local officials prescribed by the Corporation Act. The Highflyers denounced Somers's proposal. When the vote came the Lords were locked in a tie forty-six to forty-six; the bishops present voting eleven to ten against Somers's amendment. With the support of four of William's bishops (Gardiner, Hough, Jones and Moore) in addition to Sharp,[41] the Tories appeared to have carried the day; for a tie in the Lords meant a defeat for the amendment. When proxies were counted, however, the amendment was carried fifty to forty-seven.[42] A few days later the Whigs won an even greater victory by passing another amendment to reduce the penalties provided for in the new law.[43] This drastic revision of the Bill proved unacceptable to the Tory Commons so that the entire measure was subsequently dropped early the next year.

Thwarted in 1702 the High Church Party sent another Occasional Conformity Bill to the Lords in December 1703. Both the Queen and the Ministry still advocated its passage, yet it again met with defeat. Eighteen bishops were present and six more sent their proxies. This time the bishops divided thirteen to nine against the Tories. Hough and Moore switched back to the Whig side, though another of William's nominees, Stratford, joined Sharp in voting for the Bill.[44]

In opposing the Bill in 1703 Bishop Burnet and other Whigs emphasized the necessity of uniting all Englishmen against France, and of encouraging England's allies abroad. In 1704 the Highflyers devised a strategy designed to exploit Parliament's concern for the war effort; they decided to tack a third Occasional Conformity Bill on to a Supply Bill. This trick alienated the Queen, the Ministry and many moderate Tories, including some bishops. For example, though still strongly in favour of an occasional Conformity Act, Bishop Nicolson successfully lobbied against the tack among his friends in the Commons.[45] So, of course, did the Ministry—with the result that the Commons rejected the tack by a large majority and instead repassed the Occasional Conformity Bill alone. This time it met with a decisive defeat in the Upper House. Eleven bishops, however, still supported it: six of the pre-1688 appointees (Beaw, Compton, Crewe, Mews, Sprat and Trelawny); two of William's (Sharp and Stratford); and three of Anne's (Beveridge, Hooper and Nicolson).[46]

Election losses in 1705 failed to discourage the Highflyers. When Anne's second Parliament assembled the High Church Party introduced a resolution declaring the Church to be in danger. Archbishop Sharp and Bishops Compton, Hooper and Sprat all spoke in favour of the resolution along with Rochester and Nottingham. Bishops Burnet, Hough and Moore joined Somers in attacking it. As Lord Halifax expressed it: 'to speak plain, there's always a cry for the Church when a certain faction is disregarded'.[47] The Whigs soundly defeated the resolution, substituting in its stead one that declared 'that the Church of England ... established by law, as rescued by His late Majesty King William of ever glorious memory, is now in a most glorious and flourishing condition'.[48] Compton and Hooper protested against the substitute declaration along with twenty-three lay peers.[49] Since the Whig resolution passed sixty-one to thirty in a house with nineteen bishops and seventy-four lay lords present,[50] it can be assumed that most of the fourteen bishops besides the protesting two voted with the Whigs.

That same winter the High Church Party suffered another defeat over the Regency Act. They could not effectively oppose an Act to provide for an interim Government to rule between Anne's death and the arrival of the Hanoverian heir without appearing as Jacobites. They could, nevertheless, employ the opportunity to commit the regency commission (and thus by implication the House of Hanover) to the protection of the Church of England. The Lords accepted Rochester's amendment to restrain the commission from repealing or altering the Act of Uniformity, but it defeated Nottingham's proposal to guarantee the Test Act with only two bishops protesting.[51] Furthermore the bishops supported the important Whig amendment to repeal the self-denying clause of the 1701 Act of Settlement by a vote of eleven to two.[52] The vote on these two questions clearly shows that only a small minority of the bishops would invariably support the High Church Party, and even these bishops appear to have been less ardent in the Church cause than were laymen like Haversham, Rochester or Nottingham. The same situation prevailed a year later during the debates over the Scottish Union.

The issue of the union involved both of the key controversial questions of the period: the protection of the Established Church and the nation's international security. To Anglicans the prospect of giving official recognition to the schismatic Kirk, combined with parliamentary representation for its adherents, was perhaps even more distasteful than permitting occasional conformity. Yet Scotland would accept union on no other terms. Should Scotland fail to agree to union, England faced the possibility of seeing the northern kingdom become a hostile State under a separate ruler. Canon Every correctly writes that English opposition 'came in the first place from the High Church Party, and was primarily based on ecclesiastical grounds'.[53] Their opposition failed because most moderate Tories appear to have been unwilling to jeopardize national security even to ensure the Anglican monopoly. Certainly this seems to be true of the bishops. Bishop Hooper asserted that the union was thoroughly impractical, like the mixing of two different strong liquors. He was especially opposed to the admission of sixteen Scottish peers as it would further weaken the importance of the episcopal bench.[54] But most of the bishops took a less adamant position. Part of the credit for the episcopal support of the union must go to Archbishop

Tenison. Understanding how sensitive the bishops were to the treaty's guarantee of the Kirk he sought to counterbalance that undesirable provision by adding a similar guarantee for the Church of England. After consultation with several bishops Tenison drew up a Bill, as he described it, 'for the security of the doctrine, liturgy and rites of the Church of England'.[55] When he presented his proposal to the Lords the High Church Party objected because they felt they were being outmanœuvred. Nottingham angrily rebuked Tenison for not first consulting Convocation (where the High Church Party had a majority). Archbishop Sharp, always a believer in the advantages of union despite his high churchmanship, confined his efforts to amending the Bill to include a guarantee of the Test Act. But Sharp's amendment was rejected sixty to thirty-three, only Bishops Beveridge, Compton, Crewe, Sprat and Stratford voting with him.[56] Defeated on this count Sharp, Beveridge, Compton, Crewe and Hooper tried a month later to block the clause in the Treaty which confirmed the rights of the Kirk. Again they were defeated, this time fifty-five to nineteen.[57] Despite their disappointment over these setbacks Sharp and the other High Church bishops generally supported the treaty. Nicolson says that all the bishops present (Fifteen—including the Tories Beaw, Beveridge, Crewe, Compton, Sharp and Trelawny) voted for article 13 of the treaty, even though Nottingham and several lay lords opposed it.[58] Furthermore, only Hooper opposed the last seven articles, and upon the final passage of the treaty not one bishop protested.[59] Since the different provisions of the treaty passed the Lords with a majority of about three to one the position of the episcopal bench did not prove decisive as it had in some earlier controversial votes. Still, it seems more than likely that the bishops' nearly unanimous support of the union must have greatly weakened the Highflyers. Without the full assistance of at least the avowedly Tory bishops they had little chance of blocking the treaty. In this instance, as in the case of the Regency Bill, the Tory bishops proved that despite their narrow views towards Dissenters they were Englishmen before they were Anglicans. For them, even as for their Whig brethren, national security appeared essential for the protection of the Established Church, not *vice versa*. Once they no longer feared for the safety of the nation, however, they would be only too anxious to turn to the task of strengthening the Church.

By the end of 1709 British and allied successes had removed the threat of military defeat. The problem now was when and how to terminate hostilities. On that question Tories and Whigs were divided. Just at this juncture Dr Sacheverell's trial reopened the bitter struggle between the High Church Party and their Latitudinarian opponents. This *cause célèbre* so agitated public opinion that it was wellnigh impossible, for churchmen at least, to remain neutral. Sacheverell's inflammatory sermon, implicitly attacking the Revolution Settlement, presented the Whigs with a challenge they could not disregard. Conversely, the 'persecution' of a devout clergyman for preaching what they considered sound Anglican doctrine could not fail but arouse the Church Party. Actually when the case came up before the Lords only half of the bishops were present to vote. As might be expected these thirteen represented the stalwarts of both parties, and their division was along strict party lines: Burnet, Cumberland, Fleetwood, Moore, Talbot, Trimnell and Wake against the doctor; Crewe, Compton, Dawes, Hooper, Sharp and Sprat for him.[60] Though the Whigs carried the impeachment sixty-nine to fifty-two, Sacheverell's trial, coming when it did, spelled their ruin. Within a few months Anne had replaced the Whig ministry with one led by Harley and St John. In the election later that year (1710) the Tories recaptured the Commons with an impressive majority.

During the years of increasing Whig dominance many Tory bishops had proved willing to support the ministry when national interest so demanded. In like manner, while the Tories were in power from 1710–14, many of the Whig bishops, especially those who might be called Church Whigs, showed their willingness to underwrite Tory ecclesiastical legislation. Specifically they voted for the Occasional Conformity Act, The Scottish Toleration Act, the Act restoring lay patronage in Scotland, and some of them even for the more radical Schism Act. Oddly enough the first of these Bills, though it had long been a Tory policy, was not put through by the ministry. In fact, Nottingham, the most consistent High Churchman among the lay peers, engineered the passage of the Occasional Conformity Act against the wishes of Harley by making a deal with the Whigs. He won Whig support in return for agreeing to back a Whig resolution demanding 'no peace without Spain'.[61] Since Harley had refused to include him in the new ministry personal pique must have played a part in shaping his scheme, but Nottingham had other and better reasons. Unlike the extreme Highflyers Nottingham had always advocated an energetic war policy against France and had always supported the Hanoverian succession. He sought to dissociate the Church Party from any taint of Jacobite sympathy. It appears that most of the episcopal bench shared his point of view. In any event, the Occasional Conformity Act sailed through the Upper House with almost no opposition, the bishops with the exception of Crewe giving it their full endorsement.[62] Modern commentators show little sympathy with the Whig peers and bishops who thus ditched the Dissenters. Yet when Trevelyan attributes the Whigs' action solely 'to their factious desire to overthrow the ministry and the peace',[63] he is not entirely fair. As Bishop Burnet says, the Whigs well knew that the new Tory Parliament would push through an Act outlawing occasional conformity. [64] By negotiating with Nottingham they not only succeeded in passing the 'no peace without Spain' resolution, they also saw to it that the Occasional Conformity Act would be less extreme in its provisions. The Tory Bill in 1702 had included heavy penalties; the new Act reduced these to a minimum and also included a declaration guaranteeing continued toleration. Though its passage represented a retreat for the Whigs it was essentially a compromise measure worked out by the moderates in both parties. In the circumstances it is perfectly logical that it won the approval of the episcopal bench. Later when George I and his Whig ministers desired to repeal the act they discovered that most of the older Whig bishops still supported it.[65]

Unlike the Occasional Conformity Act, the Scottish Toleration Act was fathered by the Tory ministry. Episcopalians in Scotland did not enjoy, even after the Union, rights comparable to those afforded English Dissenters by the Toleration Act of 1689. Since probably a majority of the Scottish Episcopalians harboured Jacobite leanings their plight did not arouse as much sympathy from their English brethren as might otherwise have been expected. Nevertheless even Whig churchmen were galled by the manner in which the Scottish Presbyterians persecuted Episcopalians, especially after the imprisonment of Greenshields in 1709.[66] Archbishop Tenison repeatedly advocated action to relieve Scottish Episcopalians, as did Bishop Nicolson. Thus Church Whigs quite naturally approved of the Tory Act of 1712,[67] though they were instrumental in seeing that its benefits extended only to those who abjured the Pretender. The Scottish Toleration Act was almost immediately followed by a law which restored lay patronage in Scotland, despite the vigorous opposition of the Kirk. Burnet obviously disapproved of this measure as an infringment of Scottish rights under the terms of the Treaty of Union, but the Bill easily passed the Lords with only four other bishops voting against it.[68]

The passage of the Schism Act in June 1714 marked the apex of the High Church advance: the last victory of a lost cause. In depriving the Dissenters of their educational institutions the Tories' motives were fully as political as religious. The one remaining loophole in the Anglican monopoly was that, although they could not hold office, Dissenters could still vote. To the Highflyers, the Dissenting academies appeared as nurseries of whiggery as well as of schism: the tree must be cut off at the roots. In fact the Tory leader in Commons, Bromley, openly offered to abandon the Bill if in its place the Whigs would accept a law disfranchising Dissenters.[69] In view of the objectives of the Schism Act it should have been bitterly opposed by all Whigs. Among laymen it was; virtually every leading Whig peer signed the protest against it. But the Whig bishops were not so united—only five of them signed the protest (Evans, Fleetwood, Moore, Tyler and Wake).[70] Since the Bill only passed by a margin of five in a very full house (seventy-seven to seventy-two) a number of other bishops must have voted against it, yet Nicolson and probably several other Church Whigs lined up with the majority.[71] Furthermore, as in the case of the Occasional Conformity Act, a number of Whig bishops later opposed the repeal of the Act under George I.[72]

The support given by many Whig bishops to the ecclesiastical legislation enacted between 1710–14 should not be taken as evidence of their surrender to the party in power; nor was it the result of their succumbing to Tory kindness. On purely secular matters the Whig bishops opposed the ministry with gusto. For example, in January 1711, when the Tory majority in the Lords refused to entertain the petition of the Earl of Galway and Lord Tyrawley in defence of their conduct of the war in Spain, ten bishops signed the Whig protest (Burnet, Evans, Fleetwood, Hough, Moore, Nicolson, Trelawny, Trimnell, Tyler and Wake).[73] For their part the Tories, far from attempting to win over the

Church Whigs by blandishments, attacked them with vigour. In 1711 the Tory Commons censured Bishop Nicolson for meddling in the election of 1710 and a year later they ordered the public burning of a preface to a book of sermons published by Bishop Fleetwood.[74] There was certainly no let up in partisanship. Finally in 1714, as Oxford's influence waned and that of Boling-broke and the Highflyers increased, moderate Tories as well as Church Whigs became alarmed over the safety of the Hanoverian succession. When in April of that year the ministry pushed through a resolution declaring the Protestant succession *not* in danger, Archbishop Sharp 'spoke and voted with the Whig lords, ... drawing after him the whole bench of bishops, three courtiers only excepted'.[75] A week later the episcopal bench divided fourteen to two against the ministry—only Atterbury, the leader of the Highflyers, and the Caroline veteran, Crewe, siding with the Court party.[76]

The position of the bishops between 1710–14 was not as inconsistent as it might appear. On ecclesiastical matters most of them were at heart half Tory. It was not only High Churchmen like the first earl of Bathurst who felt the Dissenters were equally dangerous to Church and State.[77] A Church Whig like Nicolson could say: 'Religion and loyalty have always been looked upon as a sort of twins, perfectly coeval; such as are not only born together, but always die together.'[78] Almost all of the bishops believed wholeheartedly in the concept of a State Church and in that Church's right to a monopoly of political power. To them Anglicanism and patriotism were almost synonymous: they suspected any group, Jacobite or Nonconformist, which did not share their views. Even Burnet, probably the most radical Latitudinarian on the episcopal bench, warned the Dissenters that 'toleration does not at all justify their separation; it only takes away the force of the penal laws against them'.[79] What bishops could not agree upon was how best to preserve the existing system in Church and State. Their answer to that question depended upon which danger they felt to be greater: the threat of a Roman Catholic succession or of the growing political influence of Dissent. In the closing years of Anne's reign nearly all of the bishops came to recognize the former danger as the more serious. At the same time few of them could resist the opportunity to tighten up the laws restricting Dissenters. In the long run they could not have it both ways. At Anne's death most of the bishops could be classified as either Church Whigs or Hanoverian Tories. Though George I perhaps owed his throne to these two moderate groups they both lost their influence early in his reign. After 1714, as after 1688, conservative bishops who supported the new régime soon discovered that they had outlived their political usefulness. In February 1717, less than two years after his elevation to the primacy, Archbishop Wake lamented: 'How far my life may be of use to the Church of England, I cannot tell, but I see no prospect of my doing any good for it.'[80] In truth, politically he no longer counted.

It is evident from all that has been said that during the period 1688–1714 the bishops took an active part in the House of Lords. How significant a role did they play in the politics of the age? During no period in English history since the Middle Ages was the House of Lords more important than in the reigns of the later Stuarts. From the Restoration to the time of Walpole the masters of political leadership were, or became, peers.[81] The Commons may have already established its primacy but it had not yet attained the monopoly of power it possessed later. The leaders in the Lords owed much of their strength to their influence over parliamentary elections, and without their following in the Commons they would have been nearly powerless. Yet it was in the Upper House that the giants contended openly with one another; the Lords still rivalled the Commons as an arena for political conflict. Between 1688–1714 the Upper Chamber was so closely divided between the Whigs and the Tories that several crucial contests were decided there. By her creation of the eleven Tory peers in 1711 Queen Anne demonstrated the ultimate impotence of the Lords. Until that date, however, the Lords truly shared the legislative power with the Commons, as they likewise shared the judicial power with the Crown.

The exact relationship of the episcopal bench to the lay peers remained obscure. Generally authorities maintained that the bishops were not peers of the realm.[82] Nevertheless the Lords Spiritual voted on all questions (except impeachments which might result in the shedding of blood—but not excepting Bills of Attainder); they likewise had the right to speak on any point and to sign protests. Furthermore, bishops served on all kinds of committees.[83] Custom appears to have required that no bishop should move for adjournment,[84] but in practically every other respect the episcopal members were as free to act as their lay brethren. On the other hand, none of the bishops was as powerful as the great lay peers. Few of them now served on the Privy Council, none were Ministers. On the whole they appear to have entered less into debates, even on ecclesiastical legislation, than their numbers warranted. Their most direct contribution was their relatively regular attendance and above all their votes. At the close of James II's reign the episcopal bench constituted a seventh of the Lords (twenty-six out of one hundred and seventy-eight); in 1714, thanks to Anne's creations and the addition of the Scottish peers, the proportion had been reduced to an eighth (twenty-six out of two hundred and fourteen). Episcopal attendance was on a comparable scale. In William's reign there were an average of eleven bishops present out of a total average attendance of seventy: in Anne's reign nine out of a total of sixty-nine.[85] The figures, however, are somewhat misleading because after 1701 the bishops who came up to London for Parliament frequently attended Convocation rather than the House of Lords, when no important business was before the latter body. During critical discussions the episcopal bench often accounted for a sixth or a fifth of those present. At the time of the divisions over occasional conformity, 'church in danger', the Regency Bill, and the Scottish Union the bishops cast about a fifth of the votes. Thus the actual voting strength of the episcopal bench proved greater than its numbers warranted. Probably no significant legislation could have passed during this period without the support of at least some of the bishops. Certainly none did.

The importance of the bishops arose not only from their voting power; it also stemmed from their local influence. Professor Walcott mentions only Bishop Trelawny among the men in Anne's day whose political weight determined local elections.[86] He must be correct in assuming that no bishop controlled any parliamentary seats. Still, Compton's activities at London, Lloyd's at Worcester, and Nicolson's in Cumberland, as well as Trelawny's in the West Country, all suggest that if episcopal influence was seldom paramount it may sometimes have been decisive.[87] At a time when religion and politics were so closely intertwined few churchmen held aloof from political contests. Bishops sent letters and verbal instructions to their clergy recommending or condemning candidates. They also considered political affiliations when handing out patronage, for the lower clergy likewise exerted political influence. In 1710 Hearne attributed the election (in Oxfordshire) of 'a staunch whig, a loose debauchee', with 'little or nothing of religion', to the activities of 'the illiterate, impudent archdeacon of Oxford' and other local clergy.[88] It can scarcely be accounted mere coincidence that the Bishop of Oxford since 1699 had been William Talbot, a thoroughgoing Whig.

In addition to exerting pressure upon the lower clergy the bishops reached a wide audience through the pulpit. The political sermon was an accepted instrument of propaganda, especially on anniversaries such as that of the execution of Charles I (January 30th), the restoration of Charles II (May 29th), and above all November 5th—date of both the discovery of Guy Fawkes's plot and the landing of William III. Sacheverell's blast (November 5th, 1709) was unique only in the explosion it precipitated, not in the partisan nature of its contents. Many of these homiletic broadsides were printed and distributed for political purposes. The limited franchise of unreformed England must not blind us to significance of public opinion in contemporary politics. A number of constituencies besides the counties possessed a rather extensive electorate, among them nearly all of the cathedral cities.[89] More than that, the unenfranchised were not without political influence. Writing of the history of Anne's reign (in 1775) James MacPherson remarked:[90]

> In all States that possess any portion of public freedom the appeal to parties is always made to the people. Though the body of the nation enjoy but a very small share of any Government, they make up with their weight and numbers what they want as individuals ... The good opinion of the people is therefore the citadel, if the expression may be used, to which factions direct all their irregular attacks.

The Crown, Ministers, journalists and the public all assumed that the episcopate should take a lively part in politics, even though they often attacked individual bishops for doing so. As we have seen, episcopal appointments were recognized as at least partly political. Once elevated to the bench, bishops, like lay peers, enjoyed virtual life tenure; a factor which made for political independence. Yet many sees offered so meagre an income that at any time probably half of the bishops desired translation, just as many lay peers aspired to greater honours. The hope or promotion encouraged subservience to party leaders. Later under the Hanoverians one of the principal methods of controlling the episcopal bench was to reward party loyalty by translating deserving bishops from the poorer to the richer sees.[91] During William's and Anne's reigns, however, this practice was less common. Out of the fifty-six bishops who served during these years only eleven held more than one see during the period, although thirty-eight vacancies occurred between 1688–1714. Despite their active concern with politics the bishops certainly considered themselves something more than politicians in lawn sleeves. It will be recalled that on most important issues, such as Fenwick's Attainder, the Occasional Conformity Bills, the 'Church in Danger' resolution, the Regency Act, and the Scottish Union, the vote of a number of bishops was at variance with their party affiliation.

In other words the Lords Spiritual retained a distinct character; they counted for more than so many Whig or Tory votes in the Upper Chamber. There remained, in effect, a trace of the medieval concept of the clergy as an estate separate from the nobility.

In the last analysis, however, the genius of the British system of government lay in its ability to adapt old forms to new uses. By the seventeenth century government by estates, in the feudal sense, had been replaced by what contemporaries were wont to call 'mixed government'. What saved the English Parliament from the fate of the Continental estates was that it transformed itself into a body representing the conflicting pressure groups of a new and increasingly capitalistic society. This transformation came earlier and was more complete in the case of the Commons, but the Lords also experienced a similar change in character. The reason is obvious, it stems from the very nature of English society at the close of the Stuart era. The nobility was no longer conceived of as a separate order but rather as the top layer of a ruling class which owed its power to wealth and ability no less than to blood. Equally pronounced was the difference between the position of the clergy as contrasted with that of their medieval forebears. Although the Anglican Church had preserved ordination and the Catholic tradition of the priesthood, the Reformation had drastically altered the clergy's relationship to lay society. More and more the clergy were becoming simply men of a particular if rather unique profession. This change inevitably affected the episcopate. The bishops we have been discussing were mostly devout men and almost all of them were jealous of the rights and privileges of the Established Church, yet they shared the same political prejudices and beliefs as their lay brethren.

Most important of all, the Church came to be divided by the same partisan loyalties that divided the nation as a whole. Had the episcopal bench remained as united after 1688 as it had been before, its position in Parliament would assuredly have been attacked. So for that matter would the position of the lay peers had they represented a single-minded class of ancient privilege. The House of Lords survived the constitutional changes of the seventeenth century because it adapted itself to the new order rather than opposing it. With the rise of the centralized monarchy in the sixteenth century the barons had become courtiers; with the establishment of parliamentary supremacy they turned borough-mongers and popular politicians. A parallel change took place among the Lords Spiritual. By 1700 even the High Churchmen (dedicated though they pretended to be to the restoration of the old order in Church and State) thought and acted far more like party politicians than prince bishops. Atterbury was no more a Laud than Bolingbroke a Strafford!

Both to contemporaries and to later commentators, especially to recent historians like Namier and Walcott, the factional intrigues of the eighteenth century appear as an almost sordid substitute for the epic conflicts of the Reformation and the Civil Wars. Government by compromise provides little scope for heroics. The blood of the martyrs may be the seed of the Church but peaceful revolution requires something more than martyrdom. Between 1688–1714 the Anglican episcopate succeeded in committing the Church of England to the Revolutionary Settlement, and the new régime to the Established Church. Had they failed in this the Revolution of 1688 might not have been successful: it almost certainly would not have been bloodless.

[1] Robert S. Bosher, *The Making of the Restoration Settlement*, New York, 1951 [London, 1951], 278–83; Walter Gold Simon, 'The Bishops and the Anglican Establishment', *Doctoral Dissertation*, University of Wisconsin, 1954, 35–6, 57–62.

[2] *Ibid.*, 93, 99, 117.

[3] *Ibid.*, 196–7, 262, 270–1; Andrew Browning, *Thomas Osborne, Earl of Danby and Duke of Leeds*, 3 vols., Glasgow, 1944–51, I, 153–4; Edward Carpenter, *The Protestant Bishop, being the Life and Times of Henry Compton, 1632–1713, Bishop of London*, London, 1956, 48. The bishops' opposition to the Exclusion Bill is partially explained as a reaction to Whig attacks upon the episcopate at the time of the Popish Plot. See Walter G. Simon, 'The Restoration Episcopate and the Popish Plot', *Anglican Theological Review*, VOL. XXXIX, No. 2 (April 1957), 139–47.

[4] *The Life of Dr Henry Compton*, London, 1713, 16, quoted by Carpenter, *Protestant Bishop*, 84. Nineteen bishops were present on the day of his speech, *Journal of the House of Lords*, XIV, 86.

[5] A. S. Turberville, *The House of Lords in the Reign of William III*, Oxford, 1913, 12.

[6] William Cobbett, ed., *Parliamentary History*, v, 59; Browning, *Osborne*, I, 426–7.

[7] John Lake of Chichester and William Thomas of Worcester.

[8] The sixteen men nominated were:

> *In 1689 :* Gilbert Burnet to Salisbury, Humphrey Humphreys to Bangor, Gilbert Ironsides to Bristol (translated to Hereford in 1691), Simon Patrick to Chichester (translated to Ely in 1691), Edward Stillingfleet to Worcester, Nicholas Stratford to Chester.
>
> *In 1690 :* John Hough to Oxford (translated to Lichfield and Coventry in 1699).
>
> *In 1691 :* Richard Cumberland to Peterborough, Edward Fowler to Gloucester, Robert Grove to Chichester, John Hall to Bristol, Richard Kidder to Bath and Wells, John Moore to Norwich, John Sharp to York, Thomas Tenison to Lincoln (translated to Canterbury in 1695), John Tillotson to Canterbury.

[9] Gilbert Burnet, *History of His Own Times*, with notes, 6 vols., Oxford, 1833, IV, 212; Carpenter, *Protestant Bishop*, 180–1; George Every, *The High Church Party*, London, S.P.C.K., 1956, 67.

[10] *In 1692 :* Edward Jones to St Asaph.

> *In 1695 :* James Gardiner to Lincoln.
>
> *In 1696 :* John Williams to Chichester.
>
> *In 1699 :* William Talbot to Oxford.
>
> *In 1701 :* John Evans to Bangor.

[11] The five were: Hough, Humphreys, Ironsides, Patrick and Tenison. On Lloyd's party position see A. Tindall Hart, *William Lloyd, 1627–1717, Bishop, Politician, Author and Prophet*, London, S.P.C.K., 1952, 127–9.

[12] Turberville, *House of Lords in the Reign of William III*, 16.

[13] *Journal of the House of Lords*, XIV, 149. The average attendance of the bishops that spring was six or seven.

[14] Every, *High Church Party*, 19–25; Carpenter, *Protestant Bishop*, 156–8; Keith Feiling, *History of the Tory Party, 1670–1714*, Oxford, 1924, 264. Both the comprehension and the toleration Bills passed the Lords with little debate. Lord Macaulay, *The History of England from the Accession of James the Second*, ed. by C. H. Firth, 6 vols., London, 1914, 1385–6.

[15] Every, *High Church Party*, 28–36.

[16] *Journal of the House of Lords*, XIV, 453.

[17] E. Timberland, *History and Proceedings of the House of Lords*, 3 vols., London, 1742, I, 402; Burnet, IV, 74–5. The protesting bishops were: Beaw of Llandaff, Compton of London, Lloyd of St Asaph, Mews of Winchester, Stillingfleet of Worcester and Watson of St David's. When the Lords voted to expunge the protest another of William's appointees, Humphreys of Bangor, joined with the above. Timberland, I, 403; *Journal of the House of Lords*, XIV, 455.

[18] *Journal of the House of Lords*, XIV, 47.

[19] *Parliamentary History*, v, 1154–5; Burnet, IV, 350; G. J. R. James, ed., *Letters Illustrative of the Reign of William III 1696–1708, addressed to the Duke of Shrewsbury by John Vernon*, 3 vols., London, 1841, I, 134.

[20] Timberland, I, 463.

[21] Edward Carpenter, *Thomas Tenison, Archbishop of Canterbury, His Life and Times*, London, S.P.C.K., 1948, 197; James, *Letters ... of John Vernon*, I, 140.

[22] Carpenter, *Protestant Bishop*, 182–3.

[23] James E. Thorold Rogers, ed., *A Complete Collection of the Protests of the Lords*, 3 vols., Oxford, 1875, I, 146–58; *Journal of the House of Lords*, XVI, 623–9.

[24] Burnet, IV, 228–9; Timberland, II, 11; *Journal of the House of Lords*, XVI, 540. In 1689 five bishops protested against a Bill to restrict the marriage of minors on the grounds that marriage was a 'sacred ordinance' of God and thus could not be nullified. The protesting bishops were: Beaw, Compton, Mews and Watson (all pre-1688 appointees) plus one of William's nominees, Ironsides. Timberland, I, 399.

[25] In 1692 a list of Government supporters noted that Compton had influence 'over most of the Whig Party'. S.P. Domestic, William III, Chest 8, No. 25, printed in Browning, *Osborne*, III, 182. But as Carpenter shows Compton supported the Tories from 1689 on, *Protestant Bishops*, 83.

[26] Thomas Smith of Carlisle, an invalid, did not attend Parliament after 1690 but he exerted his influence in local elections. F. G. James, *North Country Bishop*, New Haven, 1956 [Oxford, 1957], 189.

[27] It has already been noted that Ironsides and Kidder voted with the Tories in the Fenwick case, and Stratford in the Norfolk divorce case. In 1695 Stratford was the only bishop who joined several Tory peers in protesting an act against perjury while in 1698 Fowler joined Compton, Mews and Sprat in protesting against an East India Company Bill. Timberland, I, 434; Rogers, *Protests*, I, 134.

[28] Turberville, *House of Lords in the Reign of William III*, 25, 182–3.

[29] *Ibid.*, 30.

[30] Burnet, IV, 6.

[31] William Thomas Morgan, *English Political Parties and Leaders in the Reign of Queen Anne*, New Haven, 1920 [London, 1920], 165.

[32] Every, *High Church Party*, 32. Morgan traces the High Church Party back to Laud (*Political Parties*, 23) but Canon Every shows that the real division between the High Church Party and the Latitudinarians did not come until 1688, pp. 11–18. See also Keith Feiling, *History of the Tory Party*, New York, 1924 [London, 1924], Chapter II.

[33] For example, see Historical Manuscripts Commission, *Portland MSS.*, IV, 35–6.

[34] A. Tindall Hart, *The Life and Times of John Sharp, Archbishop of York*, London, S.P.C.K., 1947, 213–17; Carpenter, *Protestant Bishop*, 185–7; G. M. Trevelyan, *England under Queen Anne*, 3 vols., London, 1930–4, I, 170–2.

[35] Morgan, *Political Parties*, 166–7, 171–2, 174, 263, 305.

[36] Queen Anne to Marlborough, September ?, 1707, printed in Beatrice Curtis Brown, ed. *The Letters and Diplomatic Instructions of Queen Anne*, London, 1925, 230–1.

[37] *In 1702*: William Nicolson to Carlisle (it is he who became a 'Church Whig').

In 1703: George Hooper to St Asaph (translated to Bath and Wells in six months).

In 1704: William Beveridge to St Asaph.

[38] *In 1705*: George Bull to St David's, William Wake to Lincoln.

In 1707: Offspring Blackhall (Tory) to Exeter, Sir William Dawes (Tory) to Chester (translated to York in 1714).

In 1708: William Fleetwood to St Asaph, Charles Trimnell to Norwich.

In 1709: Thomas Manningham to Chichester.

[39] *In 1710*: Philip Bisse to St David's (translated to Hereford in 1712), John Robinson to Bristol (translated to London in 1713).

In 1712: Adam Ottley to St David's.

In 1713: Francis Atterbury to Rochester, Francis Gastrell to Chester, George Smalridge to Bristol.

Atterbury and Smalridge were the two Highflyers.

[40] In addition to Bisse, Dawes, Hooper and Robinson, Anne also translated Trelawny to Winchester and Moore to Ely. Moore was the only Whig of the six.

[41] Nicolson Diary, Tullie House Copy, Carlisle, V, 122–3. The other bishops voting against the amendment were: Compton, Crewe, Mews, Nicolson, Sprat and Trelawny. The other ten bishops present (who thus must have all voted for the amendment) were Burnet, Cumberland, Evans, Fowler, Hall, Humphreys, Kidder, Lloyd, Patrick and Williams. *Journal of the House of Lords*, XVII, 179.

[42] Historical Manuscripts Commission, *House of Lords MSS.*, New Series, v, 157.

[43] Nicolson Diary, Tullie House Copy, v, 123. The bishops voted eight to six for the amendment with Evans this time siding with the Tories.

[44] The other bishops voting for the Bill (counting proxies) were: Beaw, Compton, Crewe, Hooper, Mews, Sprat and Trelawny. Those opposing it: Burnet, Fowler, Gardiner, Hall, Humphreys, Lloyd, Moore, Patrick, Talbot and Williams. The full division is given in Timberland, II, 69–70.

[45] James, *North Country Bishop*, 178.

[46] Nicolson Diary, Tullie House Copy, XVIII, 47.

[47] *Ibid.*, XIX, 181; Timberland, II, 154–60.

[48] Nicolson Diary, Tullie House Copy, XIX, 190–1.

[49] Rogers, *Protests*, I, 179.

[50] *Journal of the House of Lords*, XVIII, 42.

[51] Nicolson Diary, Tullie House Copy, XIX, 166–9. On the Regency Act see A. S. Turberville, *The House of Lords in the XVIII Century*, Oxford, 1927, 73–4. Only Bishop Hooper signed the protest against the defeat of Nottingham's proposal, Rogers, *Protests*, I, 175.

[52] Crewe and Hooper opposed the amendment; Compton and Sharp withdrew before the vote. Nicolson Diary, Tullie House Copy, XX, 59.

[53] Every, *High Church Party*, 121.

[54] Timberland, II, 175; Burnet, V, 294.

[55] Nicolson Diary, Tullie House Copy, XXII, 96; G. M. Trevelyan, *England under Queen Anne*, II, 283–4.

[56] Nicolson Diary, Tullie House Copy, XXII, 99–100. Crewe, Sharp and Stratford protested against Tenison's Bill, Rogers, *Protests*, I, 180.

[57] Nicolson Diary, Tullie House Copy, XXII, 112–13.

[58] *Ibid.*, XXII, 107. For the bishops present see *Journal of the House of Lords*, XVIII, 243.

[59] Nicolson Diary, Tullie House Copy, XXII, 109; Rogers, *Protests*, I, 180–1, 183–4.

[60] Timberland, II, 277.

[61] *Parliamentary History*, VI, 1035–9. Three bishops protested against the resolution: Bisse, Manningham and Robinson—all three of whom had been recently nominated. Timberland, II, 350–1.

[62] *Parliamentary History*, VI, 1045–6; C. E. Whiting, *Nathaniel Lord Crewe, Bishop of Durham (1674–1921)*, S.P.C.K., London, 1940, 228–9.

[63] G. M. Trevelyan, *England under Queen Anne*, III, 195.

[64] Burnet, VI, 84–5.

[65] Norman Sykes, *Church and State in England in the XVIII Century*, Cambridge, England, 1934, 35.

[66] James, *North Country Bishop*, 214–15.

[67] Carpenter, *Thomas Tenison*, 399–400.

[68] Burnet, VI, 107–108; *Parliamentary History*, VI, 1130.

[69] *Parliamentary History*, VI, 1350.

[70] Rogers, *Protests*, I, 221; Timberland, II, 422–8.

[71] James, *North Country Bishop*, 229.

[72] Norman Sykes, *William Wake Archbishop of Canterbury,1657–1737*, 2 vols.,Cambridge, England, 1957 [London, 1957], II, 122–7.

[73] Rogers, *Protests*, I, 200–1; Sykes, *William Wake*, II, 95, 127.

[74] *Parliamentary History*, VI, 1010–11, 1155.

[75] *Ibid.*, VI, 1335.

[76] *Ibid.*, VI, 1343.

[77] Lord Bathurst to Peter Wentworth, January 15th, 1714 in J. J. Cartwright, ed., *The Wentworth Papers*, London, P.R.O., 1883, 389.

[78] W. Nicolson, *The Great Day of Thanksgiving*, Dublin, 1719, 1.

[79] Burnet, VI, 188.

[80] Willis MSS. 36, f. 2d, quoted by Sykes, *William Wake*, II, 147.

[81] Turberville, *House of Lords in the Reign of William III*, 233.

[82] L. O. Pike, *Constitutional History of the House of Lords*, London, 1894, 138–9, 163–4, 326.

[83] Walter Simon, 'The Bishops and the Anglican Establishment', 84–5.

[84] Nicolson Diary, Tullie House Copy, XIX, 19.

[85] See tables in Andrew Browning, ed., *English Historical Documents, 1660–1714*, London, 1953, Appendix III, 956–7.

[86] And Trelawny's influence came chiefly from his family connections. Robert Walcott, *English Politics in the Early Eighteenth Century*, Oxford, 1956, 61, 64, 212–13.

[87] A. Tindall Hart, *William Lloyd* [London, 1952], 157–60; Carpenter, *Protestant Bishop*, 80; James, *North Country Bishop*, 198–203; Burnet, IV, 72–3; Norman Sykes, 'The Cathedral Chapter of Exeter and the General Election of 1705', *English Historical Review*, VOL. XLV (1930), 260–78; Feiling, *History of the Tory Party*, 378.

[88] Philip Bliss, ed., *The Remains of Thomas Hearne*, 3 vols., London, 1869, I, 184.

[89] Walcott, *English Politics*, 12 and note 3, 20 and note 2, 22 and note 2.

[90] *History of Great Britain*, II, 635 quoted by William Thomas Laprade, *Public Opinion and Politics in Eighteenth Century England*, New York [London, 1936], 1936, 28.

[91] Sykes, *Church and State*, 65–6; a similar situation seems to have existed during the reign of Charles II. W. G. Simon, 'The Bishops and the Anglican Establishment'. Doctoral Dissertation, University of Wisconsin, 1954, 44–7.

Bibliography of Wallace Notestein

BOOKS AND EDITED WORKS

* Original works are designated by an asterisk.

*A History of Witchcraft in England from 1558 to 1718.
 Awarded the Herbert Baxter Adams Prize in European History for 1909. In its original form this essay was the dissertation submitted for a doctorate in philosophy conferred by Yale University in 1908. (*Prize Essays of the American Historical Association*, 1909: Washington, The American Historical Association, 1911; London, H. Frowde, Oxford University Press, 1911 [i.e. 1912]. xiv+442 pp.)

Source Problems in English History.
 With Albert Beebe White. Introduction by Dana Carleton Munro.
 New York and London, Harper & Brothers [1915.] xv+421 [1] pp. (Harper's Parallel Source Problems.)

The President's Flag Day Address, with Evidence of Germany's Plans.
 By Woodrow Wilson. Issued by the Committee on Public Information, September 15th, 1917. The annotations were prepared by Professors Wallace Notestein, Elmer Stoll, August C. Krey and William Anderson, of the University of Minnesota, and Professor Guernsey Jones of the University of Nebraska.
 Washington, Government Printing Office, 1917. 30 pp. (U.S. Committee on Public Information. Red, White, and Blue Series, No. 4.)

Conquest and Kultur: Aims of the Germans in Their Own Words.
 Compiled with Elmer E. Stoll. Issued by the Committee on Public Information, November 15th, 1917.
 Washington, Government Printing Office, 1917. 17 pp. (U.S. Committee on Public Information. Red, White, and Blue Series, No. 5.)
 —— Edition of January, 1918.
 Washington, Government Printing Office, 1918. 160 pp.
 —— Edition of October, 1918.
 Washington, Government Printing Office, 1918. 163 pp.

Short Bibliography of American History.
 Compiled with C. R. Fish.
 London, 1920. 9 pp. (Historical Association, London. Leaflet No. 48. January, 1920.)

Commons Debates for 1629.
 With Frances Helen Relf.
 Minneapolis, University of Minnesota, 1921. lxvii+304 pp. (Research Publications of the University of Minnesota. Studies in the Social Sciences, No. 10.)

The Journal of Sir Simonds D'Ewes, from the Beginning of the Long Parliament to the Opening of the Trial of the Earl of Strafford.
 New Haven, Yale University Press, 1923. xix+598 pp. (Yale Historical Publications. Manuscripts and Edited Texts, VII.)

* *The Winning of the Initiative by the House of Commons.*
 London, H. Milford, Oxford University Press, 1924. 53 pp. (The British Academy. The Raleigh Lecture on History.) From the Proceedings of the British Academy. Read October 2nd, 1924. Published in the *Proceedings for 1924-5*. Reprinted 1949, 1951, 1959.

BIBLIOGRAPHY

*Interim Report of the Committee on House of Commons Personnel and Politics, 1264–1832.
  In collaboration with other members of the Committee.
  London, H.M. Stationery Office, 1932.
Commons Debates, 1621.
  With Frances Helen Relf and Hartley Simpson.
  New Haven, Yale University Press; London, H. Milford, Oxford University
  Press, 1935. 7 vols. (Yale Historical Publications. Manuscripts and Edited
  Texts, XIV [i.e. XV].)
*English Folk: A Book of Characters.
  New York, Harcourt, Brace and Company, 1938. [xxvii+328 pp. London,
  Jonathan Cape, 1938; 1943. 381 pp.
*The Scot in History.
  New Haven, Yale University Press, 1946. xvii+371 pp. London, Jonathan
  Cape, 1947. xvii+371 pp.
*The English People on the Eve of Colonization, 1603–1630.
  New York, Harper & Brothers, 1954. xvii+302 pp. (The New American
  Nation Series [3].) London, Hamish Hamilton, 1954. xvii+302 pp.
*Four Worthies: John Chamberlain, Anne Clifford, John Taylor, Oliver Heywood.
  London, Jonathan Cape, 1956. 248 pp. New Haven, Yale University Press,
  1957. 248 pp.

ARTICLES AND REVIEWS

*Articles are designated by an asterisk.

[A.H.R. American Historical Review. S.R.L.=Saturday Review of Literature]

*The Western Indians in the Revolution. Ohio Archeological and Historical Quarterly'
  xvi, 1907, 269–91.
*The Establishment of the Committee of Both Kingdoms. A.H.R., xvii, April 1912,
  477–95.
Elizabethan Rogues and Vagabonds. By Frank Aydelotte. A.H.R., xix, July 1914,
  886–7.
*The Career of Mr Asquith. Political Science Quarterly, xxxi, September 1916, 361–79.
*Joseph Chamberlain and Tariff Reform. Sewanee Review, xxv, January 1917, 40–56.
General Botha: The Career and the Man. By Harold Spender. A.H.R., xxiii,
  October 1917, 163–4.
Das Annexionistische Deutschland: eine Sammlung von Dokumenten, die seit dem
  4. August 1914, in Deutschland öffentlich oder geheim verbreitet wurden. By
  S. Grumbach. A.H.R., xxiii, January 1918, 394–6.
Jan Smuts: Being a Character Sketch of Gen. the Hon. J. C. Smuts . . . Minister of
  Defense, Union of South Africa. By N. Levi. A.H.R., xxiii, January 1918, 434.
Out of Their Own Mouths: Utterances of German Rulers, Statesmen, Savants,
  Publicists, Journalists, Poets, Business Men, Party Leaders, and Soldiers. A.H.R.,
  xxiii, April 1918, 699–700.
*Jan Smuts. Atlantic Monthly, cxxii, July 1918, 107–13.
Diplomacy as International Law. A Survey of International Relations between the
  United States and Germany, August 1st, 1914–April 6th, 1917. By James
  Brown Scott. Yale Review, viii, July 1919, 888–91.
*The Stuart Period: Unsolved Problems. Annual Report ... for the year 1916. American
  Historical Association. Washington, 1919, vol. i, 389–99.
Papers Relating to the Army of the Solemn League and Covenant, 1643–1647.
  Edited with an Introduction by Charles Sanford Terry. (Publications of the
  Scottish History Society, 2nd Series, vols. xvi, xvii.) A.H.R., xxv, January 1920,
  317–18.
L'Opinion Allemande pendant la Guerre, 1914–1918. Par André Hallays. A.H.R.,
  xxv, January 1920, 321.

The Ready and Easy Way to Establish a Free Commonwealth. By John Milton. Edited with Introduction, Notes and Glossary by Evert Mordecai Clark. *A.H.R.*, xxv, July 1920, 743–4.

The Life and Works of Arthur Hall of Grantham, M.P., First Translator of Homer into English. By H. G. Wright. *History*, N.S. v, October 1920, 181.

Occasional Addresses, 1893–1916. By the Right Hon. H. H. Asquith. *Political Science Quarterly*, xxxv, December 1920, 675.

Margot Asquith, An Autobiography. *A.H.R.*, xxvi, April 1921, 525–6.

Portraits of the Eighties. By Horace G. Hitchison. *A.H.R.*, xxvi, April 1921, 579.

Elizabethan Policy. (*Mr Secretary Walsingham and the Policy of Queen Elizabeth*, by Conyers Read.) *S.R.L.*, ii, February 20th, 1926, 572.

A History of the Tory Party, 1640–1714. By Keith Feiling. *History*, N.S. xi, April 1926, 69–70.

In Tudor Times. (*A History of England from the Defeat of the Armada to the Death of Elizabeth; with an Account of English Institutions during the Later Sixteenth and Early Seventeenth Centuries*, by Edward P. Cheyney. VOL. II.) *S.R.L.*, ii, May 1st, 1926, 752.

Calendar of State Papers and Manuscripts, relating to English Affairs, existing in the Archives and Collections of Venice, and in other Libraries of Northern Italy. VOL. XXIV, 1636–9; VOL. XXV, 1640–2. Edited by Allen B. Hinds. *A.H.R.*, xxxi, July 1926, 772–4.

Retrospective Reviews. (*The Life of Sir William Harcourt*, by A. G. Gardiner; *The Life of the Right Hon. Sir Henry Campbell-Bannerman*, by J. A. Spender; *My Diaries, being a Personal Narrative of Events, 1888–1914*, by W. S. Blunt; *The Life and Letters of George Wyndham*, by J. W. Mackail and Guy Wyndham; *Mr Balfour, A Biography*, by E. T. Raymond; *Contemporary Personalities*, by the Earl of Birkenhead; *Uncensored Celebrities*, by E. T. Raymond; *The Mirrors of Downing Street: Some Political Reflections by a Gentleman with a Duster*; *Pillars of State*, by Herbert Sidebotham; *The Diary of Lord Bertie of Thame, 1914–1918*, edited by Lady Algernon Gordon Lennox; *The First World War, 1914–1918: Personal Experiences of Lieut.-Col. C. A'Court Repington.*) *A.H.R.*, xxxii, October 1926, 22–33.

A Great Teacher. (*Council and Courts in Anglo-Norman England*, by George Burton Adams.) *S.R.L.*, iii, December 18th, 1926, 448.

The Life of Charles the First, the Royal Martyr. By Charles W. Coit. *S.R.L.*, iii, January 1st, 1927, 487. Unsigned.

Henry Chaplain: A Memoir. By the Marchioness of Londonderry. *New York Herald Tribune*, February 13th, 1927, 17.

Bonnie Prince Charlie. By Donald Barr Chidsey. *S.R.L.*, v, December 1st, 1928, 436. Unsigned.

The Star of Piccadilly: Memoir of William Douglas, Fourth Duke of Queensberry ... By Lewis Melville. *S.R.L.*, v, December 1st, 1928, 436. Unsigned.

Chevalier Bayard. By Samuel Shellabarger. *S.R.L.*, v., December 22nd, 1928, 539. Unsigned.

A Romantic Career. (*Montrose, A History*, by John Buchan.) *S.R.L.*, v, January 5th, 1929, 567–8.

Bellocian History. (*James the Second*, by Hilaire Belloc.) *S.R.L.*, v, January 12th, 1929, 583.

British Culture. (*The History of British Civilization*, by Esmé Wingfield-Stratford.) *S.R.L.*, v, February 23rd, 1929, 701–2.

King Henry the Rake. By Clement Wood. *S.R.L.*, v, March 16th, 1929, 783. Unsigned.

A Tragic History. (*Elizabeth and Essex*, by Lytton Strachey.) *Yale Review*, xviii, Spring 1929, 588–90.

The Dictionary of National Biography, 1912–1921. Edited by H. W. C. Davis and J. R. H. Weaver. *A.H.R.*, xxxiv, April 1929, 590–1.

Gossip of the Past. (*An Elizabethan Journal*, by George Bagshawe Harrison.) *S.R.L.*, v, April 6th, 1929, 858.

Monarch and Man. (*Henry the Eighth*, by Francis Hackett.) *S.R.L.*, v, April 13th, 1929, 875–6.

BIBLIOGRAPHY

"Living to Purpose." (*Richard Burdon Haldane* (*Viscount Haldane*): *An Autobiography*.) *S.R.L.*, v, May 25th, 1929, 1050–1.

Bibliography of British History: Stuart Period, 1603–1714. Edited by Godfrey Davies. *A.H.R.*, xxxv, October 1929, 101–2.

Wolsey and England. (*Wolsey*, by A. F. Pollard.) *S.R.L.*, vi, March 15th, 1930, 819–20.

Dwight Whitney Morrow. By Hewitt Hanson Howland. *S.R.L.*, vi, May 24th, 1930, 1075. Unsigned.

One Who Reached Posterity. (*The Life of Benjamin Disraeli, Earl of Beaconsfield*, by William Flavelle Moneypenny and George Earle Buckle.) *S.R.L.*, vi, July 12th, 1930, 1185–6.

A New History. (*England in the Nineteenth Century, 1801–1805*, by Alan Frederick Fremantle.) *S.R.L.*, vi, July 19th, 1930, 1207.

Portrait of a Churchman. (*Laud, Storm Center of Stuart England*, by Robert P. T. Coffin.) *S.R.L.*, vii, August 23rd, 1930, 67.

A Bibliography of Oliver Cromwell: A List of Printed Materials Relating to Oliver Cromwell, together with a List of Portraits and Caricatures. By Wilbur Cortez Abbott. *A.H.R.*, xxxvi, October 1930, 120–3.

The Father of the House. (*Memoirs of an Old Parliamentarian*, by T. P. O'Connor, 2 vols.) *Yale Review*, xix, Winter 1930, 420–2.

A Great Figure. (*Wolsey*, by Hilaire Belloc.) *S.R.L.*, vii, February 7th, 1931, 578.

Queen Victoria. (*The Letters of Queen Victoria*, 3rd Series, edited by George Earle Buckle, vol. i, 1886–90; *Side Lights on Queen Victoria*, by Sir Frederick Ponsonby.) *S.R.L.*, vii, February 14th, 1931, 596.

A Great Victorian. (*The Diaries of John Bright*; with a Foreword by Philip Bright; edited by R. A. J. Walling.) *S.R.L.*, vii, April 4th, 1931, 712.

*The End of an English Era. *S.R.L.*, vii, May 30th, 1931, 862–3.

A Victorian Statesman. (*Lord Rosebery*, by the Marquess of Crewe.) *S.R.L.*, viii, January 23rd, 1932, 469–70.

Frail Anne Boleyn. By Benedict Fitzpatrick. *S.R.L.*, viii, April 2nd, 1932, 639. Unsigned.

English Memoirs. (*Mary Gladstone* (*Mrs Drew*): *Her Diaries and Letters*, edited by Lucy Masterman; *Edward VII*, by H. E. Wortham; *A Roving Commission*, by Winston Churchill; *Lord Rosebery*, by the Marquess of Crewe; *Mr Gladstone*, by Walter Phelps Hall; *As We Were*, by E. F. Benson.) *Yale Review*, xxi, Summer 1932, 819–25.

The Hurts of Haldworth and Their Descendants at Savile Hall, the Ickles, and Hesley Hall, Being a Study of Social and Domestic Life in Past Times; more particularly in Hallamshire and at Nottingham during the reign of Elizabeth, at Rotherham under Cromwell, and at Sheffield in the Eighteenth Century. By Sir George Reresby Sitwell, bt. *A.H.R.*, xxxvii, July 1932, 744–6.

*History and the Biographer. *Yale Review*, xxii, March 1933, 549–58.

A Victorian Statesman. (*The Life of Joseph Chamberlain*, by J. L. Garvin, vol. i, 1836–85.) *S.R.L.*, ix, March 25th, 1933, 497–500.

The Later Victorians. (*The Victorian Sunset*, by Esmé Wingfield-Stratford.) *S.R.L.*, ix, April 29th, 1933, 560.

Lloyd George and Others. (*Essays in Biography*, by John Maynard Keynes.) *S.R.L.*, ix, May 27th, 1933, 613, 616.

Chamberlain and Hicks Beach. (*The Life of Joseph Chamberlain*, by J. L. Garvin, vol. i, 1836–85; *The Life of Sir Michael-Hicks Beach* (*Earl St Aldwyn*), by Lady Victoria Hicks Beach, 2 vols.) *Yale Review*, xxii, Summer 1933, 825–9.

The Fierce Light of Politics. (*The Life of Joseph Chamberlain*, by J. L. Garvin, vol. ii, 1885–95.) *Yale Review*, xxiii, Autumn 1933, 194–7.

Queen Bess's Glorious Days. (*Queen Elizabeth*, by John Ernest Neale.) *S.R.L.*, x, February 17th, 1934, 487.

The Stuart Monarchy. (*Charles the First, King of England*, by Hilaire Belloc.) *Yale Review*, xxiii, Spring 1934, 625–6.

Acts of the Privy Council of England, 1621–1623. (Issued by the Authority of the Lords Commissioners of His Majesty's Treasury under the Direction of the Master of the Rolls.) *A.H.R.*, xxxix, April 1934, 510–12.

The Deference due a Queen. (*The Queen and Mr Gladstone*, by Philip Guedalla.) *S.R.L.*, x, April 14th, 1934, 627.
The Life and Laughter of Sydney Smith. (*The Smith of Smiths*, by Hesketh Pearson, with an Introduction by G. K. Chesterton.) *Yale Review*, XXIII, Summer 1934, 838–40.
Cromwell the Opportunist. (*Oliver Cromwell*, by John Buchan; *Cromwell*, by Hilaire Belloc.) *S.R.L.*, xi, November 10th, 1934, 269, 274.
Creevey and Buckingham. (*Creevey's Life and Times, 1768–1838*, edited by John Gore: *James Silk Buckingham, 1786–1855*, by Ralph E. Turner.) *Yale Review*, XXIV, Autumn 1934, 183–7.
Chamberlain and the Boer War. (*The Life of Joseph Chamberlain*, by J. L. Garvin, VOL. III, 1895–1900.) *Yale Review*, XXIV, Spring 1935, 604–7.
England in the Reign of Charles II. By David Ogg. *New York Herald Tribune*, April 28th, 1935, 15.
The Gentry of Connecticut. (*Captain Nathan Hale, Major John Palsgrave Wyllys, A Digressive History*, by George Dudley Seymour.) *S.R.L.*, xii, August 17th, 1935, 11.
Ten Thousand Proverbs. (*The Oxford Dictionary of English Proverbs*, compiled by William George Smith; with an introduction and index by Janet E. Heseltine.) *S.R.L.*, xiv, August 29th, 1936, 10–11.
An Eighteenth-Century Traveller. (*The Torrington Diaries*, edited with an introduction by C. Bruyn Andrews, and a general introduction by John Beresford, VOLS. I, II, and III.) *Yale Review*, XXVI, Winter 1937, 414–17.
*History. In *On Going to College, A Symposium*. New York, Oxford University Press, 1938, 97–119.
The Amberleys and Their Friends. (*The Amberley Papers: The Letters and Diaries of Bertrand Russell's Parents*, by Bertrand and Patricia Russell.) *Yale Review*, XXVII, Spring 1938, 643–4.
An Inventory of the Historical Monuments in Westmorland. Issued by the Royal Commission on Historical Documents.
An Inventory of the Historical Monuments in Middlesex. (Royal Commission.) *A.H.R.*, XLIII, July 1938, 824–5.
The Place-names of Warwickshire. By J. E. B. Gover, A. Mawer, and F. M. Stenton, in collaboration with F. T. S. Houghton. *A.H.R.*, XLIII, July 1938, 928–9.
The "Tory Democrat". (*Letters from Benjamin Disraeli to Frances Anne, Marchioness of Londonderry, 1837–1861*, edited with an introduction by the Marchioness of Londonderry.) *S.R.L.*, xix, November 12th, 1938, 6.
British Politicians of Yesterday. (*The Captains and the Kings Depart, Journals and Letters of Reginald, Viscount Esher*, edited by Oliver, Viscount Esher.) *S.R.L.*, xix, December 10th, 1938, 12–13.
The Wisdom of Proverbs. (*Racial Proverbs*, by Selwyn Gurney Champion.) *Yale Review*, XXVIII, Winter 1939, 428–30.
Great Whig. (*Lord Macaulay, Victorian Liberal*, by Richmond Croom Beatty.) *S.R.L.*, xix, January 21st, 1939, 7.
The Dictionary of National Biography ... 1922–1930, edited by J. R. H. Weaver. *A.H.R.*, XLIV, April 1939, 633–4.
Village Hampdens. (*The British Common People, 1746–1938*, by G. D. H. Cole and Raymond Postgate.) *S.R.L.*, xx, May 13th, 1939, 16.
Calendar of the Manuscripts of the Most Honourable the Marquess of Salisbury ... Preserved at Hatfield House, Hertfordshire. Part XVII. Edited by M. S. Giuseppi. (Historical Manuscripts Commission.) *A.H.R.*, XLV, January 1940, 458.
Acts of the Privy Council of England. 1626, June–December; 1627, January–August. (The Lords Commissioners of His Majesty's Treasury under the Direction of the Master of the Rolls.) *A.H.R.*, XLV, January 1940, 458–9.
News of Seventeenth-Century London. (*The Letters of John Chamberlain*, edited with an introduction by Norman Egbert McClure, 2 vols.) *Yale Review*, XXX, Autumn 1940, 188–91.
*To England's Account. *Yale Review*, XXX, Winter 1940, 350–65.
From Chaucer to Victoria. (*English Social History: A Survey of Six Centuries*, by G. M. Trevelyan.) *Yale Review*, XXXII, Summer 1943, 792–5.

*History and the Education of Free Men. *American Scientist*, XXXII, Autumn 1944, 254–63.

The English People: Impressions and Observations. By D. W. Brogan. *A.H.R.*, LI, January 1946, 278–80.

Two Books on English History. (*The Spirit of English History*, by A. L. Rowse; *England in the Eighteen-Eighties: Toward a Social Basis for Freedom*, by Helen Merrell Lynd.) *Yale Review*, XXXV, Winter 1946, 347–9.

Two English Liberals. (*Beatrice Webb*, by Margaret Cole; *Short Journey*, by E. L. Woodward.) *Yale Review*, XXXVI, Winter 1947, 350–4.

*The English Woman, 1580 to 1650. In *Studies in Social History: A Tribute to G. M. Trevelyan*, edited by J. H. Plumb. London, 1955, 69–107.

A History of the English-Speaking Peoples. By Winston S. Churchill. Vol. I, The Birth of Britain. *A.H.R.*, LXII, October 1956, 93–5.

(The editor is grateful to Donald C. Gallup, Assistant Professor of Bibliography, Yale University, for his advice and assistance.)

INDEX

Abbot, George, Archbishop, 103
absolutism, 230; Tudor, 89, 126; comparison between Tudor and Stuart, 115–16
Admiralty Commission, 205–24
Alford, Edward, 63, 66
Anderson, Sir Henry, 138, 139
Andrewes, Launcelot, Bishop, 103, 104
Anglican Church, see Church of England
Anglican monopoly of political power, 240, 241, 243, 247, 248
Anglicans, 30, 36, 95, 103, 231, 234, 238, 243, 244
Anglo-Catholicism, 103, 104, 111, 230
Anglo-Scottish hostility, 46–8
Anglo-Scottish union, commissioners for, 49, 50, 51, 52, 53
Anne, Queen, 224, 237, 238, 239, 240, 241, 242, 243, 248, 249, 250
aristocracy, 21, 22, 23, 28, 32, 37, 38, 252
Arlington, 1st Earl of, 191, 201, 215
Arminianism, see Anglo-Catholicism
Arundels (Royalist family), 137
Ashburnham, John, 142
Ashburnhams (Royalist family), 137
Ashley, Lord, 1st Earl of Shaftesbury, 190, 191, 192, 193–4, 195, 200, 214, 215
Atterbury, Bishop, 248, 253
À Wood, Anthony, 158
Ayscough, E., 141, 146

Bacon, Francis, 48, 49, 53, 60, 71, 72, 80, 179, 182, 199
Bagshaw, Edward, 136, 144, 145
Balmerino, 1st Lord, 50
Bancroft, Archbishop, 45
Baptists, 153
Barnardiston, N., 146
Barnham, 137, 138, 141
Barrington, Sir Thomas, 135, 136, 137, 141, 144, 145, 146
Bathurst, 1st Earl of, 248
Bayntun, Sir Edward, 146
Beaw, Bishop, 236, 242, 244, 254
Beer, George Louis, 172, 173, 174, 175, 198
Belasyse, H., 81, 135, 136, 142, 145, 146
Bellingham, Sir Henry, 140
Benbow, Captain John, 212, 224

benevolences, 90, 94, 97, 117
Bennet, Sir John, 82, 85
Berkeleys (as colonists), 191
Berwick, treaty of, 113, 116, 127
Beveridge, Bishop, 242, 244
Bill of Attainder, 118, 125, 235
Bill of Rights, 20, 100, 238
bishops, 112, 127, 152, 230–55 passim
Bishops' Wars, 25, 113, 117, 127, 229
Blake, Robert, 205
Blundell, Sir Francis, 73, 81
Bodin, 177
Bolingbroke, 1st Viscount, 245, 248, 253
Book of Bounty, 59, 79, 84
Botero, Giovanni, 183–4
Bowyer, Sir Thomas, 138, 143
Breedon, Zacheus, 151, 164, 168
Brereton, Sir William, 139, 140
Brewster, Francis, 197
Brisbane, John, 216, 217, 218, 219, 220, 221, 222
Bristol, 1st Earl of, 127
Britain, James I's new name for England, 45, 49–50, 51
Bromley, William, 247
Brouncker, William, 2nd Viscount, 215, 222, 225
Brown, John, Clerk of Parliament in 1640, 79
Broxholme, John, 139, 143
Bruce, Edward, 47
Brunton, D., 24
Buckingham, 1st Duke of, 60, 63, 71–2, 79, 80, 94, 95, 96, 97, 99–100, 101, 102, 105, 106, 123, 124, 142
Bull, Stephen, 194
Burges, Cornelius, 154, 155, 157, 168
Burnet, Gilbert, Bishop, 216, 234, 235, 236, 237–8, 242, 245, 246, 247, 248, 254
Butterfield, Herbert, 18

Cage, William, 137, 139, 141, 142, 144
Calvinism, 35, 112
Calvinists, 39, 42, 43, 234
Capel, Arthur, 136, 140, 144, 145, 146
Capel, Sir Henry, 206, 215, 225
capitalism, emergence of Western, 34 (see also Protestant Reformation)
Carleill, Christopher, 175

INDEX

peerages, sale of, 21, 36
Penn, Sir William, 195, 201
Pennington, D. H., 24
Pepys, Samuel, 205, 206, 210, 211, 212, 215, 216
Petition of Right, 100–1, 105, 106, 107, 111, 117
Petty, William, 185, 199
Phelips, Sir Robert, 66, 85, 144
Pierrepont, W., 135, 136, 140, 145
political parties in the 18th century, 237, 240
Pool, Elizabeth, 152, 161–2
Pope, Mary, 152, 168
population in the 17th century, 17th-century theories of, 172, 174, 175, 176; current studies of, 174, 198; mobility of, 181; overpopulation as stimulus for emigration, 173, 174, 175; under-population, 184; experts on population, 185; population losses, 185–6; population of the colonies, 196
Powell, Robert, 179
Prayer Book, opposition of the Scots to, 112, 113
prerogative, royal, 30, 71, 76, 77, 91, 92, 93, 107, 113, 114, 118–19, 125, 229; limitations on, 101, 107
prerogative arrest, 99, 100
prerogative courts, 89
Presbyterians, 30, 151, 152, 154, 156, 157, 163, 164, 166, 167
Pride, Colonel, 150, 156
Pride's Purge, 156, 160
privileges, see parliamentary privileges
Privy Council, 20, 60, 63, 77, 78, 85, 91, 99, 115, 116, 205–6, 219, 250
property, changes in attitude towards, 21
property ownership, 28–9
property rights, 90, 91, 92, 111
Protectorate, 205, 230
Protestant Reformation, 19, 32, 46, 229, 252, 253; and the emergence of capitalism, 34–5, 39
Protestant succession, 239, 248
Protestants, 165, 191
Prynne, William, 150, 151, 152, 153, 156, 160, 161, 162, 165
Purefoy, W., 146
Puritan Independency, 26, 27, 32
puritanism, 20, 22, 26, 32, 91, 93
Puritans, 18, 22, 30, 36, 91, 92–3, 95, 103, 111–12, 132, 134, 136, 139, 153, 182, 183, 184, 189, 229, 230
Pym, John, 27, 35–6, 37, 63, 78, 118, 131, 134, 135, 136, 137, 140, 141, 142, 144, 145, 146

QUAKERS, 188, 195, 206

RADICAL MOVEMENT, 28, 31
Ramsay, Sir John, 47
referees for patent and monopoly grants, attack on, 71–2
religious conviction, power of, 33
Remonstrance of the Army, 149, 150, 151; printed rejoinders to, 150–66 passim; vindications of, 153
republican ideas, prevalence of, 151
Reformation, see Protestant Reformation
Restoration of 1660, 20, 21, 23, 29, 32, 184, 185, 187, 188, 189, 191, 230
Revolution of 1688, 23, 29, 229, 232–3, 237, 238, 253
Revolution Settlement, 230, 231, 236, 245, 253
Rich, Sir Nathaniel, 65
Richard II, 161, 163, 164
Richardson, Samuel, 153
Rigby, Alexander, 136, 142
Ripon, treaty of, 117
Rivers, James, 139
Robinson, Henry, 199
Rochester, 1st Earl of, see Hyde, Lawrence
Roe, Sir Thomas, 141
Rolle, J., 141, 143
Roman Catholicism, 103, 112, 231, 234, 248
Rooke, Captain, 224
Root and Branch Petition, 25
Roundheads, 94
royal prerogative, see prerogative
Royal Society, 185, 215
royalism, 22; —, constitutional, 29
Royalists, 24, 25, 36, 38, 114, 119, 135, 136, 137, 138, 140, 142, 143, 150, 158, 160, 165
Rudyard, B., 135, 136, 145, 146
Rump Parliament, see Parliament
Rupert, Prince, 205, 206
Rushworth, John, 82, 127, 162, 168
Russell, Admiral, 205, 223, 224
Russell, Lord William, 1st Duke of Bedford, 138
Russell, Captain Edward, 213, 217

SACHEVERELL, DR HENRY, 245, 251
Sackville, Sir Edward, 65
Sadler, Edmund, 65, 67
St John, Oliver, 134, 135, 136, 140, 141, 142, 144, 145
Salisbury, Lord Treasurer, 94, 109
Salisbury, William, 64
salus populi, 149, 157
Salvetti, 80
Sancroft, Archbishop, 232, 234
Sandys, Sir Edwin, 52, 61, 63, 66, 70, 71, 79, 83
Savage, William, 64
Savile, Sir Henry, 219, 220

270